Contents

Reveal
London

Welcome to the 2014 edition of London's greatest showcase of architecture and urban design.

London faces many challenges in the coming decades, including the increasing demand for housing, the pressure on our open spaces, and the ever-present effects of a changing climate. The pace of urban change, and the need to make our city efficient, sustainable and, not least, liveable, means that we need high-quality design more than ever.

Open House London gives you a unique opportunity to discover the creative and inspiring schemes that today's architects, engineers and landscape designers are producing to respond to these challenges, and what lessons past design teaches us.

Open House London is just one part of the work of Open-City in championing the value of well-designed places and spaces in making a liveable and vibrant city, and the role everyone plays within it. Overleaf you can find out more about what we develop and deliver as London's leading architecture education charity.

This year, as every year, we invite you to learn more about what a high-quality built environment looks like over 48 hours in September. But you can also tell us your views in this year's annual Open Debate and our new Green Debate.

Be inspired and let us have your thoughts by joining us on Facebook and Twitter **#myopenhouse**

Victoria Thornton OBE HonFRIBA
Founding Director

Open-City is a registered charity no. 1072104

  #myopenhouse
@openhouselondon

Open–City:
Making Architecture Matter

Architecture is fundamental to our society and culture.
A high-quality built environment is essential to our health, wellbeing and prosperity, and to our sense of who we are.

Yet it is not a subject that we ever learn about formally at school. To influence change in the built environment for the better, people want and need a good understanding and the means to offer their informed views.

Open-City's mission is to champion the value of well-designed spaces and places in making a liveable and vibrant city and the role that everyone plays within it.

Our main role is advocating good design and enabling people to develop the tools, skills and resources to do this themselves.

We believe that only by fully connecting '**people, place and practice**' can the best built environment for all be created. Here we explain some of the work that we do and the thinking behind it.

Get involved in the debate and follow Victoria's **blog** at **opencitylondon.wordpress.com**

Our work: People

Case study

Joseph Zeal-Henry is an architectural assistant for Urban Projects Bureau, due to resume studies at The Cass Faculty of Architecture in September 2014. He studied Part 1 of his degree at the University of Brighton.

People should be at the heart of how places are made. By learning more about the built environment, we can present our views, hopes and expectations with confidence.

Getting people interested and enthused in the long term is key. For more than 20 years the **Open House London** annual event has provided a unique annual open forum.

It enables 250,000 Londoners to debate and discuss architectural quality by experiencing London's best buildings at first hand. Our annual **Open Debate** is now extending this.

Alongside this our year-round education and skills initiatives create a legacy for learning. They inspire thousands of young people through our **Architecture in Schools** programmes and enable people to get involved with design issues in their local neighbourhoods.

How long have you been involved with Open-City?
Roughly 7-8 years in various incarnations as pupil/intern/volunteer/mentor!

How did you originally find out about Open-City?
Through a very enthusiastic design tutor, Neil Pinder at Graveney School, who introduced me to Open-City's Architecture in Schools programme.

What attracted you to working with Open-City?
It enabled me to develop as I make my way through education and the profession. Originally it was to gain experience at an office that had something to do with architecture. More recently, I see design advocacy and the work that Open-City does as an important part of my practice. I hope the work we are doing with their Accelerate programme will help to improve the profession and my own practice as an architect.

What do you think are the most important aspects for you?
I think the theme that runs through all the projects and experience I have been involved in is that the knowledge that is created through Open-City's programmes is essential to people (in my case young people). Being given that knowledge will empower them and give them confidence to get involved within the built environment as an architect or in a different profession.

What difference has working with Open-City made to your life?
Prior to studying, it gave me the confidence to study architecture. Without that experience I wouldn't have applied. I knew that I wanted to design something, but after working with Open-City I knew I wanted to design buildings.

Our work: Place

Place is much more than just individual buildings – it includes urban landscape, green spaces, streets and transport networks. These create the frameworks in which communities can thrive.

Open-City uses the physical make-up of the city as the basis for all its work. We recognised long ago that being in a space is the most powerful and direct way to understand it.

By transforming all aspects of a place we can make better cities. That is why we believe that it is essential to learn about places from every possible aspect.

Good-quality affordable housing is essential in making London liveable, not only to the individuals who live in the city, but also to the society, the economy, and the cultural life of our capital. Our community participation workshops and training provide an opportunity for all the stakeholders to be engaged, not just the professionals.

Our annual **Green Sky Thinking** initiative encourages better collaboration among professionals to create sustainable cities by looking at every point of view, from planning, development, design and construction to client, manager and end-user.

Case study

Teresa Coyle MBE is the CEO of Finsbury Park Community Hub, which has commissioned Open-City to develop and run a programme engaging local residents in regeneration.

How did you originally find out about Open-City?
Through word of mouth which is always a good sign!

What attracted you to collaborating with Open-City?
The organisation had an in-depth knowledge and experience of design and planning, as well as an excellent method of community engagement, together with an understanding of our particular needs and concerns.

Which initiative(s) have you been involved with?
Leading consultation on master planning, new build and other bespoke, innovative ideas for the Finsbury Park Community Hub.

What do you enjoy about the relationship?
No jargon, clear goals and objectives, and most of all patience, respect and understanding.

What difference has working with Open-City made to the way of working with your community?
It showed The Forum participants that the process of bespoke training, easy tools and materials can be exciting and fun, and they learned that they can really take ownership of their own development.

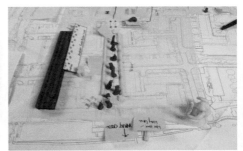

Our work: Practice

Case study

Jerry Tate set up his architecture practice in East London specialising in sustainable residential and commercial development, as well as the occasional slightly mad project!

Practice is the process by which professionals learn to hone their skills. Architects, engineers and others need a platform to showcase their work, reflect on their own knowledge and learning, and communicate their ideas.

Open House London in particular supports professionals by championing London as an international creative hub, and offers great exposure for new and recent projects.

More importantly, our education initiatives enable them to present their thinking to different audiences, including teachers and students, which helps as a training ground for their professional development.

We also enable more young people to take up career opportunities in the built environment professions through our ground-breaking **Accelerate into University** mentoring programme linking schools and universities.

How long have you been involved with Open-City?
Since 2008 when part of the My City Too! campaign.

How did you originally find out about Open-City?
I read an article about Open-City's work and was immediately impressed with their commitment.

What attracted you to working with Open-City?
We believe passionately that the quality of our built environment depends on everybody's engagement with the design debate and how architecture can shape this. Working with Open-City allows us to reach out to the public and create educational opportunities that often give surprising and inspirational outcomes.

Which initiative(s) have you been involved with?
My City Too!, Summer Architecture Academy, Architecture in Schools (both Primary and Secondary), Accelerate and Archikids Festival, and Green Sky Thinking.

What do you enjoy about the initiatives?
We really like enabling others to create, whether this is in a building workshop, or teaching within our office environment, or helping in the school classroom, and this was what we particularly enjoyed about all the initiatives.

What do you do now that you didn't do before collaborating with Open-City?
This sounds a bit serious, it has reminded us of our wider responsibility as designers in the community.

What difference has it made to your practice?
It has helped with ways of communicating, thinking about how to understand what people want and encouraging informed debate.

Opening eyes and minds

Did you learn about architecture at school?

You may know Open-City best for the Open House London Annual Event, but this is just one type of programme that we have devised and developed.

For young people especially, learning about how buildings and places are made can completely transform how they see the world. It can introduce them to new people and places, help them to develop new life skills and creativity as well as broadening their horizons.

As London's leading education charity for the built environment, **Open-City** aims to inspire young people to learn about their city. We do this through a range of initiatives inside and outside school that we have run over the past 15 years, including:

Architecture in Schools – a curriculum-linked annual programme that to date has enabled 15,000 primary and secondary state school pupils to enhance their understanding of architecture and the built environment, through inspiring building explorations and creative workshops with architects and our education team.

Archikids Festival – a festival in the City of London giving 3000 children and families every year the opportunity to explore the Square Mile's great buildings and public spaces with fun and free activities, workshops and trails.

Accelerate into University – a pioneering mentoring programme developed in association with our partners UCL's Bartlett School of Architecture and Make Architects, with the goal of widening the diversity of the architecture profession. Forty-five students from London state schools gain invaluable year-long professional mentoring and advice, and develop new skills to support their ambitions to pursue a career in the built environment.

Find out more at **open-city.org.uk/education**

"Through 'Accelerate' I learned new skills, a different way of thinking, and confidence in my own ideas has increased."

Rihana Alakija, Year 12 Accelerate into University mentee

Join our Education Fund and help us inspire more young people

Over the next 3 years we aim to enhance our role as the leading provider of architecture education for young people.
Our priorities are to:
— give every London child the opportunity to experience their city's most impressive architecture for free
— enable more disadvantaged young people to join the built environment professions
— inspire families to engage in their city in fun and innovative ways
— provide a great resource for all

As a charity we are entirely reliant on funding from individuals and companies.

We can only continue this with your support – please donate now at...

www.open-city.org.uk/educationfund

Revealing...

… the changing face of London

For more than 300 years London's skyline was dominated by the giant dome of St Paul's Cathedral – the cutting-edge architecture of its day. But in the past decade and more we've seen the capital undergo another extraordinary transformation.

As the capital's largest annual live showcase of architecture, engineering and urban landscape, Open House London has both witnessed and played a role in how London looks today. Every year it gives you the chance to explore some of London's most inspiring places and buildings at first hand, completely for free and at your own pace.

Reflecting the enormous changes that have taken place since we started more than 20 years ago, this year we are revealing a brand new version of our famous 'key' logo.

Our theme of '**Revealing**' also sheds light on the latest contemporary architecture shaping London today, as well as the role of architects, engineers and landscape designers in creating a more liveable and vibrant city.

The new Open House key

Now it features one of the latest additions to London's skyline: The Leadenhall Building, designed for co-developers and owners British Land and Oxford Properties by internationally renowned architects Rogers Stirk Harbour + Partners. This 52-storey office tower, with its distinctive angled shape, has half an acre of public space creating the largest new space in the City of London.

In Open House London you can:

— explore more than **800** buildings and places
— **rediscover** your own neighbourhood
— see how London is changing before your eyes by **visiting sites under construction**
— learn more about how **landscape design** is making London more liveable
— **talk directly** to the people designing, planning and building your city
— get a **sky high view** of the new city
— look at London's architecture afresh on foot or by bike with **our programme of walks and tours**
— join our **Open Debate** and **Green Debate** and have your say about how we can help London withstand future challenges.

Revealing: spaces to live in

"Can we design homes, or do we design houses which become homes through occupation?"

Carl Turner, Carl Turner Architects

The house is a building type that we can all relate to – we all have ideas about what makes a good home in terms of design.

With major constraints on space, demand for housing has always been one of the capital's most pressing issues. With London's population projected to change and expand in the next 20 years – with an extra 1 million people and a dramatic rise in the number of one-person households – we will need new design solutions to meet these needs.

Open House London shows you how architects are meeting this challenge, turning the constraints of limited budget, reuse of existing structures and restricted space to their advantage, to create outstanding spaces to live in – for individuals, families and communities.

Take a look at the following designs for living:

Contemporary insertions:
— **Ott's Yard** – development replacing derelict joinery workshop with two new green-roofed houses, based on the existing triangular geometry of the courtyard site (p 46)
— **Forest Mews** – 3 bespoke houses, each with a studio and courtyard, set around a communal courtyard (p 52)

Shared spaces for living:
— **The Exchange Bermondsey Spa Gardens** – new mixed-tenure housing development, designed as an urban village for modern living for Notting Hill Housing (p 62)
— **Royal Road** – new development of 100% affordable housing around a central communal garden (p 62)

Using 'leftover' spaces:
— **40a Dawlish Avenue** – award-winning sustainable private house, built on a neglected plot tucked away at the end of a suburban cul-de-sac (p 54)
— **Bateman Mews** – five houses designed as 'huts in the garden' of the large surrounding villas, with green roofs and a large shared garden (p 49)

Greening our existing homes:
— **8a Belsize Court Garages** – Victorian coach-and-horses stables transformed to architect's studio and 4-bedroom maisonette via carbon-reducing retrofit (p 22)
— **The Cedars (Span House)** – recent extension of iconic 1950s T2 house, with photovoltaic cells, solar heating of water and wood burning stove (p 59)

New housing models:
— **Mint Street** – a new development of 67 flats for Peabody, creating a new pedestrian public street (p 65)
— **Scape Greenwich** – providing 280 rooms for students at Ravensbourne College of Design and Communication and championing offsite manufacture (p 35)

Revealing: how the city works

"Can London's transport networks, housing and infrastructure cope with the forecasted 10 million Londoners?"

ice
Institution of Civil Engineers

London's infrastructure is under pressure as the city expands, while climate change presents one of the major challenges to how our city will function in the future.

Robust frameworks, services, structures and systems are essential to maintaining London's position as one of the best cities in the world to live and work in. This is where high-quality engineering is as fundamental to the architecture in creating a liveable city. We rely on engineering every day for the supply of energy and clean water to our homes and places of work, for processing and recycling our waste, for keeping our city moving, and for finding solutions to long-term problems like flood risk and pollution.

Our long-term partnership with the **Institution of Civil Engineers** continues to reveal how engineers shape the world around us and uncovers in depth some of the key issues facing our city, as well as showcasing ICE London Civil Engineering Award winning projects.
Explore the following infrastructure and engineering feats – look for orange dots ●

Upgrading our transport systems:
— **Crossrail** – Europe's largest construction project which aims to transform the rail transport network when it opens in 2018. Quiz the engineers on site at Canary Wharf, Farringdon and Moorgate (p 28, 45, 64)

— **London Victoria Railway Station** – find out more about the scheme to upgrade one of London's busiest underground stations, and get a fully guided tour of the railway station's renovated Grade II listed roof (p 73)

Training engineers of the future:
— **Royal Greenwich UTC (University Technical College)** – refurbished warehouse and new three-storey block housing a new employer- and university-led institution specialising in engineering and construction (p 34)

Ground-breaking structural achievements:
— **Connaught Tunnel** – a Victorian brick arched tunnel under the Royal Docks, originally built in 1878. Its refurbishment forms part of the Crossrail Project and will renew its life for another 120 years (p 55)
— **EDF Energy London Eye** – the world's tallest cantilevered observation wheel which has rapidly become a much-loved symbol of modern Britain (p 49)

Mitigating flood risk:
— **Salmons Brook** – a major flood alleviation scheme in a residential area that aims to store up to 134,000m³ of water in times of flood, protecting more than 1300 properties (p 33)

See London's waste transformed ... **Southwark Integrated Waste Management Facility**
Discover one of Europe's most advanced recycling facilities - a major waste treatment operation in central London. Designed for its urban residential surroundings, it showcases state-of-the-art technologies incorporating sustainable features (p 62)

The Changing Face of the Tidal Thames: Thames Estuary Partnership & ICE walk

Meet: Sat 2pm, Erith Station, Stonewood Road DA8 1TY. First come basis. Wear sturdy, comfortable footwear and rainwear and bring a drink. Max 30 on tour.
The tidal Thames Estuary is neither a wasteland nor wilderness. Not only was land intensively occupied and exploited but pressure on use is accelerating. This three-mile walk will demonstrate urban infrastructure, flood management and natural beauty, all within the M25. Tour led by Adam Guy, Thames Estuary Partnership and Roland Grzybek, ICE Fellow. Rail: Erith (for start); Slade Green (for end).

The Open Debate
'8 million and growing: Will London grind to a halt?'
Monday 15 September

In partnership with ICE, Open-City's Open Debate returns for the second year giving Londoners a voice on the issues affecting their city. 'Will London Grind to a Halt?' addresses the challenge of increased population growth and its knock-on effect on London's transport infrastructure, which is currently operating at or near capacity. Yet with challenges come opportunity. New developments and regeneration projects are springing up around transport 'hubs', creating viable new spaces in our compact city.

100 places available by ballot – see p 14 for how to enter.

Revealing: a greener city

"What does a sustainable city look like?"

SKANSKA

From above, more than half of the city is either green or blue. However, it is not just these spaces that make our city sustainable: our buildings and infrastructure should be at the forefront of delivering innovative sustainable design.

Our **Green Exemplar** strand – from large-scale regeneration projects to micro-community initiatives – highlights projects that are making significant steps in creating a sustainable city. Take a look this year at how we are making a cleaner and greener place for Londoners:

Optimizing materials:
— **The Eco-Hub at Lordship Recreation Ground** – Passivhaus, strawbale and timber-frame construction with raised floor on timber piles (p 41)
— **Hackney's Timber Buildings Walking Tour** – Visit three of the most significant timber buildings in the world just a short walk apart (p 38)

Energy:
— **73 Chester Road** – Victorian house carefully transformed in 2006 to make it fit for the 21st century, reducing its carbon footprint by over 80% (p 22)
— **Myplace Centre** – A new £4.7 million youth centre and Havering's first zero carbon building – one of only a few in the UK (p 42)

Urban greening:
— **The Dalston Eastern Curve Garden** – Community garden created on abandoned railway land in Hackney area lacking in green public space (p 38)
— **Growing Communities' Eco Classroom** – Urban garden grows zero-food-miles organic salads whilst classroom provides shelter for gardeners as well as a learning space (p 36)

Healthy learning:
— **Deptford Green School** – Winner of LABP best educational building award in 2013 with highly sustainable design (p 52)
— **Dagenham Park Church of England School** – BREEAM Excellent-rated building designed to maximise the learning and social areas by way of the building's orientation and fabrication (p 18)

Look for the Green Exemplar dot ● in the programme listings for more sustainable projects.

Sustainable thinking is a key theme for Open-City year round. If you are an architect, designer or other built environment professional, get involved in our annual **Green Sky Thinking Week** on 20-24 April 2015. It's a London-wide initiative highlighting innovative and practical solutions on how we make London's built environment sustainable. Now in its 5th year.
www.greenskythinking.org.uk

Join this year's Green Debate

London: Designed for healthy living?
Tuesday 16 September
With so much green seen from above, why is London's air pollution one of the worst in Europe? With cyclists doubling on the city's roads in the last 20 years, is there sufficient design for them? With London delivering some of the best exemplars in green construction in the world, do the majority of our buildings follow suit?

The Green Debate asks public and professional citizens alike – how healthy is London's built environment, and how can we improve it?

Join our inaugural Green Debate at the exemplar Saw Swee Hock Student Centre of the London School of Economics (p 73).

100 places available by ballot – see p 14 for how to enter.

LSE Estates Division

Revealing: places and spaces of the city

"How do we make the landscape of the city as precious as the rural landscape?"

Landscape Institute
Inspiring great places

Inspirational places and spaces are vital in creating a thriving, healthy city and improving the quality of our lives. Over the centuries the unique landscape of London has been shaped by its public spaces, including its distinctive streets, squares and parks. Open spaces are essential in making a city that we all want to live in, yet land use is coming under increasing pressure.

How do we create a sustainable landscape for the future? And how can we build beautiful places in a world where there are major challenges in managing water and other natural resources? The role of the landscape architect today is to offer creative, holistic solutions that are environmentally led, transformative and enhance the quality of human life.

Take a look at some of the projects with landscape at their heart:

Community-led open space:
— **Free Space Wenlock Barn Estate** – spend a day exploring design and local food growing initiatives led by local residents with community engagement group Fourthland (p 36)
— **Green Man (Phoenix Community Housing)** – discover a new public open space surrounded by contemporary timber-framed buildings

housing a market hall, community cafe and training kitchen (p 53)

Inspirational public realm:
— **King's Cross** – regular tours exploring this major development of the King's Cross 'railway lands', with 20 historic and 50 new buildings set in a high-quality public space and brand new urban square (p 24)
— **The Leadenhall Building** – half an acre of public space at ground level, which represents the largest new open area in the City of London (p 30)

Parks and gardens:
— **Clissold Park** – find out about the restoration of this park's design back to its original simplicity through enhanced key features and enriched biodiversity (p 38)

Large-scale transformation:
— **Further beyond the Olympic Park** – 2 expert-led walks from the Olympic Park exploring the historic hybrid landscape of the Lea Valley and one of London's least-known but most significant areas of regeneration (p 38)
— **Nine Elms Walk** – a walk and talk giving inside view on new landmark buildings and public realm at Nine Elms on South Bank, the largest regeneration zone in central London (p 69)

Look for the yellow dot ● in the programme listings for more landscape/public realm projects.

See **openhouselondon.org.uk/landscape** for more on landscape-related events. For more details on landscapes in London see **landscapeinstitute.org/openhouse**

Revealing: more ways to look at your city

"What did I like about Open House? The enthusiasm and variety. New discoveries, completely unexpected."

Open House participant 2013

With more than 800 buildings, walks, talks and tours, here are some of the ways to get ahead and make the most of your weekend:

1. FIRST, CHOOSE YOUR BUILDINGS AND PLAN YOUR WEEKEND ...

All buildings and events taking part this year are listed in the directory section of this guide from p 18. For updates see **openhouselondon.org.uk/search**.

Get the app! The invaluable tool for your weekend, the Open House London app contains the all-important map on the day, 'store your favourites' and 'buildings nearby me', as well as complete listings. August early-birds can download for only 69p until 30 August (thereafter £2.99).

Choose a hub – Burlington House

In some places you can step from one building straight to another. Burlington House is just one of these hubs. The original 18th-century mansion was home to the Earls of Burlington, but was later entrusted to the care of six learned societies and organisations. Discover the story of this unique cultural campus for arts and sciences since 1874 (see p 71).

2. DIG DEEPER ...

Find background information on most Open House buildings through free 'archifacts' sheets available at **openhouselondon.org.uk/search**. If you want to dig deeper here are some ideas ...

Buy the Open House book ... Get a copy of Victoria Thornton's book *Open House London* for an overview of 100 of some of the most architecturally inspiring buildings that have featured in the past 20+ years of Open House. Available with 15% discount by quoting the code OPENHOUSE at checkout from **open-city.org.uk/shop**

AJ Buildings Library:

View architectural photography, drawings and details of Open House London projects in the AJ Buildings Library. For more information, see online listings and the iphone app, and entries marked with the red AJ symbol ● in this guide. The AJ Buildings Library, which contains 1,900 exemplar British schemes, is free to OpenHousers in September. **AJBuildingsLibrary.co.uk**

AJ Buildings Library

Robert Elms
BBC London and Open House

Robert Elms Show Monday to Fridays 12-3pm and Saturdays 10am-1pm BBC London 94.9FM

"When Open House throws open the portals of so many otherwise inaccessible London buildings, it also opens our eyes to the surprising variety of architectural wonders in our midst and our minds to infinite possibilities of the built environment. For years now we have covered this staggeringly successful cultural event with relish on my daily show on BBC London 94.9. Every year we receive an avalanche of calls and e-mails from people eager to know more about the opportunities afforded by this unique extravaganza of the edifice. They are hungry to see behind the façades, to learn the tales and the techniques that all buildings have to tell. So yet again in nearly every London Borough, Londoners will learn a little more about the city we all share, and BBC London 94.9 will of course be with them."
Robert Elms

BBC LONDON 94.9 FM

More copies of the guide for your friends ...
Buy from: AA Bookshop, London Review Bookshop, Museum of London, RIBA Bookshop, Royal Academy, Swedenborg Society, Tate Britain, Tate Modern, V&A Museum.

3. CHOOSE A NEW ROUTE …

Get active! … Walking or cycling is the perfect way to keep fit while taking in some great architecture. With Transport for London's Legible London initiative we've created some handy central London mapguides to help you plan a walking route between buildings. Download at **openhouselondon.org.uk/legiblelondon**

Go on a road trip with Arriva … Win a place on an architectural mystery whirlwind afternoon tour on 21 Sept by historic Routemaster bus with commentary by Royal College of Art tutor and bus driver Joe Kerr. 40 places available by ballot. See p 16 for how to enter. **theheritagefleet.com**

⊘ ARRIVA

Discover architecture by night … Come with us as we head out into the night on Friday 19 Sept, discovering cultural, architectural and artistic delights, raising as much as we can to help people living with cancer. Working in partnership with Open House London, Maggie's Culture Crawl is part 15 mile night-walk, part cultural adventure. From the Foreign Office, to Fulham Palace by way of the Serpentine Sackler Gallery, you'll get exclusive access to all these buildings and many others. You'll encounter talented performers and enjoy delicious food and drink along the way. Places are limited so sign up today. Visit **maggiescentres.org/culturecrawl** or call **0300 123 1801**

maggie's
People with cancer
need places like these

4. HAVE A SAY … HAVE A VIEW

The **Open Debate '8 million and growing: Will London grind to a halt?'** Monday 15 September at 6.30pm (in partnership with the Institution of Civil Engineers). 100 places available by ballot. See p10 for further details.

Join in with our new **Green Exemplar debate 'London: Designed for Healthy Living?'** Tuesday 16 September at 6.30pm (in partnership with the London School of Economics). 100 places available by ballot. See p 11 for further details.

Apply for your places now at **openhouselondon. org.uk/ballots**. The closing date is 7 September for all ballots. See webpage for full terms and conditions.

If you prefer **competitions**, here are some great competitions with incredible prizes:

> **Leadenhall Building Sunset Tour,** Saturday 20 September. Enjoy the incredible view at sunset with a glass of champagne with 50 other guests by answering the following question: **By what nickname is The Leadenhall Building commonly known?**

"Way I see London" futurology talk on Wednesday 17 September 7.30pm – hosted by leading speakers at The View from The Shard: 10 tickets to be won by answering the question: **Which architect designed the Shard?**

View from the Shard: 100 pairs of tickets to be won for the highest vantage point in London on Saturday 20 September 9am by answering this question: **Which iconic castle is it possible to see 40 miles from The View from The Shard?**

Go to **openhouselondon.org.uk/competitions** for how to enter and full terms and conditions. Closing date 7 September. Only winners will be notified.

5. WHEN YOU GET THERE

Meet the architect … Hundreds of architects will be giving talks and tours of buildings they've designed. This is your unique opportunity to meet them in person and quiz them about their work. Look out for listings marked '**A**' (see p 16).

… and the engineer Structural engineers will also be on site explaining their role where listings have the code '**E**' (see p 16). Among these are The Sutton Life Centre (p63) engineered by **Elliott Wood**. Other Elliott Wood projects: 3floor-in2 Apartment (p 47), Jerwood Space (p 61), North London Hospice (p 33), ORTUS (p 61), Robin Grove music room & library extension (p 25). www.elliottwood.co.uk

Audio Described Tours … Blind and partially sighted people can enjoy VocalEyes audio described tours of four of London's iconic buildings: Maggie's Centre (p 39); 55 Baker Street (p 70); the Ismaili Centre (p 48); and the Old Royal Naval College, Greenwich (p 34). Tours are led by VocalEyes describers with building representatives or designers. Find out more and book at **vocaleyes.co.uk**, email **enquiries@vocaleyes.co.uk** or call 020 7375 1043. Collaboration between **VocalEyes**, the national charity providing access to the arts and Open House London, kindly supported by the Greater London Fund for the Blind.

> **How to look at a building**
> **Ken Allinson**, co-author of *London's Contemporary Architecture: An Explorer's Guide*, shares his top tip for getting more out of your building explorations:
> "Can you imagine certain qualities of the building taken away? Would that matter? What could be added to the building to improve it?" Go to **openhouselondon.org.uk/experts** for more expert top tips on how to get the most out of your weekend!

Take photos ... Enter the Open House London 2014 Photography Competition!

Take part in our photography competition in partnership with AirBnB. Send us your best shots on one of 3 themes of 'Revealing': 'my changing face of London', 'my community', or 'my building'. Submit as either a general enthusiast or professional photographer. Judging the entries will be AJ's Art Editor, The Photographers' Gallery Director and renowned architectural photographers. For full details and terms and conditions go to **openhouselondon.org.uk/competitions**

Photography competition sponsor:

Supporters:

6. GET THE KIDS INVOLVED!

Open House Junior for families ... Your kids can become architectives by joining in the exciting family activities of Open House Junior taking place throughout the weekend. Inspiring the next generation of Londoners aged 5 to 12, the programme is full of fun and free activities. Come and join us to design, draw and build London's cityscape! Highlights include:

City of a Thousand Architects
20 September, 11am-3pm
City Hall in the London Living Room
Structurally Found
20 & 21 September
Photography Treasure Hunt using twitter to capture the engineering feats of the city's structures.
Build a View Shaper!
20 Sept 11am-3pm

Part of the City of London's Sculpture in the City programme.

City Children's Trail with three carefully chosen, kid-friendly, self-guided routes – perfect for short legged walkers! Available from the City of London Information Centre, EC4M 8BX.

Check out **openhouselondon.org.uk/junior** for more great activities!

Archikids web resource ... Your intrepid architective youngsters can lead the way with the Archikids web resource, filled with fun facts and activities to keep them inspired beyond the weekend. **archikids.org.uk**.

7. SHARE YOUR ARCHITECTURE ADVENTURE

Keep up to date and share your Open House experience on Facebook and Twitter **@openhouselondon**. Tell us which buildings you liked best **#myopenhouse**

Are you a seasoned OpenHouser? Share your stories, memories and pictures from the past 20 years of Open House London at **facebook.com/openhousememorybank**

8. HELP TO KEEP OPEN HOUSE ALIVE!

Open House London can only continue with YOUR support.

Please help keep Open House weekend free for all by donating at **open-city.org.uk/donate**

What is Open House?

Open House was started in 1992 by a small charity (now called Open-City). Giving everyone the chance to explore London's great buildings helps us all to become more knowledgeable, engage in dialogue and make informed judgements on architecture.

Core to our beliefs and values is having direct experience. You can't make an informed decision just through photos and illustrations. You need first-hand knowledge of the space in question to know what the reality is.

The event is delivered by its community. Open House London is only possible with the support of hundreds of property and building owners, architects and engineers and others who give a huge amount of time and resources for free in putting on events and opening buildings. Without them, and the 6000 volunteers over the weekend, the event simply would not happen.

The concept has become so successful it has spread to more than 25 cities on 4 continents worldwide, including New York, Chicago, Dublin, Helsinki, Melbourne, Barcelona, Rome, Lisbon, Buenos Aires, Athens, Tel Aviv and Vienna. All cities are part of the Open House Worldwide Family, which shares the founding principles of the original event in London. **www.openhouseworldwide.org**

Part of the
Open House
Worldwide Family
openhouseworldwide.org

How to use this guide

This guide gives you details of all the buildings, walks, tours and special events taking part in Open House London over the weekend of 20 and 21 September. Use this guide to help you plan your visits and route.

— **Get the most up-to-date listings on our website openhouselondon.org.uk**
— **Get the iPhone (IOS7) or android app to store your favourites and use the map on the day**
— **Keep up to date and share over the weekend on Facebook and Twitter @openhouselondon #openhouselondon**

How does the event work?
The Open House London annual event is fully inclusive and admission is free to all, in line with the Open-City charity ethos of increasing wider understanding about the importance of good design.

How can I find the building(s) I'm interested in seeing?
Buildings and related events are listed geographically by borough to reflect the support of our local authority partners, and then alphabetically by name within each borough. The index (p 76) also lists buildings by type.

You can also use our online search facility at **openhouselondon.org.uk/search** and **our app** (69p until 30 August, thereafter £2.99) to find the building(s) you want. Search by building name but also by date, type, architect and area. Use the map interface to plan your route between buildings and events.

What information is given in each listing?
In this guide and on the website each listing has:
— building name
— address including postcode
— opening days and hours
— visitor access
— pre-booking details where relevant
— amenities
— nearest transport (with bus numbers at the end)

Which days are the buildings open?
Each building decides which day(s) and times it can open. Use the following key to plan your visit:
▫ Open Saturday only
▪ Open Sunday only
■ Open BOTH Saturday and Sunday

Key to the listings
Facilities on site, access information, special events, tours by architects and engineers, and highlight buildings have the following codes and icons:

A Architect on site
B Bookshop
C Children's activities
d Some disabled access
D Full wheelchair access
E Engineer on site
G Green Features
N Normally open to public
P Parking
Q Long queues envisaged
R Refreshments
T Toilets

● AJ Library Building
● Green Exemplar
● Landscape / Public realm
● Infrastructure/ Engineering

How do I get entry to a building?
Buildings taking part in Open House London are generally on **first come basis**, in line with our mission to make architecture accessible to all. Therefore you DON'T need to book except in a number of cases.

Each building selects its own method of opening, and for various reasons some decide to operate a booking system. Details can be found in each listing.

In the very few cases where bookings are required, use the contact details in these listings to book on or after 15 August ONLY – **DO NOT** try to book earlier than this as your request will not be accepted.

Terms of entry
Open House London is a free event inviting everyone to take part. Each building's opening, security arrangements and terms of entry are controlled by individual owners, and entry to each building is on terms and at times specified, on 20 & 21 September 2014. Participation in events is at your own risk. Information in this guide is provided by contributors. Open-City has taken all reasonable care to verify the information provided and cannot accept responsibility for any variation from the details published here. Please do respect building owners and their privacy, and be mindful when taking photos.

Important: see disclaimer see p 79

BALLOTS
Ballots are operated in a small number of instances for the following buildings and events:

10 Downing Street (p 70)
Antony Gormley Room at The Beaumont (p 70)
Arriva archibus mystery tour (p 14)
EDF Energy London Eye (p 49)
Gray's Inn (p 24)

Pre-Open House events:
Open Debate (p 10)
Green Debate (p 11)

The ballots will close on 7 September.
Go to **openhouselondon.org.uk/ballots** to enter. PLEASE NOTE ONLY successful applicants will be notified.

What will I find on the weekend?
Thousands of Open House volunteer guides and stewards will be showing you around and answering your questions over the weekend. Both professionals and amateur enthusiasts give their time and knowledge. In recognition of their support, their volunteer badge gives them priority access to buildings (apart from those that are pre-booking only). Email **volunteers@open-city.org.uk** if you want to find out how to become an Open House volunteer.

Keep up to date with all of Open-City's programmes by signing up to our regular **enewsletter** at **open-city.org.uk**

Please help keep Open House weekend free for all by donating at **open-city.org.uk/ donate**

Barking & Dagenham

See **openhouselondon.org.uk/barking**
to find out more about this area

Barking Abbey with St Margaret's Church
The Broadway, North Street, Barking IG11 8AS
■ Sat 10am-4pm. 10.30am & 2pm special guided tours of Abbey, Tower and Chapel (max 15 in Chapel). 11am-1pm bell ringing demonstrations (max 10). N D T B P
Grade I listed St Margaret's Church (1215 onwards) has interesting monuments, art and impressive stained glass. Includes Arts and Crafts work by George Jack, and Walker Organ (1914). Abbey dates from 666 AD and includes ruins, Curfew Tower and Chapel of Holy Rood with 12C Rood Stone. Ronald Wylde Associates (restoration 2005) 666AD onwards.
Tube/Rail: Barking; 5,62,EL1,287,366,387,EL2

Barking Central and Barking Learning Centre ●
2 Town Square, Barking IG11 7NB
■ Sat 10am-5pm/Sun 10am-4pm. Self-guided tour leaflets for Barking regeneration projects available at Barking Learning Centre reception. Further opportunities to visit the Barking bathhouse pop-up spa within the learning centre. N D T G
Formed the catalyst for Barking's regeneration projects. With a strong focus on striking architecture and high quality public realm, includes the popular arboretum and secret garden folly alongside the striking terrazzo paved colonnade with bespoke chandelier lights. RIBA Award winner 2011. Allford Hall Monaghan Morris 2007.
Tube/Rail: Barking; 5,62,287,EL1,387
www.ahmm.co.uk

Barking Enterprise Centre
50 Cambridge Road, Barking IG11 8FG
■ Sat/Sun 10am-4pm. Tours and briefings on arrival. G d
Home to 50 small office units with reception and facilities to support start-up businesses. Forming the entrance to the William Street Quarter, the brown brick building incorporates brise soleil on south elevation. Coloured panels provide visual link to Barking Central. Rated BREEAM Excellent with biodiverse roof and PV cells. Pellings 2011.
Tube/Rail: Barking; 5,62,169,238,287,366,368,387,EL1,EL2

Castle Green
Gale Street, Castle Green, Dagenham RM9 4UN
■ Sat 8.30am-1pm. Pre-book tours ONLY on 020 8724 1500. Last entry 12.30pm. Max 20 at one time. D R T P
An extended PFI school and community facility in the heart of the borough. State of the art facilities have been developed in line with new pedagogy focusing on importance of communication. architecture plb 2005. Entry: school, community theatre, sports and arts areas.
Tube: Becontree; Rail: Barking; 62,287,368

Closed Loop Recycling ● ●
16 Choats Road, Dagenham RM9 6LF
■ Sat 10am-5pm. Hourly tours, pre-book ONLY on nick.cliffe@closedloopre cycling.co.uk. Max 12 per tour. T G P d
State of the art plastic bottle recycling facility, 55,000 tonnes of waste plastic bottles recycled per year into food-grade plastic to manufacture new food and beverage packing. Many green design features with a BREEAM 'very good' rating. 2009.
Rail: Dagenham Dock; EL2

Dagenham Library
1 Church Elm Lane, Dagenham RM10 9QS
■ Sat 10am-5pm. First come basis. N D T
A contemporary flagship building situated on a newly-created 'Gateway Square' the library is a shared 2-storey public building with a Council 'One Stop Shop'. Striking glazed facade with 82 residential units above the library featuring coloured balcony panels. architecture plb 2010. Entry: public areas.
Tube: Dagenham Heathway; 145,173,174,175,364

Dagenham Park Church of England School ●
School Road, Dagenham RM10 9QH
■ Sat 10am-2pm. Architect led tours 10am, 11am and 12pm. Pre book ONLY, contact: openhouse@ahmm.co.uk. D T A G
AHMM's new building has helped to forge a strong identity for the school centred on its specialism of performing arts. Flexible classroom spaces are arranged around the performance hall at the heart of the school, with two connected atria providing open learning and social areas as well as natural light and ventilation. The BREEAM Excellent-rated building was designed to maximise the use of off-site fabrication through an integrated façade structural system as well as other key components such as building services modules. Allford Hall Monaghan Morris 2012.
Tube: Dagenham Heathway; Rail: Dagenham Dock; 145,687
www.ahmm.co.uk

Eastbury Manor House
Eastbury Square, Barking IG11 9SN
■ Sun 12pm-5pm. Regular tours, first come basis. Last tour 4pm. D R T C A P
Architecturally distinguished and well-preserved, brick-built, Grade I listed manor house, originally the residence of a wealthy Tudor gentleman. Contains 17C wall-paintings, wood panelling and a fine Tudor turret. Many original features have been restored, including east turret. Charming walled garden. Unknown/Richard Griffiths Architects (restoration) 16C/2003/2008-09. Entry: house, gardens, cafe, shop.
Tube: Upney; Tube/Rail: Barking; 62,287,368

Technical Skills Academy ●
1 Short Blue Place, Barking IG11 8FJ
■ Sat 2pm-5pm. D T
Quality education and vocational training for young people (14-19yrs) Focus on hospitality & food, hair & beauty, construction trades. Commissioned by LBBD and run by Barking and Dagenham College and a key part of the civic regeneration of Barking Town Centre. Sustainable features include combined heat and power heating system. BREEAM rated Excellent. Rick Mather Architects 2012.
Tube/Rail: Barking; 5,62,287,EL1,387

The Broadway
Broadway, Barking IG11 7LS
■ Sun 11am-5pm. Regular tours, pre-book ONLY on 020 8507 5607. D R T
Original theatre modernised with striking but sympathetic new double-height foyer space, preserving the original facade which now forms part of interior. H Jackson and R Edmonds/Tim Foster Architects (refurb) 1930/2004. Entry: foyers, auditorium, studios, offices.
Tube/Rail: Barking; 5,62,366,387,EL1

The Malthouse & Granary at the Ice House Quarter
80 Abbey Road, Barking IG11 7BT
■ Sat 10am-1pm. First come basis, access via river terrace. T d
Restoration of a 5-storey Victorian Malthouse and Granary on the River Roding with contemporary bronze clad extension, featuring low-tech approach to viable sustainability. Malthouse now an arts/creative centre. Schmidt Hammer Lassen/Pollard Thomas Edwards 2012. Entry: Granary and Malthouse terrace.
Tube/Rail: Barking

Valence House
Becontree Avenue, Dagenham RM8 3HT
■ Sat 10am-4pm. Regular tours. N D R T B P
Grade II* listed 15C manor house with medieval moat. Recently discovered late 16C wall painting & impressive oak panelling. Reopened 2010 with new galleries, archive and local studies centre with new 'passive' collection strongrooms. Feilden Clegg Bradley (refurb) 15C/2010. Entry: museum, cafe, giftshop, archives centre.
Tube: Becontree; Rail: Chadwell Heath; 150,62,128,368

WALKS/TOURS

Barking Central walk including Anne Mews and William Street Quarter Phase II ● ●
■ Meet at the entrance to Barking Learning Centre. Sat 11am-3pm. Tours 11am, 12pm, 2pm. First come basis. A
Walking tour of AHMM's groundbreaking residential-led regeneration of Barking town centre, including Barking Learning Centre, the Lemonade Building, and the borough's first new council housing for 25 years. Allford Hall Monaghan Morris 2010/2011/2014. Entry: External views only.
Tube/Rail: Barking; 5,62,238,368,387
www.ahmm.co.uk

Becontree Estate Bus Tour, Dagenham
■ Meet: Sun 10am for bus departure at Civic Centre, Dagenham RM10 7BW. First come basis. Duration approx 4 hours. Max 45 on tour. R T B P d
Built by the LCC during the 1920s and early 1930s, the estate was once the largest of its kind in Europe, with over 25,000 houses. Later building programmes extended the estate to house an estimated population of 90,000. Entry: all parts of Becontree Estate including entry to Kingsley Hall, Valence House and three vacant homes.
Tube: Dagenham East; Rail: Romford; 5,103,128,150

Revealing the Roding
■ Meet: Broadway Theatre entrance, Broadway IG11 7LS Sat tours, pre-book ONLY on keeley.gourlay@lbbd.gov.uk. Further information given upon booking. R T
Roding Riverside is a key regeneration area on the edge of Barking Town Centre which includes the Ice House Quarter – a hub for creative industries – and the Fresh Wharf development site on either side of the banks of the River Roding. A short tour of the Roding Riverside regeneration area will end with a tour of parts of the award winning Granary building – Schmidt Hammer Lassen/Pollard Thomas Edwards 2012.
Tube/Rail: Barking; 5,62,287,EL1,387

Supported by

Key. A Architect on site **B** Bookshop **C** Childrens' activities **d** Some disabled access **D** Full wheelchair access **E** Engineer on site **G** Green Features **N** Normally open to the public **P** Parking **Q** Long queues envisaged **R** Refreshments **T** Toilets

Barnet

22 Cavendish Avenue

22 Cavendish Avenue N3 3QN

■ **Sat/Sun 1pm-5pm. Regular tours, first come basis. A d**

Re-conversion of two apartments to single dwelling with enlarged extension and garden room.The deep plan and level changes between lounge and garden generate a design with an intricate section and roof as light-scoop at centre of the plan. Materials used include dark grey metal windows and roof edging and Danish bricks, to match the existing brick used at the rear. A new porch and timber windows are detailed traditionally and are sympathetic to the existing streetscape. Rozeman Architects 2012.

Tube: Finchley Central; 82,125,143,382,460,626

Friends Meeting House

North Square NW11 7AD

■ **Sun 2pm-5pm. Max 40 at one time. R T B P**

Delightful brick and tile building inspired by the famous 1688 Meeting House at Jordans in Buckinghamshire. A simple building in a tranquil setting, reflecting the Quakers' beliefs and last year celebrated its centenary. Fred Rowntree 1913.

Tube: Golders Green; H2

Golders Green Unitarians

31-and-a-half, Hoop Lane NW11 8BS

■ **Sat 10am-5pm/Sun 1pm-5pm. First come basis. D R T**

Grade II listed small interwar building with Arts and Crafts pulpit and mural by Ivon Hitchens in the tradition of Morris & Co. Reginald Farrow 1925. Entry: church, gardens.

Tube: Golders Green; H2,82,102,210,460

Hampstead Garden Suburb Free Church

Central Square NW11 7AG

■ **Sun 12.30pm-6.30pm. Last entry 15 mins before close. D R T P**

Grade I listed Nonconformist church, set in the suburb's integrally planned Central Square to balance St Jude's Church nearby, but with a low concrete dome. Distinctive interior with large Tuscan columns on high brick plinths. Sir Edwin Lutyens 1911.

Tube: Golders Green then H2 bus

Phoenix Cinema

52 High Road N2 9PJ

■ **Sun tours at 10.30am, 11.15am, 12noon, 12.45pm. Film screening at 1.30pm. Pre-book ONLY on 020 8444 6789. Max 10 per tour. R T C**

The Phoenix is one of the oldest cinemas in the country with 1910 barrel-vaulted ceiling and Art Deco wall reliefs by Mollo and Egan. Grade II listed. Birwood/Howes & Jackman/Pyle Boyd Architects/HMDW Architects 1910/1938/2002/2010. Entry: auditorium, projection room, public and private areas.

Tube: East Finchley; 102,143,234,263

22 Cavendish Avenue

St Jude on the Hill

Central Square NW11 7AH

■ **Sat 10am-5pm/Sun 12pm-5pm. Sat/Sun Guided talk on the Walter Starmer murals at 2pm. Local archives display. N R T B P**

Eccentric and magnificent Edwardian church by Sir Edwin Lutyens, Grade I listed. Described in Simon Jenkins' Thousand Best Churches as 'one of Lutyens' most distinctive creations'. England's most extensive 20C wall-painting scheme by Walter Starmer. Memorial to horses killed in WWI. Sir Edwin Lutyens 1911. Entry: nave, choir & chapels.

Tube: Golders Green then H2 bus to Heathgate

Wrotham Park

Wrotham Park, Barnet EN5 4SB

■ **Sun 10am-5pm. Tours on the hour except 1pm. Pre-book ONLY on 020 8275 1425. No children under 16. Last tour 4pm. Max 20 per tour. P d**

A privately-owned Grade II listed Palladian mansion with grand interiors restored in 1883, set in 300 acres of parkland in the midst of 2,500 acres. Built for Admiral The Hon. John Byng. Isaac Ware 1754/1883. Entry: entrance hall, dining room, drawing room, saloon, staircase hall.

Tube: Cockfosters, High Barnet; Rail: Potters Bar; 84

WALKS/TOURS

Hampstead Garden Suburb Artisans' Quarter Walk

■ **Meet: Sun 2pm and 4.30pm, Register inside St Jude on the Hill, Central Square NW11 7AH**

First come basis. Max 25 per tour.

Guided walks of 'the most nearly perfect example of the 20C Garden Suburb' (Pevsner). Informally laid out terraces and picturesque Arts and Crafts vernacular cottages. Additionally, material for self-guided walks will be available at all the Hampstead Garden Suburb Open House sites throughout the weekend. Unwin & Parker, Lutyens, Bunney, Baillie Scott & others.

Tube: Golders Green; then 82 bus; 102 to Hampstead Way

Phoenix Cinema

Wrotham Park

Gratefully supported by:

Golders Green Unitarians

Hampstead Garden Suburb Residents Association

Rozeman Architects

Phoenix Cinema 1910-2010

WROTHAM PARK

HAMPSTEAD - GARDEN - SUBURB - TRUST

Brent

See **openhouselondon.org.uk/brent**
to find out more about this area

BAPS Shri Swaminarayan Mandir
105-119 Brentfield Road, Neasden NW10 8LD
- Sat/Sun 10am-4pm. Tours on the hour. Last entry 3.30pm. Max 30 per tour. N D R T B P

Masterpiece of traditional Hindu design and exquisite workmanship that rises serenely amid London's iconic skyline. Using 5000 tonnes of Italian Carrara and Indian Ambaji marble and the finest Bulgarian limestone, it was hand-carved in India before being assembled in London. 1995. Entry: all areas except monks' quarters, admin block, kitchen, gym. NB. Respectful dress please – no shorts, short skirts, sleeveless tops.
Tube: Harlesden then 224 bus; Tube/Rail: Wembley Park then 206 bus

Capital City Academy
Doyle Gardens NW10 3ST
- Sat 10am-2pm. Regular tours, first come basis. Max 80 at one time. T P d

Foster and Partners' first school and the first new build City Academy. A glass and stainless steel building, slightly curved following the slope of the grounds surrounded with sports fields and a park. It is unique with its beautiful, clean and curved lines which reflect the sky and the green surrounding it. Foster + Partners 2003. Entry: theatre, main reception, arts areas.
Tube: Willesden Green; Rail: Kensal Rise; Tube/Rail: Kensal Green; 206,266

Christ Church, Brondesbury
Christchurch Avenue, Brondesbury NW6 7YN
- Sat/Sun 10am-5pm. First come basis, tour leaders on hand. Displays of the history of the building and blueprints. Last entry 4.30pm. N D R T

Second church to be built in North West London in the Victorian Gothic style. Converted to modern worship space, with Gothic features intact. Charles R Baker King 1866.
Tube: Kilburn; Rail: Brondesbury Park; 98,206,16

Cottrell House
53- 63 Wembley Hill Rd HA9 8BU
- Sat/Sun 10am-5pm. First come basis, queuing if necessary. Hourly tours. In house craft market, exhibition launch and live music. N D R T B C A

An enterprise space in Wembley set up by Meanwhile Space and initiated by Brent Council to support local start-up businesses and entrepreneurs with affordable workspace in a prominent, long term vacant building. The Decorators 2013.
Tube: Wembley Central; Rail: Wembley Stadium; 18,83,92,182

Ruach City Church
197-199 Kilburn High Road NW6 7HY
- Sat 10am-5pm. First come basis. N T d

Once the largest cine-variety theatre in England (over 4,000 seats). Italian Renaissance-style interior and original Wurlitzer theatre pipe organ. Grade II* listed. George Coles 1937. Entry: main hall only.
Tube: Kilburn; Rail: Kilburn High Road; Brondesbury Park; 16,16A,32,189,316,332,328

Wembley WC Pavilion

South Kilburn Regeneration
Cambridge Road/Kilburn Park Road NW6
- Sat/Sun 10am-5pm. First come basis. N A G

Redevelopment of Bronte and Fielding House at South Kilburn to create mixed tenure scheme of 229 apartments featuring CHP system. Supported by Network Housing Group. Architects will be onsite and access will include viewing platform of the development. Alison Brooks Architects/Lifchutz Davidson Sandilands 2014.
Tube: Kilburn Park; Rail: Queen's Park; 16,31,32,98,206
www.networkhg.org.uk

The Tin Tabernacle / Cambridge Hall
12-16 Cambridge Avenue NW6 5BA
- Sat/Sun 1pm-5pm. Half-hourly tours, first come basis. Last tour 4pm. Last entry 4.30pm. Max 15 per tour. N R T d

1860s corrugated iron chapel. Inside transformed after the last war into a ship by local people, complete with decks, portholes, bridge and even a bofors gun. 1863. Entry: Chapel, roperoom, classroom, wardroom.
Tube: Kilburn Park; Rail: Kilburn High Road; 31,328,316,32,206,632

Underground Bunker, Neasden
Brook Road NW2 7DZ
- Sat 8.30am-5pm. Pre-book ONLY by email on katy.bajina@ networkhg.org.uk. Comprehensive tour given. Sensible footwear and clothing should be worn. Last entry 5pm. Max 25 at one time. T P d

Underground 1940s bunker used during WWII by Winston Churchill and the Cabinet. Purpose-built of reinforced concrete, totally bomb-proof subterranean war citadel 40ft below ground, with Map Room, Cabinet Room and offices, housed within a sub-basement protected by a 5ft thick concrete roof. 1940s.
Tube: Neasden, Dollis Hill; 245,182,332,232

Wembley WC Pavilion ●●
Empire Way, Wembley HA9 0FJ
- Sat 1pm-3pm. Half-hourly tours, pre-book ONLY through info@gortscott.com. Last entry 2.30pm. T A

The public convenience has a concrete base which stands up to heavy use and supports the filigree, shiny metal screen

South Kilburn Regeneration

above. Each of its sides is subtly differentiated in response to the specific contexts. 2013.
Tube: Wembley Park; Rail: Wembley Stadium; 83,92,182,206

WALKS/TOURS

Roe Green Village
- Meet: Sun 11am and 3pm at Village Green, Roe Lane NW9 9BH. Tours of village with historian Peter Cormack FSA. N P d

Built to provide workers' housing for employees of AirCo (the Aircraft Manufacturing Company based in nearby Colindale/ Hendon), Roe Green was designed in the garden village idiom by Sir Frank Baines, principal architect at HM Office of Works. The 250 dwellings (a mixture of cottages and 'cottage flats') and their planning (around existing features such as trees and hedge divisions) clearly show the influence of the Arts & Crafts Movement. Sir Frank Baines 1918-19.
Tube: Kingsbury, Colindale; Rail: Kenton; 204,302,305,324,183

Network Housing Group won the contract to develop the second phase of South Kilburn's £600 million regeneration project at Bronte and Fielding House. United House are the developers. This development is designed by architects Lifschutz Davidson Sandilands, who were involved in the London 2012 Athletes Village, and Alison Brooks Architects, who won the prestigious Building Design Architect of the Year Award 2012. The phase comprises 126 private properties and 103 rented properties, and the designs are inspired by the local traditional mansion block facades. The scheme was shortlisted for the 2013 London Housing Design Awards.

Supported by

Key. A Architect on site **B** Bookshop **C** Childrens' activities **d** Some disabled access **D** Full wheelchair access **E** Engineer on site **G** Green Features **N** Normally open to the public **P** Parking **Q** Long queues envisaged **R** Refreshments **T** Toilets

Bromley

See **openhouselondon.org.uk/bromley** to find out more about this area

Bethlem Royal Hospital
Monks Orchard Road, Beckenham BR3 3BX
■ Sat 10am-5pm. Tours of administration building at 10am and 11am, first come basis. Last entry 4.30pm. N T B P d
The first opportunity to see the 1930 hospital administration building, currently undergoing refurbishment to open in 2015 as the Museum of the Mind. Ralph Maynard Smith/Fraser Brown McKenna 1930/2013. Entry: archives and museum, main building by tours only.
Rail: Eden Park; 356,119,194,198

Bromley and Sheppard's College
London Road (entrance via Wren Gates, no vehicle entry), Bromley BR1 1PE
■ Sat tours at 1.45pm, 2.30pm, 3.15pm, 4pm. Pre-book ONLY on 020 8460 4712. Max 20 per tour. R T d
Founded to house the widows of clergymen, the original building consisted of 20 houses built around a classically-styled quadrangle. Captain Richard Ryder – one of Sir Christopher Wren's surveyors – was in charge of design and construction. Captain Richard Ryder 1666. Entry: grounds, quadrangle, chapel.
Rail: Bromley North & South; 208,358

Bromley Parish Church
Church Road, Bromley BR2 0EG
■ Sat 10am-4pm. Tours of church spaces including the organ and the tower which offers views over Bromley and beyond. Activities include church trail and crafts for harvests. N D R T P C
J.Harold Gibbons designed the new church in 1948 to blend with the 14C tower which was heavily damaged during the war. New community rooms were added in 1982 and solar panels for energy efficiency have also been installed. J. Harold Gibbons (rebuilding) 1300s/1982.
Rail: Bromley North; 61,119,126,138,146,162,208,246

Bullers Wood
St Nicolas Lane, Logs Hill, Chislehurst BR7 5LJ
■ Sat 10am-1pm. Regular tours, first come basis. Talks every 30 mins on history of architecture. Last entry 12.30pm. Max 30 at one time. R T B
Typical mid-Victorian stucco-fronted house built on a grassy hillside, extended in 1888 by Ernest Newton whilst William Morris simultaneously redesigned the interiors. The library, formerly the drawing room, is famous for its unique William Morris hand-painted ceiling. The school was founded in 1930. Ernest Newton c1850. Entry: library, two classrooms, grounds.
Rail: Chislehurst, Elmstead Woods, Bickley; 314

Camden Place (Chislehurst Golf Club)
Camden Park Road, Chislehurst BR7 5HJ
■ Sat/Sun tours at 10am and 11am. Pre-book ONLY on 020 8467 2782. Max 25 at one time. D R T P
Early 18C mansion and home of Napoleon III 1870-80. Brick facade, early 18C Dutch wall paintings and breakfast room with exquisite original plaster ceiling by James Stuart. Golf Club from 1894. George Dance the Younger (remodelled) 1717-19C. Entry: ground floor.
Rail: Chislehurst; 269,162

Camden Place (Chislehurst Golf Club)

Keston Parish Church
Church Road, Keston BR2 6HT
■ Sun 1pm-5pm. Regular tours. Last tour 4.30pm. Max 30 at one time. D R T P
A 12C building standing on an ancient burial site. The small Victorian extension complements the beauty of this delightful medieval church together with a well appointed hall, completed in 1992. 12C.
Rail: Bromley South; 320,146,246

St George's RAF Chapel of Remembrance
Main Road, Biggin Hill TN16 3EJ
■ Sat 10am-4pm/Sun 12pm-4pm. Regular tours, first come basis. Last entry 30mins before close. Max 20 at one time. N D T B P d
Chapel building in shape of an aircraft hangar, with plain brick interior and 17 stained glass windows commemorating the spirit of WWII air and ground crew. Messrs Beasley/Harper/Williams 1951.
Rail: Bromley South; 320

St Mark's Square
McLaren Site Offices, Unit 1, Simpsons Road BR2 9AP
■ Tours on Sat at 10.30am, 11.30am and 1pm. Pre-book ONLY via Cathedral Group (Sarah Bennett – S.Bennett@cathedralgroup.com). PPE will be provided by McLaren Construction (boot size must be provided when booking). Attendees must arrive at site 15 minutes prior to start of the session. Duration approx 1 hour. Max 10 per tour.
£90m mixed-use PPP scheme to transform the southern end of Bromley Town Centre from Cathedral Group. The St Mark's Square scheme is a new residential and leisure quarter with a landscaped public square surrounded by a nine screen multiplex VUE cinema, 25,000 sq ft of cafés and restaurants, 130-bedroom hotel, 200 private and affordable apartments and a new 400 space secure underground car park. Due 2015.
Rail: Bromley South; 119,126,261

The Churchill
High Street, Bromley BR1 1HA
■ Sat/Sun 10am-5pm. Regular tours, pre-book ONLY via our box office on High Street, Bromley. Max 20 per tour. R T d
Wonderful example of a repertory theatre in style of European opera houses, with vast stage, sub-stage workshops and auditorium seating 785. Ken Wilson 1977. Entry: auditorium, stage, wings, dressing rooms, rehearsal spaces.
Rail: Bromley South, Bromley North; 119,138,208,227,726

St Mark's Square

The Keston Windmill
Heathfield Road, Keston BR2 6BF
■ Sat/Sun 12pm-5pm. Regular tours. Last entry 4pm. Max 10 at one time. R Q C G P d
A 1716 post mill and Kent's oldest surviving windmill, black and weatherboarded, on a brick roundhouse. Entry: windmill only. NB. Steep stairs.
Rail: Bromley South, Hayes; 246,146,320

The Odeon, Beckenham
High Street, Beckenham BR3 1DY
■ Sat/Sun tour 9.30am, first come basis Max 15 on tour. T d
Art Deco cinema with proscenium arch, stained glass windows and typically Deco mouldings. Robert Cromie 1930. Entry: main foyer, auditorium.
Rail: Beckenham Junction; 227,194,358,367,726,352,351

WALKS/TOURS

Self-guided Architecture of Chislehurst Walk
Organised by the Chislehurst Society.
Trail is available in printed form, free of charge, provided applicants send a Stamped Addressed envelope to The Chislehurst Society, The Old Chapel, 3 Queens Passage, Chislehurst High Street, Kent, BR7 5AP. The Trail can also be accessed as a download from www.chislehurst-society.org.uk/CATTWALK.pdf. N W
A look at some of the large houses built in the late nineteenth and early twentieth century by Ernest Newton, C H B Quennell and other noted architects.
Rail: Chislehurst; 269,162

Self-guided Chislehurst Trail
Organised by the Chislehurst Society.
Trail can be accessed online on our website, at www.chislehurst-society.org.uk/Pages/About/ChislehurstTour.html, or alternatively downloaded as a pdf at www.chislehurst-society.org.uk/HistoryBus/HistoryBuswebcopy.pdf. N W
Self-guided walk round the best examples of local architects' work, including EJ May, Ernest Newman, Somers Clarke, etc.
Rail: Chislehurst; 61,269,162

Supported by

Bromley
THE LONDON BOROUGH

Camden

See **openhouselondon.org.uk/camden**
to find out more about this area

2 Willow Road
2 Willow Road NW3 1TH
- Sat/Sun 11am-5pm. Entry via limited timed tickets only, available from house on day, first come basis. No tours, non-guided viewing only. Last entry 4.30pm. Q

Goldfinger's unique Modernist home, largely in original condition. The house, which has 3 floors at the front and 4 at the back, is designed for flexibility, efficient use of space and good day-lighting. Complete with fittings and furniture designed by Goldfinger and an impressive modern art collection including works by Marcel Duchamp, Max Ernst, Henry Moore and Bridget Riley. Ernö Goldfinger 1939.
Tube: Hampstead; Rail: Hampstead Heath; 24,46,168,268,C11

5 Pancras Square ●
5 Pancras Square N1C 4AG
- Sat 8am-8pm/Sun 11am-5pm. D R T G

Set to be one of the greenest buildings in London after achieving a BREEAM sustainable design rating of 'Outstanding', Camden's new 13 storey building combines two swimming pools, a state-of-the-art fitness gym, cafe, relocated modern library, customer access centre and office accommodation. Bennetts Associates Architects 2014.
Tube/Rail: King's Cross St Pancras; 10,30,59,205,390

8 Stoneleigh Terrace (Highgate New Town, Stage 1)
8 Stoneleigh Terrace N19 5TY
- Sun 10am-5pm. NB. Closed 1pm-2pm. Tours on the hour. Last tour 4pm. Max 25 per tour. T

Built during the golden era of Camden public housing by an architect who studied with Ernö Goldfinger and worked with Denys Lasdun. Peter Tábori, Camden Architects' Department 1972-9.
Tube: Archway; 4,C11

8a Belsize Court Garages ● ● Ⓝ
8a Belsize Court Garages NW3 5AJ
- Sat/Sun 10am-1pm. Architect-led tours every 45 mins, first come basis. Last entry 12.15. Max 10 per tour. A G

Originally a late 19C coachman's living quarters and stable, this mews house combines an award-winning architect's studio and spacious light-filled maisonette after a 2-phase retrofit. Sanya Polescuk Architects 2012. Entry: all areas.
Tube: Belsize Park, Swiss Cottage; 168,268,24,46,113

10 Brock Street
Regent's Place Estate NW1 3JL
- Sat 10am-5pm. Regular tours, first come basis. A E D T

A brand new build, completed in the summer of 2013, this 14-storey office building uses modern technology to operate in an environmentally sustainable way, looking on to Regent's Place's busy plaza. Wilkinson Eyre Architects 2013. Entry: atrium and reception lobby.
Tube: Great Portland Street, Warren Street, Euston Square; Rail: Euston; 30,24,29,108,205

20 Triton Street – Lend Lease HQ ● ● ●
20 Triton Street, Regent's Place NW1 3BF
- Sat 10am-5pm. Half-hourly tours, first come basis. Last entry 4.30pm. Max 18 per tour. D R T G

Royal College of General Practitioners

Lend Lease's EMEA HQ is a showcase for occupant health, productivity and employee engagement. First office fit-out to be awarded BREEAM Excellent. Sustainable features include a focus on indoor air quality with 3000 plants, a biodiverse green roof designed to mimic the seasons and London's largest 'insect hotel' for a commercial building. Woods Bagot 2011. Entry: office space, roof terrace.
Tube: Great Portland Street; 18,27,30

20 Triton Street, Regent's Place Estate ●
20 Triton Street, Regent's Place NW1 3BF
- Sat 10am-5pm. First come basis. E D T G

Ten-storey office complex housing a restaurant and a community theatre. The main feature of the building is the atrium, where artwork by Gary Webb is displayed. Terry Farrell and Partners/Lend Lease 2009.
Tube: Great Portland Street, Warren Street, Euston Square; Rail: Euston; 30,C2,88,108,27

32 Great James Street
32 Great James Street, WC1N 3HB
- Sat 10am-1pm. First come basis.

Two Grade II* listed Georgian properties that have been the head offices of GMS Estates for generations have been redeveloped for the 21st Century. A melee of unconnected post-war extensions and dank lower ground spaces has been replaced with two storeys of striking work space. Original 18C oak panelled rooms lead through to new bright offices with an asymmetric lofted ceiling that incorporates recessed lighting to accentuate the geometric planes. A copper bronze triangulated roof perches over this new area to the rear of the existing terrace. An old silver vault has become a meeting room with the barrelled ceiling and heavy steel door retained. Emrys Architects/Elliott Wood Partnership 1722/2013.
Tube: Holborn Tube/Rail: Farringdon; 19,38,55,243
www.elliottwood.co.uk

44 Willoughby Road
44 Willoughby Road NW3 1RU
- Sat 1pm-5pm/Sun 10am-1pm. Regular tours, first come basis. Max 20 per tour. Q G d

New-build open-plan studio house designed as a floating box with integrated gardens on each level and mesh screens for privacy and sun control. Sustainable features include heat pump, PV panels and water collection. RIBA award shortlist 2012. Mark Guard Architects 2012. Entry: all except 2 bedrooms.
Tube: Hampstead; Rail: Hampstead Heath; 268,C11,46,168

73 Chester Road ●
73 Chester Road N19 5DH
- Sat tours at 10am, 11am, 12noon, 2pm, 3pm, 4pm. First come basis. Max 10 per tour. G P

JW3-Jewish Community Centre London

Semi-detached late Victorian house, carefully transformed from 2006 to make it fit for 21C, reducing its carbon footprint by over 80%. Sustainable features include walls internally insulated, sash windows overhauled and double glazed and draught stripped, high performance windows, solar hot water and PV panels, sun tunnel, wood burning stove, water saving techniques. Sarah Harrison 1890/2006.
Tube: Archway; C2,C11,214,134,390

A Hard Working House
Grafton Way Fitzrovia, Regents Park W1T 5DB
- Sat/Sun 10am-5pm. First come basis, queuing outside if necessary. A

More-or-less public, more-or-less private, the Georgian townhouse is London's most hard working architectural typology. We pushed it to its limits, adapting the typology to provide a mixed-use socially sustainable development that provides commercial spaces, residential accommodation and a three-storey family home. The project includes a full-scale renovation, reorganisation and reinterpretation of the existing building with a light-weight rooftop pavilion and garden. Urban Projects Bureau 2013
Tube: Warren Street, Goodge Street; 134,24,29,14,390
www.urbanprojectsbureau.com

Alexandra Road ● Ⓝ
13(b) Rowley Way, Abbey Road NW8 0SF
- Sat 10am-5pm. First come basis, queuing if neccessary. Regular tours. Last entry 4.30pm. Max 4 at one time. Q

The last large social housing complex in London – a low-rise, high-density enclave. Terraced housing reinterpreted. Listed Grade II* in 1993. Flat virtually as originally designed. Neave Brown 1968-79. Entry: whole flat.
Tube: Swiss Cottage; Rail: South Hampstead; 159,139

Annroy
110-14 Grafton Road NW5 4BA.
- Sat/Sun 1pm-5pm. D R T B Q

A conversion and extension, including two extra floors, of a 1950s warehouse into photographic studio, offices and production facilities, 12 flats for sale and owner/occupier penthouse. Trevor Horne Architects 1960s/2009.
Rail: Kentish Town West; 131,214

Artchive – Philip Hughes Studio
62 Rochester Place NW1 9JX
- Sat/Sun 11am-5pm. First come basis, queuing if necessary. Max 12 at one time. A d

Private gallery and art archive. Mews workshop converted to artist's studio/summerhouse. Uses mirrors and glazed surfaces to produce theatrical distortion of spaces. Mezzanine studio carpeted in red, double-height garden room, wedge-

shaped glazing. Rear connects to garden with spa. RIBA Award Winner 2005. Hughes Meyer Studio/Sanei Hopkins Architects 2004. Entry: all areas.
Tube: Camden Town; Rail: Camden Road; C2,29,134

Bertram Street Low Energy Victorian Terrace ●
8 Bertram Street N19 5DQ
■ Sat/Sun 10am-4pm. Hourly tours, first come basis. NB. residents have a dog. No under 16s please. Last tour 3pm. Max 10 per tour. G
Low-carbon retrofit to a 3-storey Victorian terraced house in a conservation area to reduce emissions by 77%. Includes pioneering method of fitting internal wall insulation while the residents continued to live in the property. Sustainable features include vacuum glazing, MVHR, solar thermal and PV. United House with Sustainable Energy Academy, Parity Projects, LB Camden 2010. Entry: most living areas.
Tube: Archway, Tufnell Park; 4,143, C11

British Medical Association House
Tavistock Square WC1H 9JP
■ Sat 10am-5pm. Tours on the hour. Last tour at 4pm. Pre-book ONLY on 020 7383 6363. Max 20 at one time. T d
Designed for the Theosophical Society and acquired by the BMA in 1923. Extended by Wontner Smith (1928/9) and Douglas Wood (1938/50 and 1959/60). Sir Edwin Lutyens 1913/1929. Entry: council chamber, Princes room, Hastings room, library, garden.
Tube: Russell Square; Tube/Rail: Euston; 59,68,91,168

British Museum, World Conservation and Exhibition Centre ●
Great Russell Street WC1B 3DG
■ Sat 10am-1pm. Sat tours at 10am, 11am, 12noon and 1pm. Pre-book ONLY at www.britishmuseum.org. Visitors will have the opportunity to visit the building, led by a member of the project team. Max 15 per tour. R T B
The World Conservation and Exhibitions centre is an important new building that has allowed the British Museum to transform the way it displays and looks after its collection. Sir Robert Smirke/Rogers Stirk Harbour + Partners 1823-38/2014.
Tube: Tottenham Court Road, Holborn, Russell Square; Tube/Rail: Euston; 98,8,25

Burgh House
New End Square NW3 1LT
■ Sun 9.30am-5.30pm. World War One exhibition. Last entry 4.30pm. N R T B C d
Grade I listed Queen Anne house retaining original panelling and staircase with a modern gallery set in a small terrace garden. 1704. Entry: cafe, period rooms, art gallery, shop, kids' corner, Museum of Hampstead.
Tube: Hampstead; Rail: Hampstead Heath; 46,24,268,168, C11

Camden Local Studies and Archives Centre
2nd Floor, Holborn Library, 32-38 Theobalds Road WC1X 8PA
■ Sat 11am-3pm. Tours at 11am, 12noon, 2pm, first come basis. Duration 45 mins. Max 10 per tour. T
Described as 'the pioneer' of the post-war public libraries, Holborn Library has a structure of reinforced concrete, a front wall cantilevered out from internal columns and a galleried reading room; the entrance has a cantilevered canopy supported by piloti. Sidney Cook 1960.
Tube: Chancery Lane, Holborn; 19,38,55,143

Royal College of Physicians

Cecil Sharp House
2 Regent's Park Road NW1 7AY
■ Sat/Sun 11am-5pm. Hourly tours from 1pm to 4pm, first come basis. 1pm tour will focus on 60ft Ivon Hitchens mural (1954). Children's quiz for families available and temporary exhibition on Yan Tan Tethera in situ. Max 20 per tour. D R T C
Purpose built in 1930 to house the English Folk Dance and Song Society, this Grade II listed building was designed by members of the Art Workers Guild of the time. Fletcher and Pinkerton/Stillman and Eastwick-Field 1930/1951. Entry: Kennedy Hall, private gardens, Vaughan Williams Memorial Library.
Tube: Camden Town; Rail: Camden Road; 274, C2,29,253,168

Clean Break
2 Patshull Road NW5 2LB
■ Sun 10am-5pm. Displays; tours will address the experiences of women offenders and women at risk of offending and their experience of Clean Break's studios and building location. N R T A
Award-winning theatre company and charity working with women affected by the criminal justice system. Previously a factory, the building was designed as "non-institutional" in specific contrast to the prison environment, giving women offenders access to high quality, light studios and an unobserved external space. Avanti Architects 1998.
Tube: Kentish Town; Overground: Kentish Town West; 134,214,393, C2

Clearwater Yard
Inverness Street, Camden Town NW1 7HB
■ Sun 1pm-5pm. Architect led tours 2pm and 4pm. D T A
Nestling between a row of Georgian terraced houses and a primary school, Clearwater Yard's horseshoe plan wraps around a wall to create a courtyard and extends upwards to enclose three office blocks topped by a sedum roof. Allford Hall Monaghan Morris 2011.
Tube: Camden Town; 274
www.ahmm.co.uk

Conway Hall
25 Red Lion Square WC1R 4RL
■ Sat/Sun 10am-5pm. Regular tours. Exhibition from new catalogued archives. Max 40 per tour. N T d
HQ of the Conway Hall Ethical Society, a long-standing organisation renowned as a hub for free speech and progressive thought. Grade II listed Art Deco building, the interior is finished with quality materials, and remains largely intact. Frederick Herbert Mansford 1929. Entry: foyer, main hall (except if hired for event), library.
Tube: Holborn; 98,19,38,8,25

Dairy Art Centre ●
7a Wakefield Street WC1N 1PG
■ Sun tours on Sun at 2pm and 3pm, first come basis. Max 20 per tour. N T A
Jenny Jones's sensitive adaptation of Dairy Art Centre, a former milk depository highlights the building's unique raw, industrial features, which provide a vibrant space for exhibitions. Jenny Jones 1960s/2013.
Tube: Russell Square; 59,68,91,17,45

Dunboyne Road Estate (formerly Fleet Road Estate)
■ Meet: Sun 2pm, 36 Dunboyne Road, NW3 2YY Guided tour by original architect Neave Brown and contemporary architect Takeshi Hayatsu (6a Architects), pre-book ONLY on http://www.eventbrite.com/e/open-house-london-dunboyne-road-estate-tickets-12128210805?aff=estw. Max 10 per tour. A
Grade II listed low rise/high density housing scheme for London borough of Camden known as Fleet Road. No.36 is a split level maisonette retaining many of the original features such as sliding partitions and fitted joinery work. Neave Brown & LB Camden Architects Dept 1969-75.
Tube: Gospel Oak, Hampstead Heath, Belsize Park; 24,168,46, C11

Fenton House
Hampstead Grove NW3 6SP
■ Sat/Sun 11am-5pm. Entry to house and gardens via limited timed tickets only available on the day, first come basis. Last entry 4.30pm. Q d
Beautiful town house (1686) situated in 1 1/2 acres of walled gardens. Retaining many original features, it houses important decorative arts collections. Panoramic views across London from top floor balcony. 1686.
Tube: Hampstead; Rail: Hampstead Heath; 46,210,268

Freemasons' Hall
60 Great Queen Street WC2B 5AZ
■ Sat 10am-5pm. Last entry 4.30pm. N D T B
Monumental classical exterior belying elaborate and varied interior decoration: extensive use of mosaic, stained glass, decorated ceilings and lighting. Ashley and Newman 1927-33. Entry: Grand Temple and ceremonial areas.
Tube: Holborn, Covent Garden; 1,59,68,91,168,171,188

Garden Court Chambers
57-60 Lincoln's Inn Fields WC2A 3LJ
■ Sat 10am-4pm/Sun 10am-1pm. Hourly tours. Last tour Sat 4pm, Sun 1pm. Display of historical photography and architectural drawings and recent restoration works. Max 25 per tour. T Q d
Inigo Jones' design at no.59-60 intended as model for Lincoln's Inn Fields development, copied by no.57-58 with portico

and elliptical staircase added by Soane. Sympathetically refurbished by current occupiers, a barristers' chambers. Retains many original features, staircases, fireplaces, mouldings and historical associations. Inigo Jones/Sir John Soane 1640s/1700s. Entry: reception, staircases, meeting & conference rooms.
Tube: Holborn; Tube/Rail: Charing Cross; 1,59,68,91,168,171,188,243

Gibbs Building, Wellcome Trust
215 Euston Road NW1 2BE
◼ Sat 10am-5pm. Talks on Thomas Heatherwick sculpture. Activities for families including create your own London skyline. Last entry 4.45pm. Max 600 at one time. D R T C
HQ of the Wellcome Trust – a global charitable foundation dedicated to achieving improvements in health by supporting the brightest minds. Vast open plan design around a light-filled atrium featuring spectacular artwork. RIBA Award Winner 2005. Hopkins Architects 2004. Entry: ground floor atrium, 5th floor viewing gallery and art works.
Tube: Euston Square, Warren Street; Tube/Rail: Euston, King's Cross St Pancras; 18,24,29,30,253

Government Art Collection
Queen's Yard, 179a Tottenham Court Road W1T 7PA
◼ Sat/Sun 10am-5pm. Tours on the hour. Duration 45 mins. Pre-book ONLY on 020 7580 9120 or www.gac.culture.gov.uk/openhouse2014.html Last tour 4pm. Max 25 per tour. T
Guided tour of premises and behind-the-scenes look at how this major collection of British art operates. The viewing area will be hung with works marking the 100th anniversary of the outbreak of the First World War. Entry: all areas except office accommodation.
Tube: Goodge Street, Warren Street, Euston Square; Tube/Rail: Euston; 10,14,24,29,73,134,390

Gray's Inn
Gray's Inn WC1R 5ET
◼ Sun 10am-3pm. Sun tours at 10.30am, 12noon, 2pm. By ballot ONLY through Open House, see p.16 for details. Duration 1 hour. Must enter via entrance in High Holborn next to Cittie of Yorke. Max 30 per tour. T
700 year old legal collegiate institution. Hall includes 16C screen. Much of Inn redesigned in neo-Georgian style by Sir Edward Maufe after 1941 bombing. 1560/1800/1950. Entry: hall, large pension room, small pension room, chapel and the walks.
Tube: Chancery Lane, Holborn; Tube/Rail: King's Cross St Pancras, Blackfriars; 8,19,25,38,45,55,242,341

Hampstead Friends Meeting House
120 Heath Street NW3 1DR
◼ Sun 2pm-5pm. Regular tours. T d
Listed Arts and Crafts freestyle building with plain interior and many charming original features, sympathetically modernised in 1991. Entrance via listed gateway. Frederick Rowntree 1907. Entry: ground floor, 1st floor library.
Tube: Hampstead; Rail: Hampstead Heath; 268

Highgate Literary & Scientific Institution
11 South Grove N6 6BS
◼ Sun 12pm-5pm. Unrestricted entry to Victoria Hall, half-hourly tours to other rooms. Last entry 4.15pm. Max 12 per tour. T P d
Fine stuccoed building overlooking Pond Square, and home to Institution since 1840. Formed from 1790 coach house, stables and yard, with final additions c1880. 1790/1880. Entry: Victoria hall, members' room, library, Coleridge room.
Tube: Highgate, Archway; 214,210,271,143

Johnson Building ◉◎
77 Hatton Garden EC1N 8JS
◼ Sat 10am-5pm. Regular tours, first come basis. Architect talk and tours at 10am and 11am. Max 40 at one time. N T A G d
One of Derwent London's key developments in London's midtown, a part-refurbishment and part new-build centred around stunning central atrium. Sustainable features include displacement air-conditioning and 'DALI' lighting technology. RIBA Award Winner 2008. Allford Hall Monaghan Morris 2006. Entry: atrium.
Tube: Chancery Lane; Tube/Rail: Farringdon; 55,38,25,8,19
www.ahmm.co.uk

JW3-Jewish Community Centre London ◎
341-351 Finchley Road, NW3 6ET
◼ Sun 10am-10pm. First come basis, tours every 30mins until 6pm. E N D R T A G
Award winning Jewish arts, community and cultural centre. Designed to host a wide range of activities; dance, cinema, restaurant, theatre, art and cooking. Lifschutz Davidson Sandilands 2013. Entry: varies throughout the day, access to a nursery and roof garden usually closed to the public. Alex Lifschutz will be onsite.
www.jw3.org.uk
Tube: Finchley Road, West Hampstead, Finchley Road & Frognal; 13,82,113,187,268

Kentish Town Church of England Primary School ASD
Islip Street NW5 2TU
◼ Sat 10am-4pm. Regular tours, first come basis. Last entry 3pm. Max 20 per tour. N D T A
Extension and refurbishment to the existing Kentish Town Church of England Primary School, to provide a new inclusive resource base for children with Autistic Spectrum Disorders (ASD). The extension brings together new and old buildings sensitively. Haverstock 2011. Entry: open access to reception and school hall, other areas by tour only.
Tube/Rail: Kentish Town; Rail: Kentish Town West; C2,134,214,393

Kentish Town Health Centre ◎
2 Bartholomew Road NW5 2BX
◼ Sat 10am-2pm. Architect-led half-hourly tours, first come basis. Last entry 1.30pm. Max 30 per tour. D T A
Housing a GP Practice and other health facilities, this compact three storey building is inspired by the game 'Jenga'. The complex inter-relationships of all the building's uses are adjusted to create a flexible space for all the community. RIBA Stirling Prize shortlist 2009. Allford Hall Monaghan Morris/Elliott Wood Partnership 2008.
Tube/Rail: Kentish Town; C2,134,214,46
www.ahmm.co.uk | www.elliottwood.co.uk

King's Cross Public Realm ◉◎
Western Transit Shed, 11 Stable Street N1C 4AB
◼ Sat/Sun 10am-4pm. King's Cross site tours, pre-book ONLY at http://tours.kingscross.co.uk. Regular public realm tours starting at King's Cross Visitor Centre. Max 20 per tour. E D R T C A G
A mixed-use development of the King's Cross 'railway lands' (Masterplan Allies and Morrison, Porphyrious Associates + Townshend Landscape Architects, 2004). 20 historic and 50 new buildings set in high quality public space. Central St Martins Granary Building (Stanton Williams 2011) and Granary Square (Townshend 2012). Townshend Landscape Architects/Stanton Williams 2012. Entry: Visitor Centre, viewing platform and Skip Garden.
Tube/Rail: King's Cross St Pancras; 10,46,73,214,390

Robin Grove music room & library extension

London Mathematical Society
De Morgan House, 57-58 Russell Square WC1B 4HS
◼ Sun 11am-4pm. Half-hourly tours. Exhibition running. Last tour 3.30pm. Max 10 per tour. N
Two Grade II listed buildings, 4-storey yellow stock brick with a rusticated stucco base. No.57 has a further attic level with a garden at the rear. Staircases are intact and each room still retains the high ceilings and ornamental fireplaces. James Burton 1803. Entry: lower ground floor, reception, room 14, members' room.
Tube: Russell Square; Tube/Rail: Euston, King's Cross St Pancras; 188,91,168,7

London School of Hygiene & Tropical Medicine ◎
Keppel Street WC1E 7HT
◼ Sat 10am-5pm/Sun 10am-3pm. Tours on the hour, first come basis. Exhibition on history of building. Last tour Sat 4pm, Sun 2pm. Max 20 per tour. T d
Beautiful Grade II listed Art Deco building with highly decorated facade, period library, north courtyard extension and new south courtyard building. P Morley Horder & Verner O Rees/Devereux Architects 1929/2003/2009. Entry: entrance hall, library, north and south courtyard buildings.
Tube: Goodge Street; Tube/Rail: Euston, King's Cross St Pancras; 10,24,29,73,134

Lullaby Factory, Great Ormond Street Hospital for Children
Great Ormond Street WC1N 3JH
◼ Sat 1pm-5pm. Tours at 1pm, 2pm, 3pm & 4pm. Pre-book ONLY on gocreate@gosh.nhs.uk Max 10 per tour. Duration 20 mins. D R T A
Studio Weave and Great Ormond Street Hospital have transformed an awkward exterior space landlocked by buildings into a secret world that cannot be seen except from inside the hospital and only heard from a few special listening pipes. Studio Weave 2012.
Tube: Holborn, Russell Square; 38,59,91,168,243

Lumen United Reformed Church and Cafe ◉◎
88 Tavistock Place WC1H 9RS
◼ Sat 10am-6pm. Hourly tours, first come basis. Artist will be present. Last tour 5pm. Max 10 per tour. N D R T

St Pancras Chambers and Clock Tower

Created within the shell of an existing 1960s United Reformed church, Lumen is a Christian worship space but open to people of all faiths and none. Redesign includes a cafe clearly visible from the street through a dramatic 8m high window, a new extension housing three rooms, a reflective space the 'Shaft of Light': a white-rendered spectacular conical intervention which reaches through the full 11m height of the building to a single roof-light. The courtyard garden is a quiet oasis with a fountain designed by revered artist Alison Wilding RA, who also designed the font, and drinking fountain. The front window is adorned by a magnificent bronze sculpture designed by emerging artist Rona Smith. RIBA Award Winner 2009. Theis + Khan 2009.
Tube: Russell Square; Tube/Rail: King's Cross St Pancras; 46,45,7,205,30,73,390

Montpelier Community Nursery ◯
115 Brecknock Road N19 5AH
■ Sun 1pm-5pm. First come basis, queuing outside if necessary. Last entry 4.45pm. D T A G
New-build community nursery providing affordable childcare for 24 2-5 year olds. The energy efficient cross laminated timber building maximises daylight and has an excellent relationship with the treescape of the secluded public gardens within which it is situated. 2013 RIBA National Award and Stephen Lawrence Prize Winner. AY Architects 2012.
Tube: Kentish Town, Tufnell Park; Rail: Kentish Town; 390,393,134,29

Regent's Place Estate
Regent's Place Estate NW1 3HF
■ Sat 10am-5pm. Regular tours, first come basis. E N D
Multi-use corporate estate in the West End, with exterior space landscaped for workers use, outdoor events and to display various pieces of artwork. Terry Farrell Partnership 2013. Entry: main building areas.
Tube: Great Portland Street, Warren Street, Euston Square; Tube/Rail: Euston; C2,30,88,27

Robin Grove music room & library extension
8 Robin Grove, London N6 6NY
■ Sat 1pm-6.30pm. Regular tours, first come basis. Last tour 6.30pm. Max 40 per tour. A G

Extension of house along the entire north edge over 2 floors creating idealised views into the woods. The extension into the garden is as auditorium – a place for performance listening or slumber, it projects its volume into the garden and is lit with 3-sided natural light. Andrew Pilkington Architects/Elliott Wood Partnership 2011. Entry: ground floor of house, garden.
Tube: Archway, Highgate; Rail: Gospel Oak, Hampstead Heath; 214,C11,210,143,603
www.elliottwood.co.uk

Royal Academy of Dramatic Art
62-64 Gower Street WC1E 6ED
■ Sat tours at 11am, 11.30am, 12noon, 12.30pm. Pre-book ONLY at boxoffice@rada.ac.uk (Lorna O'Leary). Max 25 per tour. D T
Theatres, public bar and first class teaching facilities with large glass curving bay and terracotta grid of cleverly disguised flytower, and shaft of daylight from roof through glass floor to workshops in basement. RIBA Award Winner. Avery Associates Architects 2001.
Tube: Euston Square, Goodge Street; Tube/Rail: Euston; 10,24,73,134,390

Royal Asiatic Society
14 Stephenson Way NW1 2HD
■ Sat 2pm-4pm. Talks on history and collection of Society followed by architect-led tours, at 1pm, 2pm, 3pm, 4pm. Exhibition on the building and its neighbourhood. Last entry 4pm. Max 20 per tour. A N R T d
An original 1880s warehouse converted by the architects Jestico + Whiles for their offices. Featuring an atrium with an up-and-over full height glazed screen fronting the mezzanine floor. In 2007 the RAS purchased the building and remodelled it to house its collection and facilitate its activities. 1880s. Entry: 3rd floor studio, 2nd floor council room, 1st floor reading room, ground floor lecture theatre.
Tube: Euston Square, Warren Street; Tube/Rail: Euston, King's Cross St Pancras; 10,14,24,27,390

Royal College of General Practitioners
30 Euston Square NW1 2FB
■ Sat 12pm-5pm/Sun 12pm-4pm. Tours every 30 mins, also specialist architect-led tours describing restoration process. Pre-book ONLY via openhouse@rcgp.org.uk. Max 20 at one time. D R T A
Grade 2* listed building designed by Arthur Beresford Pite. Recently restored to showcase magnificent Edwardian faiencing tile work, rust glass mosaic floor and other historic features in transformed modern surroundings that now provides the new headquarters of the Royal College of General Practitioners. Arthur Beresford Pite/Harmsen Tilney Shane 1908/2012. Entry: Roof Terrace, state of the art auditorium and boutique bedrooms.
Tube/Rail: Euston, Euston Square

Royal College of Physicians ◯
11 St Andrew's Place, Regents Park NW1 4LE
■ Sun 10am-5pm. Regular architectural and garden tours bookable on the day. Lecture titled 'the architecture of Sir Denys Lasdun' will start at 2.15pm and will be given by Dr Barnabas Calder. Children's activities and family quiz. Special exhibition celebrating building's 50th anniversary, including Lasdun's building models lent by RIBA. Last entry 3.30pm. N D R T B C
Dramatic interior spaces and white mosaic exterior elevated on piloti. Grade I listed and one of London's most important post-war buildings. Sir Denys Lasdun 1964/1996. Entry: main hall, theatres, library, Osler Room, Censors' Room, council chamber, treasures, physic garden.

Tube: Warren Street, Great Portland Street, Regents Park; Tube/Rail: Euston, King's Cross St Pancras; C2,18,27,30,88,205,453
www.rcplondon.ac.uk

Shopfront Apartment at 280 Gray's Inn Road
280 Gray's Inn Road WC1X 8EB
■ Sat 10am-6pm. First come basis, queuing outside if necessary. Tours every 10mins. Last entry 5pm. Max 8 per tour. A G d
Conversion of former commercial units into a modern two-storey apartment within the Bloomsbury Conservation Area. Living spaces balance privacy with shopfront interaction, whilst the basement bedroom is a peaceful daylit retreat. Daykin Marshall Studio 2011. Entry: Ground floor and basement.
Tube: King's Cross; 17,45,46,63,259

Sir John Soane's Museum
No.13 & 14 Lincoln's Inn Fields WC2A 3BP
■ Sat 10am-4.30pm. Last entry 4.30pm. N T Q C A
No.14 Lincoln's Inn Fields, built by Sir John Soane in 1824 and let out in his lifetime as a private house, is a rare and beautiful example of the architect's late work with a number of fine interiors. The building, restored in 2006-7 by Julian Harrap Architects (RIBA Award Winner 2009), houses an education centre and research facility. Sir John Soane/Julian Harrap Architects (refurb) 1812 & 1824/2008. Entry: No.14 Lincoln's Inn Fields; 2nd floor of No.13 (small groups only). Please note: No access to main museum.
Tube: Holborn; 1,8,19,25,38

St George's Bloomsbury
Bloomsbury Way WC1A 2SR
■ Sat 10am-6pm/Sun 12pm-5pm. Regular architect-led tours. Hawksmoor and Bloomsbury exhibition in Undercroft. N D R T A
Last of Hawksmoor's six London churches and consecrated in 1730, St George's is regarded for its majestic portico and stepped tower with lion and unicorn sculptures. The nave is now graced with a magnificent late 17C chandelier, which once hung in the grand entrance of the V&A. The interior and exterior re-lighting scheme concludes the restoration project coordinated by World Monuments Fund Britain. Nicholas Hawksmoor 1720s.
Tube: Tottenham Court Road, Holborn, Russell Square; Tube/Rail: Euston; 8,19,25,38,55

St Giles-in-the-Fields
60 St Giles High Street WC2H 8LG
■ Sat 10am-5pm/Sun 12pm-5pm. N D T
Grade I listed Palladian church by architect of Woburn Abbey, with one of London's best preserved early Georgian interiors. Recently restored 17C/18C historic organ. Many interesting memorials and associations with Maryland, Sydney and Melanesia. Henry Flitcroft 1730-34.
Tube: Tottenham Court Road; 1,7,8,10,14,19,24,25,29,38,55,73,98, 134,176,242

St Pancras Chambers and Clock Tower ◯
The Forecourt, St Pancras Station, Euston Road NW1 2AR
■ Sat/Sun 10am-5pm. Regular tours, every 20 minutes. Pre-book ONLY on https://openhouselondon2014stpancras. eventbrite.co.uk Last entry 4.40pm
Former Midland Grand Hotel, now St Pancras Renaissance Hotel and Chambers apartments. Includes hotel lobby and clock tower. George Gilbert Scott 1868-1873.
Tube/Rail: King's Cross St Pancras; 10,30,63,91,390

St Pancras International ●●

Meet at special assistance meeting point (next to Starbucks) Euston Road N1C 4QP

■ Sat/Sun 10am-4pm. Tours on the hour. Pre-book ONLY through www.kingscrossandstpancras.com/walking-tours. Last tour 4pm. Max 20 per tour. N D T

A unique Grade I listed Victorian railway station completed in 1868, with the original station hotel following in 1873. After a £800 million transformation, St Pancras International, home of HS1, has redefined railway stations for the 21st Century and is a destination in its own right. The tour will include an architectural history of the iconic station. Barlow/Gilbert Scott/Foster + Partners/Lansley 1868/2007. Entry: grand terrace, arcade, circle.
Tube/Rail: King's Cross St Pancras; 10,30,59,205,390

St Pancras Old Church

Pancras Road NW1 1UL

■ Sat 9am-5pm/Sun 11am-5pm. Regular tours, first come basis. N R B d

Dating from 11/12C and standing on oldest site of Christian worship in London (3C). Inside is much 17C ornamentation and outstanding 6C Altar Stone, reputed to have belonged to St Augustine. Surrounding Churchyard, containing tombs of Sir John Soane, Mary Wollstonecraft and others, has been extensively restored and recently refurbished. 12C.
Tube: Mornington Crescent, Camden Town; Tube/Rail: King's Cross St Pancras; 46,214

Store

31-32 Alfred Place, WC1E 7DP

■ Sat/Sun 10am-5pm. First come basis, queueing if necessary. Workshops and children's activities taking place. N T B C A d

Store is an association of artists and architects based in London. From its headquarters in the heart of Bloomsbury, Store runs a design and art practice, equipped with workshop facilities; it curates exhibitions, invites residencies and organises events open to the public. The large empty office block was given over to Store in April 2013 by a property development company on a rolling short tenancy. Alfred Place was once the place of work for the architect Cedric Price. Store.
Tube: Goodge Street, Tottenham Court Road; 10,24,29,73,390

Swiss Church London

79 Endell Street WC2H 9DY

■ Sat 11am-3pm. Renovation video screening. N D R T

Grade II listed community/cultural venue and reformed church which has undergone a major renovation. A transparent structure using glass and mirrored panels to highlight features of the 19C architecture has been inserted with a freestanding structure right above the entrance that offers additional office and exhibition space. Christ & Gantenbein (refurb) 2010.
Tube: Tottenham Court Road, Covent Garden, Holborn; Tube/Rail: Charing Cross; 24,29,176,19,38

Swiss Cottage Library

88 Avenue Road NW3 3HA

■ Sat 10am-5pm/Sun 11am-4pm. Regular tours focusing on the library's original architect Sir Basil Spence. N D R T B C P

Grade II listed building by renowned Modernist, which has been refurbished and remodelled whilst protecting the building's landmark status. Sir Basil Spence/John McAslan and Partners (refurb) 1963/2003. Entry: public areas and basement reserve stock area.
Tube: Swiss Cottage; 31, C11,82,13,268,187,46

The Art Workers Guild

6 Queen Square WC1N 3AT

■ Sat 12pm-6pm/Sun 12pm-5pm. Exhibition of work by current members.

1713 terraced house with hall at rear. Notable renovated Arts and Crafts interior. Portraits of Guild Masters since 1884. FW Troup 1713/1914. Entry: hall, committee room and library.
Tube: Russell Square, Holborn; Rail: King's Cross St Pancras; 59,68,91,168,188

The Coach House ●

2a Belsize Park Gardens NW3 4LA

■ Sun tours at 10am, 11am, 12noon, 2pm, 3pm, 4pm. Pre-book ONLY on http://www.superhomes.org.uk Max 10 per tour. NB. Children over 12 only. G

Victorian house retrofitted to save 70% carbon, features internal and external insulation, high performance double glazing, integral draught stripping, LED low energy lights. New for 2014: energy savings and pay backs. 1860.
Tube: Belsize Park, Swiss Cottage, Finchley Road; 168,268,13,46,113

The Horse Hospital

Colonnade, Bloomsbury WC1N 1JD

■ Sat/Sun 12pm-5pm. First come basis. N T d

Unspoilt example of purpose built 2-storey urban stable with many unique features. One floor is a gallery, the other holds the Contemporary Wardrobe, Europe's largest public-access street fashion collection. James Burton 1797. Entry: upstairs and downstairs gallery, collection space. NB. Exhibition of photographs, memorabilia and ephemera from lost, rock-star studded, cult 60s film.
Tube: Russell Square; Tube/Rail: Euston; 7,19,38,55,68,168,243

The Swedenborg Society

20-21 Bloomsbury Way WC1A 2TH

■ Sat 1pm-4pm. Talks on the history of the society and the building. Last entry 3.45pm. Max 20 at one time. R T B d

Grade II listed Georgian domestic building c1760, formerly part of Bedford Estate. Interior refurbished 1925-6 to form lecture hall, library and bookshop. Oak woodwork and green Doulton tiles line the staircase. c1760/1926. Entry: hall, Wynter room, Gardiner room, bookshop. Wheelchair access on request.
Tube: Holborn; Tube/Rail: King's Cross St Pancras; 8,19,25,38,55

The Wiener Library

29 Russell Square WC1B 5DP

■ Sun 1pm-4pm. Half-hourly tours. Last entry 3.45pm. Max 10 per tour. N R T d

Sensitive yet bold refurbishment of historic Grade II listed townhouse for The Wiener Library including dramatic first floor reading room, new mezzanine and ground floor exhibition spaces. Barbara Weiss Architects (refurb) 2011. Entry: Wolfson Reading Room, exhibition, archive stores.
Tube: Russell Square; Rail: Euston; 7,59,168,188

UCH Macmillan Cancer Centre ●

Corner of Capper Street and Huntley Street WC1E 6DH

■ Sat 1pm-5pm. Half-hourly tours, first come basis. Last tour 4.15pm. Max 8 per tour. D T A

The building makes clever use of its tight urban site by incorporating a highly flexible layout with a series of stacking, light-filled atria which lend a feeling of spatial generosity. A variety of art commissions are located on the building's exterior. RIBA National Award winner 2013. Hopkins Architects 2012.
Tube: Warren Street, Euston Square; Tube/Rail: Euston, King's Cross St Pancras; 10,18,30,73,134

Victorian Waterpoint ●

St Pancras Cruising Club, Camley Street N1C 4PN

■ Sat/Sun 10am-5pm. Last entry 4.30pm. Max 50 at one time. R T

At around 9m x 6m and 3 storeys high, the top floor originally contained a vast 70 cubic metre capacity cast iron water tank. This tank now forms an impressive viewing gallery; the ornate brickwork and elaborate detailing is an indication of the importance of engineering to the Victorians. Sir George Gilbert Scott 1872. Entry: ground, first and second floors (viewing platform).
Tube/Rail: King's Cross St Pancras; 30,63,73,205,214

Waterlow Park

Highgate Hill, N6 5HG

■ Sun 10am-5pm. Tour at 11.30am with Peter Barber. Last entry 4.45pm. Max 30 per tour. N D R T C P d

Grade II* listed building in Waterlow Park dating from c1580. Original Tudor wooden framework extended and 'modernised' by successive owners over the centuries. In 1889 it was given by Sir Sydney Waterlow along with the park to a trust for public benefit. Now the house is run primarily as an arts and education centre. C16. Entry: Lower, upper and long galleries and restaurant revealing the trompe l'oeil on the staircase which is usually hidden.
Tube: Archway; Rail: Upper Holloway; 143,210,214,271,W5

Working Men's College

44 Crowndale Road NW1 1TR

■ Sat tour at 10am followed by tour of neighbouring building, Theatro Technis. First come basis. Max 30 on tour. D T A

Grade II listed building (1905) has recently been revitalised with work including a new library with mezzanine internet café, reconfiguration of a gymnasium into performance space, computer/graphics studios and improved accessibility. Paul Murphy Architects (refurb) 2005/2012. Entry: library, hall, foyer, canteen.
Tube: Mornington Crescent, Kentish Town; Tube/Rail: King's Cross St Pancras, Euston; 24,46,134,214,253

WALKS/TOURS

Four Bloomsbury Squares ○

■ Meet: Sun 11am at centre of Bloomsbury Square Gardens WC1A 2RJ. Landscape tour, duration 1.5-2 hours.

Tour by LUC (Land Use Consultants) who led on the redesign and redevelopment of the garden square 17C concept within Bloomsbury Squares. Restoration would see Russell Square, Woburn Square, Gordon Square and Bloomsbury Square returned to being vibrant green spaces within the city. Landscape Institute Award winner. LUC.
Tube: Russell Square; Holborn Rail: Euston 7,59,68,168,188

Virginia Woolf in Bloomsbury ○

■ Meet: Sat 10am outside 29 Fitzroy Square W1T 6LQ First come basis, duration approx 1 1/2 hours.

A guided walk of the squares associated with Virginia Woolf and the Bloomsbury Group.
Tube: Great Portland Street, Warren Street; 18,27,30,73,88,205

Supported by

Key. A Architect on site **B** Bookshop **C** Childrens' activities **d** Some disabled access **D** Full wheelchair access **E** Engineer on site **G** Green Features **N** Normally open to the public **P** Parking **Q** Long queues envisaged **R** Refreshments **T** Toilets

City of London

See openhouselondon.org.uk/cityoflondon
to find out more about this area

1 Finsbury Circus
1 Finsbury Circus EC2M 7EB
■ Sat/Sun 10am-1pm. Half-hourly tours, first come basis. Last tour 12.30pm. Max 20 per tour. N D T A
This Lutyens Grade II listed building has been comprehensively redeveloped to provide a high quality contemporary interior, with a fully glazed spectacular atrium roof to maximize daylight and aspect. Edwin Lutyens/Gaunt Francis (refurb) 1925/2009. Entry: reception, listed staircase, atrium, 8th floor, basement, listed boardroom.
Tube/Rail: Liverpool Street, Moorgate; 43,76,100,141,205

4 Bayer House ●
Golden Lane Estate EC1Y 0RN
■ Sun 11am-5pm. Half-hourly tours, first come basis. Closed between 1pm and 2pm. Last tour 4.30pm. Max 10 per tour.
Part of Golden Lane Estate which was the first public housing to be listed. A maisonette with many of the original detailing and finishes. Chamberlin, Powell & Bon 1957. Entry: all rooms.
Tube: Barbican; Tube/Rail: Farringdon, Liverpool Street; 4,55,56,153,243

30 St Mary Axe (The Gherkin) ●
30 St Mary Axe EC3A 8EP
■ Sat/Sun 8am-3pm. Groups of 30 people every 10 mins, strictly 20 mins duration in total, first come basis. High security with bag and body scans. Bring photo ID. Open House volunteer priority entry not valid. Last tour 2.30pm. D T Q
30 St Mary Axe, affectionately known as the 'Gherkin', is a landmark curvilinear 40-storey office building in the heart of London's financial centre and is unlike any other ever conceived. With distinctive tapering form that minimises its footprint and effect on the London skyline and eco-friendly glazed skin with lightwells, the building also has a glazed dome at the top with spectacular 360-degree views across the city. RIBA Stirling Prize Winner 2004. Foster + Partners 2003. Entry: foyer, top of the building.
DLR/Tube: Bank; Tube: Aldgate; Tube/Rail: Liverpool Street; 4,8,25,100,149
www.30stmaryaxe.com

100 Victoria Embankment – 'Unilever House' ●
100 Victoria Embankment EC4Y 0DY
■ Sat 10am-5pm. First come basis, queuing outside if necessary. Last entry 4.30pm. Max 200 at one time. D T
Landmark curved Grade II listed building which has been transformed to give it a new lease of life. RIBA Award Winner 2009. James Lomax Simpson/Kohn Pedersen Fox Associates 1930/2007. Entry: lobby and ground floor atrium.
Tube/Rail: Blackfriars; 63,100,388,45

Apothecaries' Hall
Black Friars Lane EC4V 6EJ
■ Sun 10am-3pm. First come basis. Last entry 2.45pm. Max 100 at one time. Q
A courtyard building with some of the best-preserved 17C livery hall interiors, on the site of the Blackfriars Priory on which the original hall burnt down in 1666. Thomas Locke 1672. Entry: parlour, court room, great hall.

Tube: Monument; Tube/Rail: Blackfriars; 4,11,15,23,26,45,63,76,172

Bank of England
Threadneedle Street EC2R 8AH
■ Sat/Sun 9.30am-4pm. Regular tours ending in museum, many steps. Duration 30 mins. Strictly first come basis, Open House volunteer priority entry not valid. High security: bag & body scans. Last entry 4pm. D T Q
Originally by George Sampson, Robert Taylor & John Soane; rebuilt 1925-39 by Herbert Baker in imperial classical style. Soanian remnants: screen walls and reconstruction of 1793 Stock Office in Museum. Sir Herbert Baker 1925-39.
DLR/Tube: Bank; Tube/Rail: Liverpool Street; 8,11,26,43,76,133,242

Barber-Surgeons' Hall
Monkwell Square, Wood Street EC2Y 5BL
■ Sat/Sun 10.30am-4.30pm. First come basis, queuing outside if necessary. Last entry 4pm. N D T Q
The current Hall was rebuilt following the destruction of the previous building in WWII. Much larger than its predecessor it incorporates cellars and domestic offices in addition to the Great Hall, a Court Room, a Library, the Charter Room, a Reception Room and quarters for the Master. Kenneth Cross and Laurence King & Partners 1969. Entry to five rooms including the Great Hall. NB. Exhibition on history and activity of Barbers' Company, with input from the Medical Artists' Association.
Tube: St Paul's, Barbican; Tube/Rail: Moorgate, Liverpool Street; 100,56

Barbican Centre ●
Silk Street EC2Y 8DS
■ Sat tours at 12noon, 1pm, 2pm, 3pm by Barbican Tour guides, pre-book ONLY on 0845 120 7500. Meet at Advance Box Office Level G. NB. Barbican general opening hours Sat 9am-11pm/Sun 12noon-11pm. Max 20 per tour. N R T B C d
An exploration of the Barbican via the Highwalks, the history of the site, the original design and the ideas that inspired it. RIBA Award Winner 2007. Chamberlin Powell & Bon/Allford Hall Monaghan Morris (refurb) 1963/2006.
Tube: Barbican, Bank; Tube/Rail: Moorgate, Liverpool Street; 4,243,47,78,11
www.ahmm.co.uk

Bells and Belfries at St Botolph Aldgate
Aldgate High Street EC3N 1AB
■ Sat/Sun 10am-4pm. Bell ringing demonstrations and limited belfry tours on Sat only (10am-12noon & 2pm-4pm). Max 20 in belfry. Last entry 3.30pm. N R T d
Rare opportunity to see the bells and belfry of this church by the architect of Mansion House, with demonstrations taking place. Inside is London's oldest organ. George Dance the Elder 1744.
Tube: Aldgate; Tube/Rail: Liverpool Street; Rail: Fenchurch Street; 42,78,100,67,15

Billingsgate Roman House and Baths
101 Lower Thames Street EC2R 6DL
■ Sat/Sun 11am-4pm. Museum of London curators on site. T
Some of London's best Roman remains, comprising late 2C house with a 3C bath house built within its courtyard. First discovered in 1848.
Tube: Monument; Rail: Fenchurch Street, Blackfriars; 15,35,40,43,47,48,78

Bishopsgate Institute
230 Bishopsgate EC2M 4QH
■ Sat/Sun 11am-5pm. Tours by archivist on the hour, first come basis. Displays of original plans for Institute and images through time. Last tour 4pm. N R T B

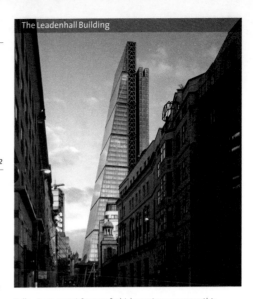

The Leadenhall Building

Following a recent £7.2m refurbishment programme, this beautifully restored historic Grade II* listed building combines elements of Arts & Crafts/Art Nouveau/Victorian architecture. Charles Harrison Townsend/Sheppard Architects (restoration) 1894/2011. Entry: library, great hall, boardroom (restricted access)
Tube/Rail: Liverpool Street; 8,26,35,42,47,48,78,149,242,344,388

Broadgate City of London: Behind the Scenes ●
Broadgate Welcome Centre, Finsbury Avenue Square, Broadgate EC2M 2PA
■ Sat 10am-5pm. First come basis. Rooftop tours of 10 Exchange Square 10.30am-3pm. Duration 15min. Max 6 per tour. E D T C
Broadgate is home to an outstanding series of buildings designed by renowned architects including Skidmore, Owings & Merrill, Arup and Make Architects and forms a unique environment in the city with public art, event spaces, shops, bars and restaurants. Current Broadgate development is due for completion in 2016 and Broadgate Circle in 2015. Arup Associates and SOM 1984-90. Pick up guide to Broadgate's architecture and see an interactive model of the campus in the Broadgate Welcome Centre. The lobbies of 155 Bishopsgate, One Broadgate and 201 Exchange House will also be open for viewing.
Tube/Rail: Liverpool Street, Moorgate, Bank; 8,11,26,35,42,47
www.broadgateestates.co.uk

Broadgate Tower ● ●
201 Bishopsgate, Primrose Street EC2M 3AB
■ Sat 10.30pm. Pre-book ONLY on www.broadgate.co.uk/openhouse Max 30 only. A
Unique opportunity to meet and hear from the Broadgate Tower architects, Skidmore, Owings & Merrill. Tour will include access to the top two floors – level 32 and 33. This 540ft high building offers London views through floor to ceiling glazing. Skidmore, Owings & Merrill 2008. Entry: 201 Bishopsgate: ground floor reception; Broadgate Tower: ground floor reception, 17th floor.
Tube/Rail: Liverpool Street; 8.35,42,47,48,149,242
www.broadgateestates.co.uk

Butchers' Hall
87 Bartholomew Close EC1A 7EB

Haberdashers' Hall

■ Sat 10am-4.30pm. First come basis. Last entry 4.30pm. N D T G d

The sixth Butcher's Hall and second on this site (1883 to present) following considerable damage from Zeppelins in 1915 and bomb damage twice during WWII. A chance to see the Hall before closure in 2015 due to major redevelopment of Barts Square. Howard Kelly 1959. Entry: Hall, Court Room, Great Hall.
Tube: Barbican, St Paul's; 4,8,25,56,242

Casper Mueller Kneer Studio, Barbican
Podium Unit, Shakespeare Tower, Barbican EC2Y 8DR
■ Sat 10am-5pm. First come basis. Last entry 4.45pm. Max 15 at one time. A

The practice's Barbican studio will be open and will display ongoing formal and material explorations, including the recent collaboration with fashion house Celine. Casper Mueller Kneer 2011. Entry: ground floor, mezzanine.
Tube: Barbican; Tube/Rail: Moorgate; 4,243,47,78,11

Chartered Accountants' Hall
Moorgate Place EC2R 6EA
■ Sat 9am-3pm. Regular tours every half an hour. Last tour 2.30pm. R T d

Late Victorian neo-Baroque building with modern-style 1970 extensions supporting 5 storeys of offices over the Great Hall. John Belcher/William Whitfield Architects 1893/1970. Entry: main and small reception rooms, great hall.
Tube/DLR: Bank; Tube/Rail: Liverpool Street, Moorgate; 76,100,133,153,214,271

City of London School
Queen Victoria Street (main entrance on river walkway nr Millennium Bridge) EC4V 3AL
■ Sat 10am-7pm/Sun 10am-4pm. Last entry half hour before close. D R T B

Founded in 1442, the new building was designed by the City architects' department on the site of the 15C Baynard Castle. Includes much Victorian art. Stuart Murphy & Tom Meddings 1986. Entry: 'Public' rooms, new theatre, Great Hall with Walker organ and model railway room. Wheelchair access via public inclinator on Peter's Hill next to Millennium Bridge.
Tube: Mansion House, St Paul's; Tube/Rail: Blackfriars; 4,11,15,26,45,63,76,100,172

CityPoint (Simmons & Simmons' offices only)
Ropemaker Street EC2Y 9SS
■ Sat 1pm-5pm. Tours at 1.15pm, 2pm, 2.45pm, 3.30pm, 4.15pm. Pre-book ONLY on http://www.ow.ly/y7v9C Please arrive 15mins before tour start.

Built in 1967 for BP, CityPoint was the first building in the City of London taller than St Paul's Cathedral. The building was refurbished in 2000, and its height increased to 127 metres. F. Milton Cashmore and H.N.W. Grosvenor/Santiago Calatrava/Sheppard Robson 1967/2000.
Tube: Moorgate, Barbican; Tube/Rail: Liverpool Street; 47

Clothworkers' Hall
Dunster Court, Mincing Lane EC3R 7AH
■ Sat/Sun 11am-4pm. Regular tours. Archive displays and design bookbindings. Max 30 per tour. D T

Home to The Clothworkers' Company, founded in 1528, Clothworkers' Hall is the sixth livery hall to stand upon the site. The interiors evoke the history of English Classicism from Wren to the present day and include portraits of notable Clothworkers – including Samuel Pepys – and a stunning set of 18C Brussels tapestries. Herbert Austen Hall 1955-58. Entry: all ceremonial rooms.
Tube: Bank, Monument, Tower Hill; Rail: Fenchurch Street; 15,25,40

Crossrail Moorgate Construction Site ●
Crossrail Moorgate site office, Moorfields EC2Y 9DT
■ Sat/Sun 10am-5pm. Hourly tours, pre-book ONLY at www.crossrail.co.uk/openhouse. Last tour 4pm. Max 20 per tour.

Crossrail experts will focus on works at the Moorgate site. Quiz the engineers and get a platform viewing of the 55m deep shaft. Mott Macdonald due 2018. ICE
Tube: Moorgate; 21,100,43,76,141
www.crossrail.co.uk/openhouse. www.mottmac.com

Custom House
20 Lower Thames Street EC3R 6EE
■ Sat/Sun 9.30am-3.30pm. Possible security bag checks. Various displays. Detection dog displays 10.30am, 12noon & 1.30pm. Last entry 3.15pm. T d

Elegant late-Georgian building partly rebuilt by Smirke after subsidence. The 58m long neo-classical Long Room was the central reporting point for all London Customs business in the 19C. David Laing/Sir Robert Smirke 1813-17/1825. Entry: west reception ground floor, main hall, long room, robing room, quay.
Tube: Tower Hill, Monument; Rail: Fenchurch Street; 15,25

Dr Johnson's House
17 Gough Square EC4A 3DE
■ Sat 11am-6.30pm. Regular short talks on architectural features of the house. Last entry 6pm. Max 80 at one time. N T B

Fine example of early 4-floor town house with original panelling, open staircase and famous 'swinging panels' on the open-plan first floor. Johnson compiled his famous 'Dictionary of the English Language' (1755) here. c1700. Entry: all areas.
Tube: Chancery Lane; Tube/Rail: Farringdon, Blackfriars; 15,26,76,341,45,63,100,172

Drapers' Hall
Throgmorton Street EC2N 2DQ
■ Sat 10am-4pm. First come basis, queuing outside if necessary. Last entry 3.30pm. T

Livery hall first built in the 1530s, twice destroyed by fire and rebuilt (1666 & 1772). Late 19C facade and opulent Victorian interior. H Williams and Sir T G Jackson 1868. Entry: principal function rooms.
DLR/Tube: Bank; Tube/Rail: Moorgate, Liverpool Street, Cannon Street; 21,26,76,242,388

Fishmongers' Hall
London Bridge EC4R 9EL
■ Sat 10am-5pm. Tours at 10am, 12noon, 2pm, 4pm. Pre-book ONLY on http://fishhallopenhouse2014.eventbrite.co.uk Max 30 per tour. Duration 30 mins.

Fishmongers' Hall is a rare example of a Greek Revival town building featuring an arcaded granite base and a riverside terrace. Designed by the architect Henry Roberts, a student of Sir Robert Smirke, the Hall's classical simplicity is contrasted by the magnificence of its interior rooms. Henry Roberts 1831-5.
Tube: Monument; Tube/Rail: London Bridge; 17,43,21,149,521

Golden Lane Estate ● ⓐ
EXHIBIT Gallery, Golden Lane Estate, 20 Goswell Road EC1M 7AA
■ Sat 10am-5pm. N D T B

Golden Lane is a Grade II listed estate, an early exemplar of British modernist architecture originally intended as accommodation for key City workers. Chamberlin, Powell & Bon 1957 onwards.
Tube: Barbican, St Paul's; Tube/Rail: Farringdon, Liverpool Street; 4,55,56,153

Gresham College – Barnard's Inn Hall
Barnard's Inn Hall, Holborn EC1N 2HH
■ Sat 10am-3pm. First come basis, queuing if necessary. D T d

Barnard's Inn dates back to at least the mid 13C. Hall contains three wooden bays dating from 15C with later linen fold wood panelling added in the 1600s. The Mercers Company organised repairs in 1932. Roman fragments below medieval hall contain unique roof timber structure. Renovated in 1990 to become the home of Gresham College. 14C.
Tube: Chancery Lane; 8,17,25,45,46,242,341,521

Guildhall
Gresham Street EC2V 7HH
■ Sat/Sun 10am-5pm. Last entry 4.30pm. d

The City's seat of municipal government since 12C. Grade I listed, rare example of medieval civic architecture with post-war extensions and rebuilding. John Croxton/George Dance the Younger 1440/1789. Entry: Great Hall.
Tube/DLR: Bank; Tube: St Paul's, Mansion House; Tube/Rail: Moorgate, Liverpool Street; 8,76,100,133,242

Guildhall Art Gallery
Guildhall Yard EC2V 5AE
■ Sat/Sun 10am-5pm. Half-hourly tours Sat 10.30am-4pm, Sun 10.30am-3pm, first come basis. N D T B

Purpose built art gallery housing City of London's art collection, built over remains of London's 2C Roman amphitheatre. Front facade is sympathetic to the Grade I listed Guildhall neighbour and uses same traditional materials – Portland stone and Collyweston stone slates. Interior uses fine finishes of marble, American elm, damask wall coverings. The newly opened City of London Heritage Gallery, built within the Guildhall Art Gallery will display some of the City's finest archival treasures and will have as its centrepiece during Open House the City's 1297 Magna Carta. This is widely acknowledged as the finest of only 17 surviving examples of the document from the 13th century. Richard Gilbert Scott 1999. Entry: art gallery and Roman amphitheatre.
Tube/DLR: Bank; Tube: St Paul's, Mansion House; Tube/Rail: Moorgate, Liverpool Street; 8,100,133,21,149

Guildhall Library
Aldermanbury EC2V 7HH
■ Sat 9.30am-5pm. Half-hourly tours 10am-3.30pm lasting 45mins, first come basis.

Purpose built over 5 floors to house printed books and manuscripts. Features include old pneumatic tubes system and 56 listed translucent pyramid roof lights. Sir Giles Scott, Son + Partners 1974. Library and basement stores.
Tube: Bank, St Paul's, Mansion House; Rail: Liverpool Street; 8,100,133,21,149

Guildhall School of Music & Drama, Milton Court
Milton Court, 1 Milton Street EC2Y 9BH
- ■ Sun 11am-6pm. Regular tours to front of house and backstage areas, first come basis. First tour 11.15am, last tour 5pm. Some performances taking place. N D R T A G

Milton Court is the Guildhall School's world-class new building, which opened in September 2013. State-of-the-art facilities include a concert hall, two theatres (proscenium arch and studio), rehearsal and foyer spaces. RHWL Arts Team and David Walker Architects 2013.
Tube: Barbican; Tube/DLR: Bank; Tube/Rail: Moorgate, Liverpool Street; 4,43,64,76,100,153

Haberdashers' Hall ●
18 West Smithfield (opposite Bart's Hospital by traffic barrier under flagpole) EC1A 9HQ
- ■ Sat 10am-4.30pm. Last entry 4pm. Max 350 at one time. D B A

Opened by the Queen in 2002 as one of the first new livery halls in the Square Mile for nearly 40 years, this is a brick building with traditional lime mortar and handsome lead roof, standing around a peaceful courtyard. American oak panelling and old artefacts and pictures provide internal finishes. Hopkins Architects 2002.
Tube: Barbican, St Paul's; Tube/Rail: Farringdon; 8,25,56,242,521

King's College London, The Maughan Library
Chancery Lane WC2A 1LR
- ■ Sat/Sun 1.30pm-5pm. Last entry 4.30pm. D R T

London's first fireproof building, built to house records of the Court of Chancery. Now renovated to house a fine university library. J Pennethorne and Sir John Taylor/Gaunt Francis Associates 1851/2001. Entry: Round room, Rolls chapel (now Weston room), some library areas.
Tube: Chancery Lane, Temple; Tube/Rail: Charing Cross; 11,15,26,172,341

Lloyd's of London ●
One Lime Street EC3M 7HA
- ■ Sat 10am-4pm. First come basis, queuing if necessary. R T Q G d

Lloyd's is the world's specialist insurance market which celebrates its 326th anniversary in 2014. Its roots can be traced back to 1688 when London's importance as a trade centre was dramatically rising. The Lloyd's building is world renowned, and a key example of British High-tech architecture. A RIBA Award Winner, the building design contained many energy efficient elements for its time which have been improved upon in recent years. Richard Rogers Partnership 1986. Entry: ground floor, lifts, 11th floor gallery, Adam room escalators.
DLR/Tube: Bank; Tube: Monument; Tube/Rail: Liverpool Street; Rail: Fenchurch Street; 25,40,35,48,344

Lloyd's Register Group ●
71 Fenchurch Street EC3M 4BS
- ■ Sat 10am-5pm. First come basis, queuing outside if necessary. Last entry 4pm. Max 250 at one time. T Q A d

Sumptuous building with many original decoration and architectural features. Sympathetically extended by Richard Rogers Partnership whose glass and steel structure soars above as a fine example of high-tech architecture. RIBA Award winner. Thomas E Collcutt/Richard Rogers Partnership 1901/2000. Entry: Rogers building entrance and reception, Collcutt building reception, library, General Committee room.
DLR: Tower Gateway; Tube: Aldgate, Tower Hill; Rail: Fenchurch Street, Liverpool Street; 40,25,15,35,47

Luckham Apartment
8 Basterfield House, Golden Lane EC1Y 0TN

- ■ Sun 1pm-5pm. Guided tours every half hour. Architect Ros Diamond on-site.

Duplex apartment in the listed Golden Lane Estate, meticulously restored, upgraded to modern living standards. Diamond Architects 1957/2013.
Tube: Barbican; 55,56,149,243,4

Mansion House
Walbrook EC4N 8BH
- ■ Sat/Sun 9am-5pm. Sat/Sun tours at 9am, 10am, 11am, 12noon, 2pm, 3pm, 4pm. Pre-book ONLY. Apply in writing by 5 Sept to Mansion House Tours, Public Relations Office, City of London Corporation, Guildhall, PO Box 270, EC2P 2EJ. Indicate preferred tour times in order. Max 4 tickets per booking. Give names of all attendees in application. Tickets allocated by draw; successful applicants notified in writing. T d

Residence of the City of London's Lord Mayor, retaining its 18C character, with superb plasterwork and wood carving. Dance, George the Elder 1739-52. Entry: public areas of house on ground & 1st floors.
Tube/DLR: Bank; Tube: Mansion House; Tube/Rail: London Bridge, Liverpool Street; 8,11,21,25,26,149,15

Masonic Temple, Andaz Liverpool Street (former Great Eastern Hotel)
Entrance on Bishopsgate EC2M 7QN
- ■ Sun 10am-4pm. Half-hourly tours. Last tour 3.30pm. Max 20 per tour. T

Grade II listed grand Victorian railway hotel refurbished with stylish contemporary interiors. Greek Masonic Temple with magnificent Grade I listed interior of marble and mahogany, built 1912 at immense cost. Charles Barry/Conran & Partners and Manser Practice 1884/2000. Entry: Temple only.
Tube/Rail: Liverpool Street; 8,11,26,35,42,47,48,78,100,133,141,149,153,214,242

Middle Temple Hall
Middle Temple Lane EC4Y 9AT
- ■ Sun 1pm-5pm. Last entry 4.30pm. Max 500 at one time. Head Gardener will lead regular tours of the award winning gardens (weather permitting). D R T B

London's finest surviving Elizabethan Hall (1562), 101ft long and 41ft wide, highly atmospheric, with double hammerbeam roof, screen and notable paintings. 17C and 20C additions. 1562. Entry: Hall.
Tube: Temple; Tube/Rail: Blackfriars; 4,11,15,26,76,341

New Street Square ○
5 New Street Square EC4A 3BF
- ■ Sat 10am-4pm. Architect will be on site to answer questions. Max 10 at one time. T A G

A dynamic destination between High Holborn and Fleet Street serving the 'mid-town' area of the City, with a substantial group of new buildings set around a public square and hosting a programme of public art and performance. RIBA Award Winner 2009. Bennetts Associates 2007/8.
Tube: Chancery Lane; Tube/Rail: Farringdon; 4,11,15,26,76,341,45,63,100,172

One New Change
One New Change EC4M 9AB
- ■ Sat 10am-6pm/Sun 12noon-6pm. First come basis. N D R T

A new retail destination and office space creating a multi-purpose commercial powerhouse for the Square Mile. Spectacular views of St Paul's on the way up in the scenic lifts, and from the roof terrace itself, the view of the Cathedral's eastern aspect is stunning. RIBA Award Winner 2011. Ateliers Jean Nouvel/Sidell Gibson Architects 2010. Entry: retail space, roof terrace.

Tube: St Paul's, Mansion House; Rail: City Thameslink; 4,8,25,56,100,172,242,521

Osborne House
12 Devonshire Square EC2M 4TE
- ■ Sat/Sun 10am-4pm. Last entry 3.30pm. Max 30 at one time. B d

Fine Grade II listed mid-Georgian house, well preserved internally with beautiful ornate cornices and plasterwork. Now headquarters of National Association of Flower Arrangement Societies. c1700. Entry: ground floor, 1st floor, lower ground floor.
Tube/Rail: Liverpool Street; 8,11,48,149,23

Painters' Hall
9 Little Trinity Lane EC4V 2AD
- ■ Sun 10am-3pm. Informal talks given by past Masters, Clerk, and Beadle. Max 80 at one time. D T

Acquired in 1532 and rebuilt in 1670 after the Great Fire, the Hall was partially destroyed in 1941 by enemy action and rebuilt in a neo-Georgian style in 1960. The original charters are of particular interest. H D Searles-Wood/Harrington (restoration) 1915/1961. Entry: court rooms, livery hall, painted chamber.
Tube: Mansion House; Rail: Blackfriars; 4,11,15,25,26,76,100,172,344

Pipers' City of London Model at The City Marketing Suite
City of London's Marketing Suite, within Guildhall Complex (entrance at 80 Basinghall Street, leading from Gresham Street) EC2V 5AR
- ■ Sat/Sun 10am-4pm. D

An overview of the latest developments and architecture in the City of London via the interactive 1:500 scale Piper model that shows the future skyline with all of the proposed new towers.
DLR/Tube: Bank; Tube: Mansion House, St Paul's; Tube/Rail: Moorgate, Liverpool Street; 43,8,21,76,133,100,242

St Botolph Building
183 Houndsditch, EC3A 7AR.
- ■ Sat/Sun 10am-5pm. First come basis, queue outside if necessary. Last entry 3.30pm. D R T

Grimshaw's design creates a highly adaptable commercial building for developers Minerva. The upper 11 floors house high specification offices, while the first and second levels provide more flexible office space with the potential to become dealing floors. The St Botolph Building is the first major office building in the UK to use TWIN® lift technology, with 16 lifts operating independently in eight shafts within the central atrium. Grimshaw 2010. Entry: Ground floor and 13th floor.
Tube: Aldgate, Aldgate East; Tube/Rail: Liverpool Street; 25,205,15,115,254

St Bride Foundation
Bride Lane, Fleet Street EC4Y 8EQ
- ■ Sat 10am-1pm/Sun 1pm-5pm. Half-hourly tours, first come basis. Display on 100 years of printing and Fleet Street's social history. Max 15 per tour. R T B d

Built as a printers' institute in the Anglo-Dutch style, with sandstone dressings, steeply pitched tiled roof and gables; many original features remain including the swimming pool and library. Robert C Murray 1894. Entry: backstage, library, theatre, bar and selected meeting rooms.
Tube: Temple, St Paul's; Rail: Blackfriars; 4,11,15,45,63,26,76,172

St Paul's Cathedral – Triforium Tour
Access is via a registration desk in the Cathedral crypt (entry via north west crypt door) EC4M 8AD
- ■ Sat 10am-4pm. Tours on the hour. Pre-book ONLY at http://www.eventbrite.com/e/open-house-london-cathedral-

triforium-tour-tickets-11682146615?aff=estw. Max 15 per tour. Duration 45mins. R T B

The tour includes: The eighteenth-century Cathedral Library; Sir Christopher Wren's first model and designs for the new Cathedral; the stunning view down the nave from the West Gallery. The tour to these special areas is via 160 steps only. We recommend that those with pre-existing medical conditions, mobility difficulties or concerns with heights do not attempt this climb. Sir Christopher Wren 1710. Entry: Triforium.
Tube: St Paul's, Mansion House; Rail: City Thameslink, Blackfriars; 242,25,4,11,15

The City Churches

There are 42 churches within the City of London. The range of styles includes Norman, pre-Great Fire medieval, Wren's masterpieces and modern re-workings, and some of the largest enclosed spaces in the Square Mile. Four churches are listed here. A full list is available from the City of London Information Centre, St Paul's Churchyard EC4M 8BX and from each church during the weekend.

St Helen Bishopsgate
Great St Helen's EC3A 6AT
■ Sat 10am-5pm/Sun 10am-5.30pm. Regular tours outlining the changing face of St Helen's building over the centuries. Quiz for children. Open House Guest Services on Sun at 10.30am and 4pm. N D R T B C
One of the few City buildings to survive the Great Fire of London and dates from 1210 onwards. Unusual double nave with the best pre-Great Fire collection of monuments in any London parish church. Damaged by two terrorist bombs in the 1990s, then extensively and controversially reordered by Quinlan Terry in 1993.
Tube: Bank; Tube/Rail: Liverpool Street

St Mary Abchurch
Abchurch Yard EC4N 7BA
■ Sat 10am-5pm. N T
A medieval church destroyed in the Great Fire was replaced by Wren with the present building, begun in 1681 and completed five years later. An internal dome forty feet across was painted in 1708 by William Snow depicting the worship of Heaven. The church fittings are mainly 17C woodwork attributed to Grinling Gibbons. Sir Christopher Wren 1686.
Tube: Bank; Tube/Rail: Liverpool Street

St Mary-le-Bow
Cheapside EC2V 6AU
■ Sat/Sun 10am-5pm. Guided tours, Sat/Sun 11am, 12.30pm, 2pm, 3.30pm. N T d
Founded by William the Conqueror's Archbishop Lanfranc in 1080 (of which the highly significant crypt largely survives), St Mary-le-Bow was rebuilt several times, most notably by Wren after the Great Fire and again by Laurence King in 1964 after WWII destruction of Wren's design. This year the church celebrates its 50th anniversary since rebuild. Home of the Bow Bells. Sir Christopher Wren/Laurence King 1670/1964.
Tube: Bank, St Paul's, Mansion House

St Stephen Walbrook
Walbrook EC4N 8BN
■ Sat 10am-5pm. N R T
Wren's own parish church with the building personally supervised by him in 1672. Within a rectangular outline is nested a square space defined by twelve columns and covered by a huge dome. Central stone altar by Henry Moore installed in 1987. Birthplace of the Samaritans. Sir Christopher Wren 1672.
Tube: Bank, Monument

The Leadenhall Building ●
122 Leadenhall Street, EC3
■ Sat 10am-5pm/Sun 10am-4pm. First come basis, queuing if necessary. Separate opening for 50 on Saturday evening via competition. Please see page 14 for details. Last entry 4pm (Sat), 3pm (Sun). T Q
This elegant office tower developed by British Land and Oxford Properties has a distinctive angled shape that has earned it the nickname 'The Cheesegrater'. At 224 metres high it is the tallest building in the City, including 46 floors of office space. It includes half an acre of public space at ground level, which represents the largest new open area in the City. Rogers Stirk Harbour + Partners 2014. Entry: lobby, lifts, level 40.
Tube/Rail: Liverpool Street 4,8,25,100,149
www.theleadenhallbuilding.com

The Salvation Army International Headquarters
101 Queen Victoria Street EC4V 4EH
■ Sat 10am-5pm. Architect-led half-hourly tours, first come basis. Max 10 per tour. Last entry 4pm. Max 70 at one time. N D R T B A
A transparent and welcoming working environment with full-height glazing and feature steel columns. Brief was to create a space 'modern in design, frugal in operation and evangelical in purpose'. Sheppard Robson 2004. Entry: Cafe 101, board and conference rooms, 1st floor chapel.
Tube: Mansion House, St Paul's; Tube/Rail Cannon Street, Blackfriars; 388,4,11,15,17,26

The Temple Church
Fleet Street, EC4Y 7BB
■ Sun 1pm-5pm. First come basis. Last entry 4.30pm. N D B
Built by the Knights Templar, the order of crusading monks. The Church is in two parts: the Round and the Chancel. The Round Church was consecrated in 1185, its circular design is reminiscent of the Church of the Holy Sepulchre at Jerusalem. Restored by Wren after 1666 and later Smirke and Burton, the walls and ceiling being decorated in the high Victorian Gothic style.
Tube: Temple; Rail: Blackfriars, Charing Cross; 4,11,15,26,76,341

Tower 42
25 Old Broad Street EC2N 1HQ
■ Sat 10am-3pm. Tours every 45 minutes. Pre-book ONLY on www.tower42.com/news.php. Last tour at 2:30pm. Max 20 per tour. T d
The City of London's tallest occupied building, consisting of three hexagonal chevrons, at 601ft was the first to break previous restrictions on tall buildings in London. During a comprehensive refurbishment in 1995, a new glass and steel entrance hall was built on Old Broad Street and the external steel cladding was replaced. Richard Seifert & Partners/GMW Partnership/Fletcher Priest 1981/1995. Entry: ground floor entrance, level 42.
DLR/Tube: Bank; Tube/Rail: Liverpool Street

Trinity House
Tower Hill EC3N 4DH
■ Sat 10am-1pm. Last entry 12.30pm. Max 60 at one time. D T
Fine late Georgian exterior with interior painstakingly reconstructed after destruction by incendiary bomb in 1940. Good fittings, statues and works of art from original building. Samuel Wyatt/Albert Richardson 1796/1953. Entry: 1st floor ceremonial rooms.
Tube: Tower Hill; Rail: Fenchurch Street; 25,15,40

Watermen's Hall
18 St Mary-at-Hill EC3R 8EF
■ Sat tours at 9am, 10.30am, 12noon, 1.30pm. Pre-book ONLY in writing enclosing SAE to The Assistant Clerk giving name(s), address & tel no. Max 2 tickets per application. State tour time preferred. Tickets sent by post. Max 30 per tour. d
Only remaining Georgian Hall in the City of London, and perfect example of domestic architecture of the period. William Blackburn 1780. Entry: Parlour, Freemen's room, Court room, Silver room, hallway.
Tube: Monument; Rail: Fenchurch Street; 15,25,35,45

WALKS/TOURS

City Alleyways
Meet: Outside Guildhall Art Gallery, Guildhall Yard EC2V 5AE
■ Sat/Sun 10.30am-3.30pm. Regular departures every 45minutes from 10.30am. Duration approx 2 hours. First come first served. Last tour 3.30pm. Max 30 per walk.
A walk through some of the old alleyways of the City of London, passing Wren churches, Livery Halls and many little known historical places, finishing at the Monument. Walk led by qualified City of London guide.
DLR/Tube: Bank; Tube: Barbican, St Paul's; Tube/Rail: Moorgate; 8,21,23,25,43,133,141,242

Sculpture in the City 2014 ●
■ Meet: Sat 10am or 12noon at corner of 99 Bishopsgate and Wormwood Street EC2M 3XF. 2 tours, pre-book ONLY on pro.events@cityoflondon.gov.uk. Duration 1½ hours. www.cityoflondon.gov.uk/sculptureinthecity. Max 25 per tour.
Sculpture in the City is an urban sculpture park of over 10 contemporary art installations by leading international artists set within the iconic towers of the City of London.
Tube/Rail: Liverpool Street; 149,344,35,48,8,26

St Paul's Cathedral and Paternoster Square ●
Meet: Outside Guildhall Art Gallery, Guildhall Yard EC2V 5AE
■ Sat/Sun 10.30am-3.30pm. Regular departures every 45minutes from 10.30am. Duration approx 1½ hours. First come first served. Last tour 3.30pm. Max 30 per walk. T Q
A walk past St Mary-le-Bow church to St Paul's Cathedral, Temple Bar and Paternoster Square ending at St Martin's Ludgate on Ludgate Hill. Walk led by qualified City of London guide.
DLR/Tube: Bank; Tube: Barbican, St Paul's; Tube/Rail: Moorgate; 8,21,23,25,43,133,141,242

The City and the River Thames
Meet: Outside Guildhall Art Gallery, Guildhall Yard EC2V 5AE
■ Sat/Sun 10.30am-3.30pm. Regular departures every 45minutes from 10.30am. Duration approx 2 hours. First come first served. Last tour 3.30pm. Max 30 per walk. T Q
A walk down to the river Thames at Southwark Bridge, and then along the riverside path under London Bridge and through the former Pool of London to the Tower of London. Walk led by qualified City of London Guide.
DLR/Tube: Bank; Tube: Barbican, St Paul's; Tube/Rail: Moorgate; 8,21,23,25,43,133,141,242

Supported by

CITY
OF
LONDON

Key. A Architect on site **B** Bookshop **C** Childrens' activities **d** Some disabled access **D** Full wheelchair access **E** Engineer on site **G** Green Features
N Normally open to the public **P** Parking **Q** Long queues envisaged **R** Refreshments **T** Toilets

Croydon

See openhouselondon.org.uk/croydon
to find out more about this area

Whitehorse Manor Infant and Junior Schools

Airport House
Purley Way, Croydon CR0 0XZ
■ Sat/Sun 11am-3.30pm. Regular tours of Croydon Airport Visitor Centre, first come basis. Facilities at adjacent 1928 Aerodrome Hotel also open to public. N R T C P d
Unique Grade II listed 1928 building with rusticated features. Entrance facade features three 1 1/2 storey arched windows. Booking hall with glass domed atrium. Earliest example of an air traffic control tower. 1928.
Rail: East Croydon, West Croydon, Purley; 119,289 to Croydon Colonnades/Croydon Airport

Bernard Weatherill House ●
8 Mint Walk, Croydon CR0 1QQ
■ Sat 9am-5pm. Half-hourly tours, first come basis. Max 12 per tour. T R D G
New public service building provides 20,000sqft of BREEAM Excellent accredited modern commercial accommodation spread over 13 storeys combined with a public access facility at ground floor in the heart of the building. Features include energy efficient twin-skin glazed facades, occupiable roof terraces and exposed internal concrete soffits. 2013. Entry: Ground Floor, 8th and 12th floor.
Rail: East Croydon, West Croydon; 60,166,405,412,466

Connected Croydon – On Site ●
Pick up a map at Croydon Visitor Centre, adjacent to East Croydon Station CR0 1LF
■ Sat 11am-3.30pm. Architects and designers connected with Croydon projects on site at various locations as per map.
Connected Croydon is a £50m programme of public realm and infrastructure projects currently being delivered in central Croydon, transforming London's biggest borough. Design teams involved including East, John McAslan and Partners, Hassell, We Made That, muf, Project Centre, Studio Weave, Jan Kattein, Allies and Morrison.
Rail: East Croydon, West Croydon; 60,166,405,412,466

Croydon Town Hall and Clocktower complex
Katharine Street CR9 1ET
■ Sat 10am-1pm. Access to Town Hall by timed tour only at 10am, 11am, 12pm, 1pm. Duration 45mins. Last tour at 1pm. D R T C
Guided tours of the original Town Hall built 1895 (Henman), including Council Chamber and meeting rooms. Clocktower complex opened in 1993 (Tibbalds) and Museum of Croydon, including creative family workshop, opened in 2006 (FAT) open to the public, 10.30am – 5pm. Charles Henman/Tibbalds/FAT 1895/1993/2006. Entry: Town Hall including Council chambers and meeting rooms, Clocktower and Museum of Croydon.
Rail: East Croydon, West Croydon; Tram: 1,2,3; 109,119,154,197,466

Fairfield Halls
Park Lane CR9 1DG
■ Sat tours at 9.15am, 11am, pre-book ONLY by email to johnspring@fairfield.co.uk. Duration 1 1/2 hours. Max 16 per tour. T d
One of the few surviving examples of a major early post-war concert hall and arts centre in the country and is reputed for its excellent acoustics. Built in a style similar to the Royal Festival Hall, it houses a 1794 seat concert hall and 763 seat theatre. Robert Atkinson & Partners 1962.
Rail: East Croydon; 50,109,166,264,312

Old Palace, Croydon
Old Palace Road, Old Town CR0 1AX
■ One Sat tour at 11am. First come basis. Max 30 per tour. T P
Grade I listed manor house, former summer residence of Archibishops of Canterbury from 13C-18C. Elizabeth I and other monarchs regularly visited. Contains one of the finest great halls with its original roof from 1440s. 13C.
Tram: Church Street, Reeves Corner; Rail: East Croydon, West Croydon

Priory School
Hermitage Road SE19 3QN
■ Sat 10am-5pm. Hourly tours. Last entry 4.30pm. D R T A G
School for 132 students of secondary age with severe/complex needs on a lovely wooded site with teaching and therapy facilities. Cafe and gallery, life skills flat, and woodland creative arts hub. Curl la Tourelle Architects 2014. Entry: All main teaching spaces and grounds.
Tube: Crystal Palace; Rail: Gypsy Hill; 196,249,417,432,450,468

Quaker Adult School Hall
60 Park Lane, Croydon CR0 1JE
■ Sat 11am-4pm/Sun 2pm-5pm. R T B
Constructed and opened in 1908, this Grade II listed building was designed for educational purposes by William Curtis Green, who later contributed designs for Hampstead Garden Suburb and the Dorchester Hotel. The building is notable for its innovative open roof structure and simplicity of design. It remains in a remarkably original condition. William Curtis Green 1908.
Rail/Tram: East Croydon; 60,64,190,197,405

Shirley Windmill
Postmill Close, Upper Shirley Road, Croydon CR0 5DY
■ Sun 12pm-5pm. Regular tours, first come basis. Duration 1 hr. Last tour 4pm. N R T B P d
The present brick tower windmill was built in the mid 1850s to replace a post mill destroyed by fire. Now renovated to near-working condition, it is the only surviving windmill in Croydon. 1854-5. Entry: windmill.
Rail/Tram: East Croydon; 466,130,119,194,198

St Matthew Croydon
Chichester Road, Croydon CR0 5NQ
■ Sat 2pm-5pm. First come basis. Last entry 4.45pm. N D R T P
Church centres on striking panels of stained glass by John Hayward – a brilliant wall of colour which depicts various parables. David Bush 1965-72. Entry: Church and foyer.
Rail: East Croydon 64, T33

The Stanley Halls
12 South Norwood Hill SE25 6AB
■ Sat 10am-5pm. Tours taking place, first come basis. Max 10 per tour. Last entry 4.45pm. Max 20 at one time. R T d
A public hall, theatre and gallery in grand Edwardian style. Grade II listed, Stanley made fun of the Victorian style with grand ornamentation. William Ford Robinson Stanley 1903. Entry: full access including behind the stage.
Rail: Norwood Junction; 75,157,196,197,410

Thornton Heath Library ●
109 Brigstock Road, Thornton Heath CR7 7JB
■ Sat 9am-5pm. Tours 12noon, and 2pm, first come basis. Max 20 per tour. N D T
A Carnegie library (1914) with some fine original architectural features that has been recently refurbished to create a light, welcoming and spacious environment whilst its dramatic facade now makes a bold statement upon the High Street. A new white concrete and glass pavilion provides a highly visible reading area complemented by rich oaking flooring and comfortable seating. On the lower level a rejuvenated children's library leads to a community garden. FAT (pavilion) 1914/2010.
Rail: Thornton Heath; 198,250,450

Whitehorse Manor Infant and Junior Schools ●
Whitehouse Road, Thornton Heath CR7 8SB
■ Sat 10am-1pm. Half hourly tours, first come basis. Last entry 12.30pm. A D T
A stunning gold-fronted expansion to an existing primary school. The design builds on the character of the existing Victorian school building and brings togther a fragmented site with a series of inventive material and formal interventions. Hayhurst and Co 2014. Entry: classrooms, grounds.
Overground: Norwood Junction; Rail: Thornton Heath

Whitgift Almshouses
North End, Croydon CR9 1SS
■ Sat tours at 10.30am, 11.45am, 2pm, 3.15pm, pre-book ONLY on 020 8680 8499. Last tour 3.15pm. Max 30 per tour. T
Tudor almshouses dating from 1596 and founded by the Archbishop of Canterbury John Whitgift. Chapel and Courtyard with original 16C clock. 1596. Entry: courtyard, chapel, audience chamber.
Rail: East Croydon; tram/buses to central Croydon

WALKS/TOURS

The Seven Hills of Croydon
■ Meet: Sun 12noon at new Landsdowne Walk entrance, East Croydon Station CR0 1LF. First come basis. A
After WWII, Croydon transformed from a market town on London's outskirts into a 20C super suburb. This architect-led tour offers a walk around England's Alphaville via its 7 hills.
Rail/Tram: East Croydon, West Croydon; 50,109,154,194,197

Supported by

CROYDON
www.croydon.gov.uk

Ealing

See openhouselondon.org.uk/ealing
to find out more about this area

Ealing Abbey
Charlbury Grove W5 2DY
■ Sun 1pm-5pm. Tours on the hour. Last tour commences at 4pm. Exhibition also available for visitors. N D R T B P
Building began in 1897 and a century later is almost completed. Architects include F and E Walters (1897 – the nave), Stanley Kerr Bates (1960 – transepts), and Sir William Whitfield (1997 – choir and apse). Entry: church, adjacent centre.
Tube/Rail: Ealing Broadway; E2,E9,297

Ealing Town Hall, Council Chamber and Mayor's Office
New Broadway W5 2BY
■ Sun 11am-4pm. Tour, talk and refreshments with past Ealing Mayors, approx every 30mins. Last entry 3.30pm. Max 20 per tour. E D R T P
Late Victorian ragstone Gothic with sumptuous Imperial staircase. Recently restored. Charles Jones (West Wing) 1888. Entry: Council Chamber, Nelson room, Mayor's parlour.
Tube/Rail: Ealing Broadway; 65,83,112,207,297,E1,E2,E7

Horizons Education and Achievement Centre for Care Leavers
15 Cherington Road, Hanwell W7 3HL
■ Sun 10am-5pm. Half-hourly tours, first come basis. Last entry 4.30pm. Max 10 per tour. D R T A G
Developed from the refurbishment of derelict former depot buildings, a unique project providing a community resource for young people leaving the care of Ealing Council. RICS London Building of the Year 2008. Gavin Leonard 2007.
Tube: Hanwell, Ealing Broadway; 207,607,427,E3,83

Magic Box
44 Mount Park Road W5 2RU
■ Sun 10am-5pm. Half-hourly tours. Last entry 4.30pm. Max 15 per tour. A G
Dramatic and energy-efficient transformation of a large double-fronted house in a conservation area. A 2-storey contemporary 'magic box' penetrates the rear of the building. Scandinavian inspired cedar cladding and shutters create a dynamic facade opening to the garden. Double-height atrium floods light into heart of house. Finishes include long board flooring, exposed brick and polished concrete. KSKa Architects 2013. Entry: ground floor, garden.
Tube/Rail: Ealing Broadway; 207,607,E2,E9
www.kska.co.uk

Notting Hill & Ealing High School
2 Cleveland Road W13 8AX
■ Sun 10am-1pm. Last entry 12.45pm. R T G P d
6-storey extension with underground sports hall and large double-height flexible performance/assembly/drama zone, plus dance studio. Remodelling works to ground floor entrance, reception and library forming clear, light and open route leading s to 3 storey high foyer. Sustainable features include sedum roof, solar power. Ellis Williams Architects 2013.
Tube/Rail: Ealing Broadway; 297,E10

Pitzhanger Manor House
Walpole Park, Mattock Lane W5 5EQ
■ Sat/Sun 11am-5pm. Sat tours 12noon 'Plans for Pitzhanger Manor', 3pm 'Historical Tour'. Sun tours 12noon, 3pm 'Maid's Tour', 2pm 'Historical Tour'. First come basis. E N T C G d
Former country residence designed by Sir John Soane for his own use, set in the grounds of Walpole Park. Grade I listed building, expressing Soane's idiosyncratic architectural style with its stripped classical detail, radical colour schemes and inventive use of space and light. 1800-10. Entry: Manor House.
Tube/Rail: Ealing Broadway; 65,83,207,427,607

South Acton Children's Centre
Castle Close, off Park Road North W3 8RX
■ Sat 10am-3pm. Tours every 45 mins. Last tour 2.30pm. D T P
Reworking of two existing 1960s nursery schools creates an integrated children's centre in partnership with Sure Start, providing new playroom extensions, foyer, community and staff facilities, centred on a new landscaped play area. Llowarch Llowarch 2006. Entry: all areas except offices.
Tube: Acton Town; Rail: South Acton; 266,E3,207,607,440

St Mary the Virgin Perivale
Perivale Lane, Perivale UB6 8SS
■ Sat/Sun 10am-5pm. Regular tours. Sat 11.30am & 3pm talk by Professor Alan Gillett OBE on history of church and the town of Ealing. Max 30 at one time. N D R B A
Grade I listed 12C church with later additions, now an arts centre run by The Friends of St Mary's. 12C.
Tube: Perivale; Tube/Rail: Ealing Broadway; E2,E9

The White House
46 Park View Road W5 2JB
■ Sat/Sun 10am-5pm. Half-hourly tours, queuing outside if necessary. Last entry 4pm. Max 14 at one time. R T Q A P d
Louis XV Palace set in own private gardens, based on owner's grandmother's palace in Poland. 'Marble Arch' entrance – the first in London for 200 years. Extremely opulent interiors with marble, gold cornices and chandeliers. John Zylinski 2009.
Tube/Rail: Ealing Broadway; 207,83,112,607

Villa Caroisla
25C Montpelier Road W5 2QT
■ Sat/Sun 1pm-5pm. Hourly tours, first come basis. Last entry 4.30pm. Max 10 per tour. A G d
Contemporary take on backland living in Ealing, 4 bedroom eco-home is built using timber framing and passive solar design techniques. Nick Baker Architects 2012.
Tube/Rail: Ealing Broadway; 226
www.nickbakerarchitects.co.uk

Westside Young People's Centre
Churchfield Road, Ealing W13 9NF
■ Sun 10am-5pm. Tours. Last entry 4.30pm. D R T A G
Westside is a pioneering facility, evolving the concept of a creative ideas 'factory', to bring together innovative programmes that support young people in every aspect of their lives. RIBA London Award Winner 2013. Gavin Leonard MA, DipArch 2012. Entry: all areas.
Rail: West Ealing; 207,607,427,83,E2,E3

WALKS/TOURS

A Ruskinian Walk Through Shared Heritage
■ Meet: Sat 12noon, Sun 2.30pm at Chiswick Business Park, Building 3, 566 Chiswick High Road W4 5YA. 2 hrs. Led by South Acton Residents Action Group. R T G d W
Walk begins at RIBA Award-winning and wildlife-themed Chiswick Park (RSH+Partners 2000). Other focal points are

Magic Box

homes of William Willett, builder and originator of Daylight Saving Time, and Richard White, Co-founder of Law Society; resident governed South Acton Estate, birthplace of painter Patrick Caulfield, with its Children's Centre (Llowarch Llowarch 2006), 'Stamford Brook' to view Woodlands Park Ice House.
Tube: Chiswick Park, Acton Town; Tube/Rail: Gunnersbury

Brentham Garden Suburb ●
■ Meet: Sat/Sun 10.30am at The Brentham Club, 38 Meadvale Road W5 1NP. Duration approx 2 hours. N R T P
Britain's first co-partnership garden suburb, first houses built 1901. Parker and Unwin's plan introduced 1907, mainly Arts and Crafts style, organised by The Brentham Society.
Tube: Hanger Lane; Tube/Rail: Ealing Broadway; E2,E9

Ealing Common Walk
■ Meet: Sat 2.30pm at Hanger Lane end of Inglis Road by the Open House Banner W5 3RN. Duration up to 2.5 hours. Cancellation if heavy rain. R d
Walk across Ealing Common taking in the range of architectural styles. Highlights: the home of a Wimbledon champion and the death mask of a prime minister.
Tube: North Ealing, Ealing Common; Tube/Rail: Ealing Broadway; 83,112,207,427,607

Hanwell Flight of Locks & Three Bridges ●
■ Meet: Sat/Sun 1pm, 2pm, 3pm, 4pm at The Fox pub, Green Lane W7 2PJ. Duration 1 hour. N D R P
Restored flight of locks at Hanwell is a scheduled ancient monument, while Three Bridges is a unique stacked intersection of road, rail and canal, and Brunel's last major railway project. Walks led by experts in local waterway history. Isambard Kingdom Brunel 1859.
Tube: Boston Manor; Rail: Hanwell; E8,83,207,195

Walpole Park and Rickyard ●
Walpole Park, Mattock Lane W5 5EQ
■ Sun 12-3pm, tour at 11am of the park with Landscape Architect J+L Gibbons and architects from Jestico + Whiles. First come basis meeting at Pitzhanger Manor. Last entry 2.45pm. A D G T
Newly restored Walpole Park with reinstated Regency landscape, setting for Sir John Soane's Pitzhanger Manor and new facility, the Rickyard. Jestico + Whiles/J+L Gibbons 2014.
Tube/Rail: Ealing Broadway; 65,83,207,427,607

Supported by

Ealing
www.ealing.gov.uk

Key. A Architect on site B Bookshop C Childrens' activities d Some disabled access D Full wheelchair access E Engineer on site G Green Features
N Normally open to the public P Parking Q Long queues envisaged R Refreshments T Toilets

Enfield

See **openhouselondon.org.uk/enfield**
to find out more about this area

Chickenshed Theatre
Chase Side, Southgate N14 4PE
- Sat 2.30pm-6pm. Entry via hourly tours on the half hour, first come basis. Last tour 5.30pm. Max 20 per tour. E D T P

Modern, accessible purpose-built theatre, housing the unique, inclusive Chickenshed. Building houses Rayne Theatre auditorium, Studio Theatre, dance studio, restaurant, backstage and wardrobe areas, with amphitheatre & garden outside. Renton Howard Wood Levin Partnership 1994/1999.
Tube: Cockfosters, Oakwood; 298,299,307,699

Christ Church Southgate and the Minchenden Oak Garden
Waterfall Road, Southgate N14 7EG
- Sat 11am-6pm/Sun 11am-6.30pm. Hourly tours, first come basis. Material available for self-guided tours. Children's activities in the church and choral evensong on Sunday at 6.30pm. D R T C P

Grade II listed church and grounds with fine collection of pre-Raphaelite stained glass windows by Morris & Company. Minchenden Oak Garden – containing ancient Pollarded oak more than 800 years old. George Gilbert Scott 1861-1862.
Tube: Arnos Grove, Southgate; Rail: New Southgate, Palmers Green; 121,298,299, W6

Forty Hall & Estate ●
Forty Hill, Enfield EN2 9HA
- Sat 11am-4pm. First come basis. N D R T B C G P

Recently fully refurbished in partnership with HLF, this Grade I listed Carolean mansion hall 1629-32 is set in a fine estate within the Forty Hill village conservation area. Home of Sir Nicholas Rainton, Lord Mayor of London 1632-33, Master of the Haberdashers' Guild. Last private owners were the Parker-Bowles family. Now fully accessible with gift shop and cafe. Landscape restoration to start Dec 2013. Changing programme of high quality arts and crafts exhibitions. 1629-32. Entry: ground & 1st floors.
Rail: Enfield Town; 191 (10 mins walk)
www.fortyhallestate.co.uk

Friends Meeting House & Burial Grounds
Winchmore Hill Quaker Meeting, 59 Church Hill N21 1LE
- Sat/Sun 2pm-5pm. Last entry 4.15pm. Max 20 at one time. R T P d

Established 1688, the present Grade II listed building of yellow stock brick dates from 1790. A simple building with central double door under a bracketed cornice hood, flanked by large sash windows, with delicate glazing bars. Panelled interior. Curved entrance wall allowed carriages to turn in the narrow lane. Notable burials in the grounds. Entry: ground floor.
Tube: Southgate; Rail: Winchmore Hill; 125,329, W9

King George V Pumping Station ●
Swan & Pike Road, Enfield EN3 6JH
- Sat/Sun 10am-5pm. Regular tours, first come basis. Last entry 4pm. P

Designed to pump water from the River Lee into the George V reservoir, the building houses three old disused gas Humphrey pumps, and two electric pumps currently in service. William Booth Bryan 1913.
Tube: Turnpike Lane then 121 bus; Rail: Enfield Lock

North London Hospice

Lamb's Cottage
Church Street N9 9DY
- Tours Sunday at 11.00am, 12noon, 2.00pm, 3.00pm, first-come basis. P d

Late 17C timber-frame house with early 18C facade and period features. Grade II* listed. Last home of Charles and Mary Lamb. 17C/18C. Entry: house, garden.
Rail: Edmonton Green; 102,144,149,192,259, W6, W8

Myddelton House
Bulls Cross, Enfield EN2 9HG
- Sat 10am-4pm. First come basis. Last entry 3.30pm. N D R T

Neo-classical yellow Suffolk stock brick villa with mid 19C extension to north and west front. Victorian conservatory to side. Adam style ceilings to ground floor. George Ferry and John Wallen 1818. Entry: ground floor only, selected rooms, tearoom, museum, gardens. NB. Does not include entry to contemporary buildings.
Rail: Turkey Street; 217,317

North London Hospice ●
Barrowell Green, Winchmore Hill N21 3AY
- Sat 10am-12.30pm. Architect-led tours every 30mins. Pre-book ONLY, contact Tanith Slay: openhouse@ahmm.co.uk. Max 20 per tour. D T A P

The hospice offers specialist palliative care for people with life limiting illnesses. By using brick, timber floors, slim window profiles and mute colours, it is designed to feel airy and instil a domestic sense of wellbeing. Sustainable features include ground source heat pump and solar collection. Civic Trust 2012 Special Award for Sustainability. RIBA National Award 2013. Allford Hall Monaghan Morris/Elliott Wood Partnership 2012.
Tube: Southgate; 125,329
www.ahmm.co.uk | www.elliottwood.co.uk

Parish Church of St Andrew Enfield
Market Place, Enfield EN2 6LL
- Sat 9.30am-3.30pm/Sun 12pm-3pm. First come basis. N D R T

Listed church with fine organ case and monuments. 13C-19C.
Tube: Oakwood; Rail: Enfield Town, Enfield Chase; 121,191,192,231, 307,310,313,317,329,377

Priory Hospital North London
Grovelands House, The Bourne N14 6RA
- Tours taking place on Sat. Pre-book ONLY via nickhazell@priorygroup.com. Last tour 12noon. Max 30 per tour. E N R T G P d

Grade I listed neo-classical villa designed for Walker Gray. Grounds laid out by Repton. Elegant trompe l'oeil breakfast room. John Nash 1797. Entry: main house, ground and 1st floors, ice house.
Tube: Southgate; Rail: Winchmore Hill; 121,125,299, W6

Suburban Studio

Royal Small Arms Factory
RSA Island Centre, 12 Island Centre Way, Enfield (off A1055 Mollison Avenue) EN3 6GS
- Sat 10am-5pm. Regular tours, first come basis. Former Arms Factory employees present to answer questions. N T P d

Grade II listed arms factory closed to public for 170 years, buildings on site included a church (the original font is displayed in the central courtyard at the Centre) a police station and a school. Now restored as mixed-use village and commercial centre. Clock c1783. Shepheard Epstein Hunter (refurb) 1854-58/2000.
Rail: Enfield Lock; 121,491

Salmons Brook ●
Montagu Recreation Ground, Montagu Road N9 0EU
- Sat 10am-1pm. First come basis. Short presentation and guided tour. There will be a health and safety visitor induction. Please wear appropriate footwear. E N G d

Landscaped river improvement as part of a major flood alleviation scheme. Up to 40,000 cubic metres of water storage on the recreation ground in times of flood and raised defences on the upstream river reach, Salmons Walk. River corridor habitat and public realm improvements. Further flood storage upstream in Grange Park. CH2M HILL 2014.
Tube: Tottenham Hale

St Mary Magdalene Church
Windmill Hill, Enfield EN2 8QH
- Sat 10am-5pm. First come basis. D R T P

Fine Victorian Gothic church with impressive windows and painted chancel. Paintings by Buckeridge and Westlake 1897 and restored 2012. William Butterfield 1883. Entry: church & vestry.
Tube: Oakwood; Rail: Enfield Chase, Enfield Town; 121,307,377,313

Suburban Studio
11 Second Avenue, Bush Hill Park EN1 1BT
- Sat/Sun 1pm-5pm. Architect-led tours at 3pm. Last entry 4pm. Max 12 per tour. D T A G P

Timber-clad garden studio and refurbishment to Victorian house, with stunning garden – a courtyard addressed by 'floating' studio and house. Garden is a folded timber landscape with heated paddling pool, a sand pit and a fire pit. Sustainable features include a green roof. Winner of the NLA Don't Move, Improve Award for best home extension 2011/12. Ashton Porter Architects 2011. Entry: studio, garden, library.
Rail: Bush Hill Park

Supported by

●AJ Library Building   ●Green Exemplar   ●Landscape/Public realm   ●Infrastructure/Engineering   ■Open Saturday   ■Open Sunday   ■Open Saturday and Sunday

Greenwich

See **openhouselondon.org.uk/greenwich**
to find out more about this area

21st Century Span House
2 Corner Green, Blackheath SE3 9JJ
- Sat 10am-5pm. Pre-book ONLY on
  friend@friendandcompany.co.uk. Please note you will
  be required to remove shoes before entering the house.
  Last entry 4.30pm. E A
50th anniversary reimagining of 1959 Eric Lyons interior via a
modern timber/glass design along original Span principles.
Exhibited at the RA and NLA, published in Wallpaper*,
Architects' Journal. Friend and Company 2009. Entry: House,
garden, tea house.
Rail: Blackheath; 54,89,108,202,380

Charlton House
Charlton Road SE7 8RE
- Sun 10am-4pm. Self guided tours. Last entry 4pm. D R T P
London's only surviving great Jacobean mansion, set in
Charlton Park, red brick with white stone dressings and
beautifully proportioned hall. A Newton/Norman Shaw
(restored) 1607-12/late 19C. Entry: Minstrel Hall, Long Gallery,
Grand Salon, White Room, Newton, Prince Henry & Dutch
Rooms, Old Library, grounds.
Rail: Charlton; 53,54,422

Devonport Mausoleum
National Maritime Museum, Romney Road SE10 9NF
- Sat/Sun 10am-4pm. Timed tours, meet at the grand
  square. Visitors to follow signage placed outside National
  Maritime Museum main entrance to collect/register for
  ticket. d
Handsome mausoleum (1750) in former Royal Navy cemetery,
restored 1999 by the University of Greenwich. Many
interesting plaques. 1750. Entry: cemetery and mausoleum. NB.
See also Old Royal Naval College & Dreadnought Library.
*DLR: Cutty Sark for Maritime Greenwich; DLR/Tube: Canary
Wharf; Rail: Greenwich, Maze Hill; 177,180,188,199,286*

Dreadnought Library
West Gate (King William Walk), or East Gate, (Park Row), and
Romney Road crossing, Maritime Greenwich Campus SE10 9LS
- Sat/Sun 11am-4pm. Ticketed hourly tours, meet at the
  grand square. Last tour 4pm. Max 10-15 per tour. T d
Formerly Dreadnought Seamen's Hospital, now library and
computer centre of the University of Greenwich. Glazed
corridors with fine views, and steel and glass courtyard roof.
James 'Athenian' Stuart/Dannatt Johnson (refurb) 1764-
68/1999. Entry: guided tour routes only. NB. See also Old Royal
Naval College & Devonport Mausoleum entries.
*DLR: Cutty Sark for Maritime Greenwich; DLR/Tube: Canary
Wharf; Rail: Greenwich, Maze Hill; 177,180,188,199,286,386*

Eltham Lodge
Royal Blackheath Golf Club, Court Road SE9 5AF
- Sun 10am-12.30pm. Tours on the hour, first come basis. Last
  tour 12noon. Max 25 per tour. N R T P
Grade I listed Caroline mansion built for Sir John Shaw.
Refurbished 18C with fine plaster, ceilings and staircase. Club
house of Royal Blackheath Golf Club since 1923. Hugh May
1664. Entry: main hall, lounges, staircase, dining room, Glennie
room, O'Shea room.
Rail: Mottingham; 124,126,161

Emirates Air Line tour with ICE ●
Meet: Emirates Greenwich Peninsula, Emirates SE10 0DX
- Sat 10am-1pm. Sat tours at 10am, 11am, 12noon. Pre-book
  ONLY by email on EALgroups@macemacro.com. Max 18
  per tour. E D R T
Tour exploring the civil engineering achievements of the
construction of the cable car and the regeneration of the Royal
Docks. Led by the Emirates Air Line project director and ICE
regeneration and sustainability expert.
Organised by ICE. 2012. **ice**
Tube: North Greenwich

Greenwich Heritage Centre
Artillery Square, Royal Arsenal, Woolwich SE18 4DX
- Sat 9am-5pm. First come basis. N D R T B C P
The Heritage Centre houses information about Greenwich,
past and present. Exhibition about the Royal Arsenal site, its
history and buildings.
Rail/DLR: Woolwich Arsenal; 53,54,180,161,422

Greenwich Yacht Club
1 Peartree Way SE10 0BW
- Sat/Sun 1pm-4pm. Regular architect-led tours, first come
  basis. Club members available for discussion. Annual art
  show and members' bar. Max 40 at one time. N R T A P d
Contemporary timber and aluminium building using existing
pier, offering unique views of the river, The O2 and Thames
Barrier. Frankl + Luty 2000. Entry: main club house, sail loft,
boat yard. Outbuilding adapted as art show venue with
panoramic river views.
*DLR: Cutty Sark for Maritime Greenwich; Tube: North
Greenwich; Rail: Greenwich then 161,177,180,472,486, 108,
286,422*

Old Royal Naval College
**Admiral's House, King William Court, Painted Hall & Chapel,
Queen Anne Court, Queen Mary Court**
West Gate (King William Walk), or East Gate (Park Row) and
Romney Road crossing. Entry from pier via Cutty Sark Gardens
SE10 9NN
- Admiral's House, Sat/Sun 10.30am-4pm. Half-hourly talks.
  T d. King William Court. Sat/Sun 11am-4pm. Access via hourly
  tours only. Meet on Grand Square. Last tour 3.30pm. Max
  20 per tour. d. Painted Hall, Chapel, Discover Greenwich.
  Sat/Sun Tours at 12noon & 2pm and 'Meet Hawksmoor'
  12pm,1pm, 2pm, 3pm. Meet on Grand Square for tours. N T d.
  Queen Anne Court. Sat/Sun 11.30am-4pm. Access via hourly
  ticketed tours only. Meet on Grand Square. Last tour 3.30pm.
  Max 20 per tour. d. Queen Mary Court. Sat/Sun 11.30am-4pm.
  Access via hourly ticketed tours only. Meet on Grand Square.
  Last tour 3pm. Max 20 per tour. d
  Audio Described Tours taking place as part of our VocalEyes
  partnership, see p.14 for details.
Admiral's House – Designed by Wren in 1695, finished by
Hawksmoor and Vanbrugh as the Royal Hospital for Seamen
and later the Royal Naval College (1873-1998). Managed by the
Greenwich Foundation, housing Trinity Laban Conservatoire of
Music and Dance. Grade I listed.
Designed for Charles II in 1661 with later works by Wren
and John Webb, the Admiral's House has been undergoing
extensive refurbishment since 2001. John Webb 1672/1696.
Bookshop and refreshments only available in Discover
Greenwich.
King William Court – Wren-designed building completed
under the direction of Hawksmoor and Vanbrugh, 1698-1712.
Original wood panelling, refurbished by Dannatt Johnson
in 2001 for University of Greenwich. Wren/Hawksmoor/
Vanbrugh/Dannatt Johnson (refurb 2001) 1698-1712/2001.

Painted Hall, Chapel, Discover Greenwich – Painted Hall
ceiling by Sir James Thornhill 1708-27. Neo-classical Chapel
designed by James 'Athenian' Stuart 1789. Sir James Thornhill/
James Stuart/Sir Aston Webb/Wren 1712/1789. Entry: Painted
Hall, Chapel, 'Discover Greenwich' Visitor Centre featuring an
exhibition on the architecture of the site.
Queen Anne Court – Wren & Hawksmoor building, completed
1749 when Thomas Ripley built the pavilions facing the river.
Highlights include council board room, grand staircase and
restored Portland stonework. Refurbished in 2000 by Dannatt
Johnson for University of Greenwich. Wren & Hawksmoor/
Dannatt Johnson (refurb 2000) 1749/2000.
Queen Mary Court – Last major building on the site (1751).
Original layout, timber panelling, barrel vaulting and Portland
stone. Refurbished in 2000 by Dannatt Johnson for University
of Greenwich. Dannatt Johnson (refurb) 1751/2000.
*DLR: Cutty Sark for Maritime Greenwich; Rail: Greenwich, Maze
Hill; Riverboat: Greenwich Pier; 177,180,188,199,286,386*

Painting Studio ●
86 Greenwich South Street SE10 8UN
- Sat 1pm-5.30pm. First come basis. Last entry 5.30pm. A d
A painting studio for Joan Burr and a permanent exhibition
space for ceramics by Graham Burr set at the rear of an 1840s
house within the Ashburnham Triangle Conservation area.
Howel-Evans and Opher Architects 2013.
Tube: Greenwich DLR, Deptford Bridge DLR; Rail: Greenwich

Rachel McMillan Nursery School and Children's Centre
McMillan Street, Deptford SE8 3EH
- Sat 10am-2pm. First come basis. T d
Opened in 1914, Rachel McMillan pioneered the benefits of an
open-air environment for children. Named by English Heritage
as the most significant nursery school of its date in England.
London County Council Architects with Herbert Baker
designed memorial 1914-33.
Rail: Deptford; DLR: Deptford Bridge; 188,199,47

Ravensbourne ● ●
6 Penrose Way, Greenwich Peninsula SE10 0EW
- Sat 10.30am-3pm. Tours at 10.30am, 11.30am, 1pm, 2pm,
  3pm, first come basis. Children must be accompanied by an
  adult. Max 30 per tour. D T
In this stunning new location at Greenwich Peninsula, an
inspirational new learning and teaching environment, over
a series of interlinked floors around an impressive central
atrium. Opened in September 2010 it houses the latest digital
media and design technologies, an HDTV studio, prototyping
facilities and collaborative workspaces. BREEAM Excellent
status with sustainable features including green roof, solar
hot water and biomass boiler. RIBA Award Winner 2011. Foreign
Office Architects 2010. Entry: all areas.
*Tube: North Greenwich; Thames Clipper Riverboats;
188,108,129,161,486,422,472*

Royal Greenwich UTC ●
765 Woolwich Road SE7 8LJ
- Sat 1pm-3pm. Tour taking place at 1.15pm. Cindy Walters
  onsite. D T A
Royal Greenwich UTC offers GCSE, A-level and technical
courses and specialises in engineering and construction. It
consists of a refurbished warehouse and new three-storey
block with photovoltaics visible on the roof. Walters & Cohen
Architects 2013.
*DLR: North Greenwich, Woolwich Arsenal; Rail: Charlton,
Woolwich Dockyard; 12A,161,177,180,472*

Key. A Architect on site **B** Bookshop **C** Childrens' activities **d** Some disabled access **D** Full wheelchair access **E** Engineer on site **G** Green Features
N Normally open to the public **P** Parking **Q** Long queues envisaged **R** Refreshments **T** Toilets

Royal Greenwich UTC

Royal Museums Greenwich: Queen's House
National Maritime Museum, Park Row SE10 9NF

■ Sat/Sun 10am-5pm. Regular tours, first come basis. Last entry 4.30pm. Max 20 per tour. N D T
The opulent summer villa of Charles I's queen, Henrietta Maria, this is the first purely classical Renaissance building in Britain which reflected a turning point in English architecture. Much of the original splendour of the house is retained, including the 'grotesque-style' painted ceiling of the queen's bedchamber, the 'Tulip Stairs', original painted woodwork of the Great Hall and its finely laid 1635 marble floor. Inigo Jones 1637. Entry: Queen's House, including the great hall and orangery.
DLR: Cutty Sark; Rail: Greenwich, Maze Hill; Riverboat: Greenwich Pier; 177,180,188,199,286,386

Ruins of Garrison Church – RA Barracks
Grand Depot Road SE18 6XJ

■ Sat 10am-5pm. Last entry 4.45pm. Max 40 at one time. T
Built to serve the Royal Artillery community posted at Woolwich. Bombed in 1944 and now a ruin. It is the VC memorial for the Royal Artillery and has some very fine mosaics. Thomas Wyatt 1863.
DLR/Rail: Woolwich Arsenal

Scape Greenwich
Bear Point, 2 East Parkside SE10 0FQ

■ Sat 10am-4pm. First come basis. Architect-led tours at 10am, 12pm and 2pm. T D A
Scape Greenwich provides 280 rooms for students at Ravensbourne College of Design and Communication. The precast concrete-clad building champions offsite manufacture, using repetition to maximise character and construction efficiency. Allford Hall Monghan Morris 2014.
Tube: North Greenwich; Rail: Emirates Greenwich Peninsula; 108,129,132,422,486
www.ahmm.co.uk

Severndroog Castle
Castle Wood, Shooters Hill SE18 3RT

■ Sun 10am-4pm. Tours every 30mins, first come basis. Duration 25 mins. R T P
Grade II* listed triangular brick Georgian tower with Gothic windows sited in Oxleas Woods. Standing 63ft tall in woodlands it offers spectacular panoramic views across the capital. Built to commemorate the 1755 conquest of the Malabar Coast by Sir William James. Twenty five years after closing its doors to the public, restoration work has been completed and the newest visitor attraction in Greenwich and London has re-opened its doors. Richard Jupp 1784.
DLR: Woolwich; Rail: Eltham, Woolwich Arsenal, Welling; 89,122,161,244,486

St Alfege Church, Greenwich
Greenwich Church Street SE10 9BJ

■ Sat 9.30am-4pm/Sun 12pm-4pm. Sat: 11.30am and 2.30pm crypt tour. 1.05pm lunchtime recital. Sun: 12noon and 2pm crypt tour. Crypt tours pre-book ONLY on 020 8853 0687. D T
Magnificent Baroque church, Grade I listed, gutted by fire in 1941 and restored by Sir Albert Richardson to original design. Many original features. Burial site of Thomas Tallis, organist/choirmaster (1505-85). Nicholas Hawksmoor 1714. Entry: ground floor (not tower or crypt).
DLR: Cutty Sark for Maritime Greenwich; Rail: Greenwich; 177,180,188,199,286,386

Thames Barrier & Information Centre ●
1 Unity Way SE18 5NJ

■ Sat/Sun 10.30am-5pm. Special display – How the Thames Barrier was designed, built and how it works. Last entry 4.30pm. Max 40 at one time, entrance subject to availability. R T
Information centre sited by the dramatic Thames Barrier (1984), explaining its function, construction and future. Rendel, Palmer and Tritton 1984. Entry: information centre only.
Tube: North Greenwich, then 161,472; Rail: Charlton, then 177,180,472,161

The Fan Museum
12 Crooms Hill SE10 8ER

■ Sat 10am-5pm. Max 50 at one time. N D R T B C
Carefully restored Grade II listed early Georgian town houses, retaining the principal original domestic scale and character and architectural features, including elegant facades, staircase with 'barley sugar' baluster, panelled rooms, and front courtyard with wrought iron railing and gates. It now houses the only museum devoted to the art and craft of fans. John Savery/John Griffiths (conversion) 1721.
Entry: museum, Orangery.
DLR: Cutty Sark for Maritime Greenwich; Rail: Greenwich, Maze Hill; 177,180,188,286,386,199

Trinity Hospital
Highbridge SE10 9PS

■ Sat 10am-4pm. First come basis. R T B
Early 17C riverside almshouse. Quadrangle with battlemented entrance facade and early 19C tower. (Organised by the Warden of Trinity Hospital.) 1613 and early 19C.
Entry: courtyard, chapel.
Tube: North Greenwich; DLR: Cutty Sark for Maritime Greenwich; Rail: Maze Hill; 177,180,188,199,286,386

Tudor Barn and Gardens
Well Hall Pleasaunce, Well Hall Road SE9 6SZ

■ Sat/Sun 10am-5pm. Tours 11.30am, 2.30pm, first come basis. N R T P d
16C restored barn set in grounds with medieval moat, only surviving building from 'Well Hall', home to Margaret Roper, daughter of Sir Thomas More, Lord High Chancellor of England under Henry VIII. Now a function venue, restaurant and cafe set in beautiful gardens. Former home of children's author E Nesbit. Civic Trust award-winner. c1525.
Rail: Eltham; 286,161,132

University of Greenwich, Stockwell Street ●
Stockwell Street, Greenwich SE10 9JN

■ Sat/Sun 11am-4pm. Tours taking place, pre-book ONLY by emailing conferences@grc.ac.uk. Max 20 per tour. D R T
Shortly home to departments including architecture and landscaping, it features one of the largest landscaped roofs in the world. Heneghan Peng Architects 2014. Entry: whole building and roof gardens.
DLR: Cutty Sark; Rail: Greenwich; 286,177,180,188

Winter Gardens Avery Hill
University of Greenwich, Mansion Site, Bexley Road, Eltham SE9 2PQ

■ Sat/Sun 10am-4pm. Ticketed tours every hour, tickets available on the day on site. N T P
Built in 1889 this Grade II listed glass house is second only to the Palm House at Kew in size and height. T W Cutler 1891. Entry: Winter Gardens only.
Rail: Falconwood, New Eltham; 132,286

Woolwich Arsenal Clock Tower ●
Duke of Wellington Avenue SE18 6SS

■ Sat/Sun 1pm-5pm. Regular talks/tours with engineer and architect of restoration, first come basis. Max 10 per tour. E A
When the historic clocktower at the Royal Woolwich Arsenal suffered almost total destruction, Ramboll's conservation engineers employed analysis and traditional detailing to maximise its restoration. 3D modelling, repair and testing of salvaged elements allowed over 85% of the original materials to be restored and reinstated. A&Q Partnership/Ramboll (restoration) 2011.
DLR/Rail: Woolwich Arsenal
www.ramboll.co.uk

Woolwich Town Hall
Wellington Street SE18 6PW

■ Sat 9am-4pm. First come basis. N D T d
Florid Edwardian Baroque design with domed entrance hall, grand staircase and stained glass windows, a great example of civic architecture of the time belonging to the Classical tradition rather than the Gothic Revival favoured outside London. Alfred Brumwell Thomas 1906. Entry: Victoria hall, council chamber, committee rooms, public hall.
Rail/DLR: Woolwich Arsenal; 51,53,54,96,99,122,161,380,422

Supported by

ROYAL borough of GREENWICH

visit**GREENWICH**

Hackney

See **openhouselondon.org.uk/hackney**
to find out more about this area

30 Crown Place ●
30 Crown Place EC2A 4ES
■ Sat/Sun 10am-5pm. Hourly tours, first come basis. Last tour 4pm. Max 10 per tour. D T A
Striking 16-storey glass landmark office building with 3 terraces. An unusual form with a distinctive profile. Sustainable features include PV cells at roof level and ground floor geo-thermal heat source. Horden Cherry Lee Architects 2009. Entry: ground, 7th, 14th, 15th & 16th floors.
Tube/Rail: Liverpool Street; 23,149,214,242,271

51 Southborough Road
51 Southborough Road E9 7EE
■ Sat 10am-5pm. First come basis. Informal tours taking place. Last entry 5pm. T A G
A full renovation and side extension to a Victorian terrace. ZCD Architects 2013.
Tube: Mile End; Rail: Homerton, Hackney Central; 277,425

52 Whitmore Road
52 Whitmore Road N1 5QG
■ Sat 1pm-5pm. Practice Director Andrew Waugh on site. Last entry 4pm. A G d
This mixed use building on Regents Canal illustrates capabilities of the cross-laminated timber structure. The vast column-less, double-height photography studio which stretches 9mx23m will be open, as will the canalside walkway and deck. Within the studio there will be an opportunity to explore an installation by artist Dan Tobin Smith. Waugh Thistleton Architects 2012. Entry: photographer's studio.
Tube/Rail: Old Street

Adelaide Wharf
118/120 Queensbridge Road (at junction Whiston Road) E2 8PD
■ Sat 10am-4pm. Hourly architect-led tours. Pre-book ONLY on Megan.van-niekerk@firstbase.com. N.B no tour at 1pm. Last tour 3pm. Max 20 per tour. D T A G
A pioneering mixed tenure residential scheme with some workspace extruded into a prototype block, folded to create a U-shaped court. Each apartment has an outdoor room part hung, part cantilevered out over the streets, courtyard or canal. The facade is composed of layers of roughly sawn larch that makes reference to the warehouses of packing crates that once occupied this site. RIBA Award Winner 2008. Allford Hall Monaghan Morris 2008.
Rail: Hoxton, Haggerston; 26,48,55,394
www.ahmm.co.uk

Arcola Theatre
24 Ashwin Street E8 3DL
■ Half-hourly tours. Sat 10am-1.30pm & 5pm-6pm, Sun 12pm-5pm. Last entry Sat 1pm, 5.30pm, Sun 4.30pm. Max 8 per tour. N R T G
Multi-award winning professional theatre with a strong community and sustainability ethos relocated to an emerging Hackney cultural quarter. Sustainability features include minimal intervention, large scale materials reuse and renewable energy technology. Refurbishment client-led with support from Cragg Management 1868/2011. Entry: Studio 1/2 (professional theatre), Bloomberg Arts Lab, Arcola Energy Lab.
Rail: Dalston Kingsland, Dalston Junction; 149,242,38,277,243

Balcorne Street
53 Balcorne Street E3 7AY
■ Sat 1pm-10pm/Sun 1pm-5pm. First come basis, queuing outside if necessary. Sat evening drinks with architect and owner. Last entry 9.45pm (Sat) and 4.45pm (Sun). A
Timber frame rear extension to traditional Victorian terraced house, designed to make good use of cheap materials within a tight budget. Tom Kaneko 2013. Entry: ground floor and garden.
Tube: Mile End, Hackney Central; 277,425,55,26,48
www.tomkaneko.com

Calouste Gulbenkian Foundation
50 Hoxton Square N1 6PB
■ Sat 10am-5pm. Queuing outside if necessary. N T G d
The Foundation's artistic and social interests are at the heart of the design. A dramatic intervention to the first floor slab allows natural light from the rooflight above to permeate into the ground floor. Sustainable features include exposed concrete structure to provide thermal mass. Theis + Khan 2009. Entry: ground floor.
Tube/Rail: Old Street; Overground: Hoxton; 21,26,35,43,47

Cardinal Pole Catholic School
205 Morning Lane E9 1LG
■ Sat 10am-3pm. Half-hourly tours, first come basis. Displays. Last entry 2.30pm. D R T A G
New-build school on challenging new inner-city site which unites school on one site for the first time in its 54-year history. Sustainable features include PV panels, air-source heat pump. RIBA Awards Shortlisted 2013. Jestico + Whiles 2012.
Tube: Hackney Wick, Homerton

Clapton Girls' Academy
Laura Place E5 0RB
■ Sat 10am-12.30pm. Half-hourly tours. Talks/displays on history of Academy and its buildings. Last tour 12noon. Max 25 per tour. R T d
New and sensitively refurbished Edwardian buildings providing an enhanced physical environment. Sustainable features throughout. Hackney Design Award winner 2010. Also open Clapton Portico (Brady Mallalieu Architects 2006) – significant Grade II listed local landmark refurbished into a new teaching school. Jestico + Whiles 2010.
Tube: Clapton; 38,48,55,56,106,253,254,308,425,488

Clissold House
Clissold Park, Stoke Newington Church Street N16 9HJ
■ Sun 11am-4pm. Last entry 3.30pm. D R T C
Recently restored elegant late 18C brick villa with six-column Doric veranda on the west facade, set in parkland and a rare survivor of its type. Built for Jonathan Hoare by his nephew. Joseph Woods/Richard Griffiths (refurb) 1793/2012. Entry: house interior, function rooms, reception spaces.
Tube: Manor House, Finsbury Park; Rail: Stoke Newington, Canonbury; 141,341,106,393,73

Clonbrock Road
33 Clonbrock Road, N16 8RS
■ Sat/Sun 1pm-5pm. Hourly tours. Max 10 per tour. A
Internal reconfiguration, refurbishment and 2-storey front brick cantilevered extension to 1957 yellow stock residence. Lipton Plant Architects 2014.
Overground: Dalston Junction, Dalston Kingsland, Canonbury; 73,476,149,349

Dalston C.L.R. James Library & Archives
Dalston Square, Dalston Lane E8 3BQ
■ Sat 9am-5pm/Sun 1pm-5pm. Tours Sat 11am & Sun 2pm, duration 1 hour, first come basis. Archives closed Sun except for tour. Max 15 per tour. N D T
4-storey multi-purpose, state of the art library and archives building. Earle Architects 2011. Entry: quick picks, adult, children's and study areas.
Rail: Dalston Junction, Dalston, Kingsland; 30,38,56,242,277

Free Space Wenlock Barn Estate ● ●
■ Meet: Sat/Sun 12noon for tours outside Wenlock Court, New North Road N1 7PL. 12pm-5pm. A day of open gardens including estate tours and film screening. Tour begins at 12noon and screening at 3pm. Hosted by community engagement group Fourthland, includes discussion on community-led design. Max 25 per tour. R A G
3 growing initiatives on the Wenlock Barn Estate. Each celebrate the long term benefits of growing food locally, the use of local materials and the importance of resident led design and construction.
Tube/Rail: Old Street; 76,394,141,21,271

Gingerbread House ●
104 Balcorne Street E9 7AU
■ Sat 10am-5pm. Tours every 45 mins. Last entry 4.45pm. Max 20 per tour. A d
Award-winning new build house on site of former box factory with clever use of volumes and daylight, despite the physical constraints of a small urban plot. Laura Dewe Mathews 2012.
Tube: Hackney Central, Mile End; 277,425,388,26,30

Growing Communities' Eco Classroom ● ●
Allen's Gardens, corner of Bethune and Manor Roads N16 5BD
■ Sun 10am-5pm. Last entry 4.30pm. Max 30 at one time. N T C G d
Wooden building with green roof, water harvesting, composting toilet and warmcell insulation, set in an organic market garden with a deck over pond and wildlife area. Garden grows zero-food-miles organic salad leaves for local community-led box scheme whilst classroom provides shelter for gardeners as well as a learning space. Constructive Individuals (Peter Smithdale) 2004. Entry: main building, surrounding organic market garden.
Tube: Manor House; Rail: Stoke Newington; 106,67,76,73,149

Hackney Empire
291 Mare Street E8 1EJ
■ Pre-book tours ONLY and visit www.hackneyempire.co.uk for further details. Max 20 per tour. D R T
Exuberant Grade II* listed auditorium and the most perfect example of Edwardian variety theatre remaining in London. Refurbishment restored the interiors, added to the fly-tower and provided new back-stage areas, topping it off with the sign 'Hackney Empire' in massive terracotta 6.4m tall capital letters. Frank Matcham/Tim Ronalds (refurb) 1901/2004. Entry: foyer, auditorium, stage door, annex.
Tube: Bethnal Green; Rail: Hackney Central; 253,106,30,48,55

Hackney Marshes Centre
Hackney Marshes, off Homerton Road E9 5PF
■ Sat tours at 4pm & 5pm with project design director, first come basis. Max 20 per tour. N D R T A P
Community hub for Hackney Marshes comprising changing rooms, cafe and education facility. Housed in a welcoming, inclusive structure that is embedded within the landscape, culture and history of the marshes. RIBA, Civic Trust and Hackney Design Award Winner 2012. Stanton Williams 2010.
Rail: Hackney Wick, Homerton; W15

Key. A Architect on site **B** Bookshop **C** Childrens' activities **d** Some disabled access **D** Full wheelchair access **E** Engineer on site **G** Green Features **N** Normally open to the public **P** Parking **Q** Long queues envisaged **R** Refreshments **T** Toilets

Haggerston School
Weymouth Terrace E2 8LS
- Sat 1pm-4.30pm. Hourly tours from 1.30pm, first come basis. Tours led by parents who are architects. Presentation running in the hall and visuals of the school from past and present. Last tour 3.30pm. Last entry 4pm. Max 10 per tour. D T G

Grade II listed school, retaining many original features. Distinctive for large amount of timber used in construction and contains some of Goldfinger's most handsome public interiors, including bush hammered concrete and coffered ceilings. Major refurbishment recently completed as part of BSF programme. Erno Goldfinger & Hubert Bennett/Avanti Architects 1963-65/2011. Entry: main hall, reception areas, some classrooms, grounds.
Tube: Hoxton; Tube/Rail: Liverpool Street; 48,55,242,243

Kingsland Basin Moorings
Kingsland Basin Moorings (via towpath) N1 5BB
- Sun 10am-5pm. Regular tours, first come basis. Max 5 per tour. N R T G d

Small is beautiful! 6-foot narrowboats provide individual design solutions for living and working. A unique community and shared open space, and a sustainable living concept. 1984. Entry: communal areas, interiors of 3-4 individual boats.
Rail: Haggerston, Dalston Junction; 67,149,242,243,394

Lauriston School
Rutland Road E9 7JS
- Sat 10am-3pm. Regular tours, first come basis. Last tour 2.45pm. Max 15 per tour. D R T A G P

New build primary school. The raised bridge structure maximises external space for play on this restricted site and creates a large covered all-weather area. Ann Griffin with Meadowcroft Griffin Architects 2011.
Tube: Bethnal Green, Mile End; Rail: Hackney Central; 388,425,277

Levitt Bernstein Studio
1 Kingsland Passage E8 2BB
- Sat 2pm-5pm. Regular tours around studio by Levitt Bernstein staff, with models on display from arts, educational and residential sectors. Last entry 4.30pm. T A d

Levitt Bernstein are architects, landscape architects and urban designers and are opening the doors to their Dalston studio. Levitt Bernstein. Entry: reception area.
Tube: Dalston Junction, Dalston Kingsland; 38,56,30,277

National Centre for Circus Arts
Coronet Street N1 6HD
- Sun 10am-5pm. Tours every 45mins with presentation on history of circus architecture, first come basis. Last entry 4.30pm. Max 12 per tour. T C d

Housed in the former Shoreditch Electricity Generating Station. Opened in 1896 it was the first to successfully generate electricity from the destruction of domestic waste. Converted in 1994, an extension was added in 2006. E Manville/ Philip Lancashire (conversion)/ Tim Ronalds (extension) 1896/1994/2006. Entry: circus training halls.
Tube/Rail: Old Street, Liverpool Street, Shoreditch High Street; 55, 26,243,35,47,48,67,78,149,242

Oto Projects
1-7 Ashwin Street, E8 3DL
- Sat/Sun 10am-5pm. First come basis. Designer Frances Edgerley onsite with daytime material experimentations. Music performances throughout the weekend. N D R T A G

Oto project space is a rehearsal and performance space for the experimental music venue cafe OTO. The building occupies an unused site in Dalston and, uses the rubble found onsite to create a monolithic single space. Assemble 2013.
Tube: Dalston Junction, Dalston Kingsland; 30,149,242,76,56, 243,67,236,488,277

Our Lady's Convent High School
6-16 Amhurst Park, N16 5AF
- Sat 10am-1pm. First come basis, queuing outside if necessary. Last entry 12.30pm. T A

The four-storey building – complete with a roof-top multi-use games area above the sports hall – not only maximises the available external play spaces but also accommodates significant level changes across the site. The design also facilitated the two-phase construction process, which was required to make the required decant scenario possible. The chapel and its lightwell are clad in timber to highlight the significance of the space. Jestico + Whiles 2012.
Tube: Manor House, Seven Sisters; Rail: Stamford Hill, Tottenham Hale

Restored Historic Almshouse at the Geffrye Museum
Kingsland Road E2 8EA
- Sat 10.30am-4pm. First come basis. NB Closed 12:30-2pm. Last entry 4pm. Max 16 at one time. T B C

Grade I listed 18C almshouse restored to original condition. Richard Halsaul and Robert Burford/ Branson Coates Architecture 1714/1998. Entry: almshouse, museum, gardens. NB. Disabled access to museum & gardens only.
Rail: Hoxton; 67,149,242,243,394

Rivington Place
Rivington Place EC2A 3BA
- Sat 12pm-6pm. Hourly tours, first come basis. Last entry 5.30pm. Max 15 per tour. N D R T B

First permanent visual arts space dedicated to global diversity and home to Iniva (Institute of International Visual Arts) and Autograph ABP, inspired by African art and architecture as well as contemporary art and music. RIBA Award Winner 2008. Adjaye Associates 2007. Entry: ground, 1st & 2nd floors.
Tube/Rail: Old Street, Liverpool Street, Shoreditch High Street; 43,48,55,149,205,242,243

Round Chapel
Lower Clapton Road (junction with Glenarm Road) E5 0LY
- Sun 11am-4.30pm. Last entry 4.15pm. Max 30 at one time. D R T B

Grade II* listed Nonconformist chapel for 1,000 people. Described by Pevsner as 'one of the finest Nonconformist buildings in London'. Horseshoe plan, innovative cast-iron columns and tracery, restored as a centre for the performing arts. (Organised by Hackney Historic Buildings Trust.) Henry Fuller & James Cubitt 1875.
Tube: Bethnal Green; Rail: Hackney Downs, Hackney Central; 38,48,55,106,253, 242,254,394,488

Saint Barnabas Mission Hall and Church
Shacklewell Row E8 2EA
- Sat 10am-5pm/Sun 10am-1pm. Mission Hall redevelopment architects Pete Jennings and David Cawston of Piercy and Co Architects. T A d

Refurbishment of 1890 church hall building comprising new kitchen, toilets and mezzanine and extensive repair and restoration of the building fabric and ground floor hall spaces. Sir Charles Reilly/ Piercy and Co Architects 1890/2013.
Rail: Dalston Kingsland, Dalston Junction; 67,76,149,242

Self-built Straw Bale Building, Hackney City Farm ●
Hackney City Farm, 1a Goldsmith's Row E2 8QA
- Sat/Sun 11.30am-4pm. Last entry 3.45pm. R T G d

Built with a 'no-compromise' policy, all materials used are environmentally sound. Straw bale walls, lime and clay render; other components are reclaimed/recycled materials. Also see 'Magnificent Container', a NLA award-winning project space for Magnificent Revolution and competition-winning Sill to Sill scaffold board shop extension. 2007. Entry: farm site.
Tube/Rail: Bethnal Green, Liverpool Street; Rail: Cambridge Heath, Haggerston; 26,55,48

St Augustine's Tower
The Narroway, off Mare Street E8 1HR
- Sat 11am-5pm. Architectural exhibition. N R B d

Grade I listed, remaining tower of parish church, with working late 16C/early 17C clock. New exhibition of Hackney's history. Extensive views from roof. Organised by Hackney Historic Buildings Trust. 13C. Entry: all areas including clock chamber and roof. NB. Very narrow winding stairs.
Tube: Bethnal Green; Overground: Hackney Central; 30,38,48,55, 106,236,242,253,254,276,277,394,D6,W15

St Mary's Old Church, Stoke Newington
Stoke Newington Church Street N16 9ES
- Sat/Sun 10am-5pm. First come basis, displays on the history of the building. Last entry 4.30pm. N D R T C A

16/19/20C fabric, with 18C monuments. Redeveloped in 2013 as a community arts centre by Matthew Lloyd Architects. Sir Charles Barry 1829. Entry: church, graveyard. Sun: live music plus creative activities for all ages.
Tube: Manor House, Arsenal; Tube/Rail: Finsbury Park; Rail: Stoke Newington; 73,106,141,393,476

Stoke Newington School Media Arts and Science College
Clissold Road N16 9EY
- Sat 10am-1pm. Regular tours. pre-book ONLY on Dianne. thompson@sns.hackney.sch.uk Last entry 12.45pm. Max 8 per tour. N T C d

Recently refurbished as part of the BSF programme and designed in collaboration with SNS students. The design provides new facilities including new window installations for better lighting, exterior canopies with integrated photovoltaic cells and restored flooring in classroom settings. Shepheard Epstein Hunter 2003.
Overground: Dalston Junction, Dalston Kingsland; Rail: Stoke Newington; 73,106,475,493

Sutton House, The National Trust
2 & 4 Homerton High Street E9 6JQ
- Sat/Sun 12pm-5pm. Tours at 1pm, 2pm and 3pm. Last entry 4.30pm. Max 25 per tour. R T B d

Rare example of Tudor red-brick house in East End. 18C alterations and later additions. Many early features including original linenfold panelling. Sir Ralph Sadleir 1535.
Tube/Rail: Bethnal Green, Hackney Central; 30,38,48,55,253

The Bridge Academy, Hackney
Laburnum Street E2 8BA
- Sat 10.30am-3.30pm. Hourly architect-led tours, 11am-3pm, first come basis. Informal talks and Q&A sessions with teaching staff, educationalists and students planned. E D T A

Situated on a brownfield site adjacent to the Regents Canal, the innovative vertical school concept is shaped in response to its microclimatic setting. Conceived as a wrap of teaching spaces shaped around a multi-level 'heartspace', the design uses open galleries rather than corridors to promote social

cohesion, natural daylight and ventilation together with magnificent roof spaces for performance, learning and play. BDP 2008.
Tube/Rail: Old Street, Haggerston; 67,243,149,242,394

The Castle Climbing Centre
Green Lanes N4 2HA
■ Sat/Sun 10am-7pm. Tours at 1pm, 2pm and 3pm, first come basis. Last entry 6.30pm. N R T B G P d
Water-pumping station built in the Scottish Baronial style, converted for use as an indoor climbing centre. William Chadwell Mylne/Cook Townsend 1856/1995/2013. Entry: centre, tower (normally closed).
Tube: Manor House; Tube/Rail: Finsbury Park; 141,341

The Dalston Eastern Curve Garden ●●
13 Dalston Lane E8 3DF
■ Sat/Sun 11am-6pm. Tours Sat/Sun: 2pm and 4pm. Last entry 5.45pm. Max 20 per tour. N R T G
Popular community garden in area lacking in green public space featuring biodiversity planting. Created on abandoned railway land, includes large wooden pavilion for events and workshops. Hackney Design Award Winner 2010 & 2011, Landscape Institute President's Award 2011. muf/J & L Gibbons/EXYZT 2010. Entry: garden, pavilion, pineapple house.
Rail: Dalston Junction; 30,56,277,38,242

The Garden School Hackney
The Garden, Wordsworth Road N16 8BZ
■ Sat/Sun 1pm-5pm. First come basis, queuing if necessary. Last entry 4.30pm. D T A
New SEN school for LB Hackney, designed around two courtyards. RIBA Regional Award Winner 2014. Gollifer Langston Architects 2013.
Rail: Dalston Kingsland; 30,38,67,73,76

The Redundant Architects Recreation Association ●
Unit 2, Grosvenor Way, Clapton E5 9ND
■ Sat 1pm-6pm. Half-hourly tours, first come basis. Max 20 at any one time. Sat 5pm speakers from The Mill, a RARA community project and the Boat Building Colony. Model-making for children. Max 20 at any one time. R T C A G P d J
This industrial unit in East London provides flexible and affordable workspace to the downtrodden creative. The RARA offers an antidote to the 9-5 – total creative freedom. Green design features include allotment, water recycling, home-brewed ale. East London Design Bureau 2008. Entry: workshop, sleeping pod, spillout space, brewery, the colony corner, cinema.
Rail: Clapton; 38,48,55,253,425

The Studio
2 Nevill Road N16 8SR
■ Sat 11am-5pm. Regular tours, first come basis. Last entry 4.30pm. Max 5 per tour. Q A G
A unique mews property which has undergone a complete retrofit where both architects designed and built the entire scheme themselves. The small house has a surprising amount of playful elements with sliding walls, hidden storage and contrasting materials. Bradley Van der Straeten Architects 2013. Entry: all areas.
Tube/Rail: Highbury & Islington; 73,476,149

Village Underground
54 Holywell Lane EC2A 3PQ
■ Sat 9.30am-6.30pm. First come basis, queuing outside if necessary. T Q A G
Recycled tube train carriages make affordable artists' studios on reclaimed land on top of an abandoned railway viaduct.

Sustainable features include solar power. Auro Foxcroft & Nicolas Laurent 2007.
Tube/Rail: Liverpool Street, Old Street, Shoreditch High Street; 149,243,67,55,8

Waddington Studios ●
127 Church Walk N16 8QW
■ Sun 1pm-5pm. Hourly tours, pre-book ONLY by email on benedetta.r@featherstoneyoung.com. Max 8 per tour. T A d
New build development of artist and photographic studios within a mews streetscape. The design, developed in close collaboration with the artist and owners, enhances the industrial aesthetic of the mews through its form and use of patterned Corten steel panels. Featherstone Young Architects 2013. Entry: studios only.
Tube: Highbury & Islington; Rail: Dalston Junction; 73,476

Writer's Shed ●
53 Greenwood Road E8 1NT
■ Sat 10am-5pm. First come basis, architects onsite. Last entry 4.30pm. A
Designed for a children's author and illustrator, the Writer's Shed is conceived as a fairytale hut at the bottom of the garden. Weston Surman & Deane 2013.
Tube: Dalston Junction; 38,242,277

WALKS/TOURS

Clissold Park ●
■ Meet: Cafe seating area (Ground Level), on South side of Clissold House N16 9HJ. Sat tour 10am, pre-book ONLY on marketing@lda-design.co.uk/0207 467 1470. Max 30 per tour.
The restoration returned the park's design to its original simplicity by enhancing key features, introducing new areas to meet modern expectations and enriching its biodiversity.
Tube: Manor House, Finsbury Park; Rail: Stoke Newington, Finsbury Park; 67,73,106,141 From Brownfield to Green Fields: A Walking Tour
■ Meet: Sat 10am outside 17-19 Great Eastern Street, EC2A 3EJ First come basis, tour led by architectural designers Laura Rowland and Claire Beard. Max 20 on tour. D A G
The streets of London are dominated by grey manufactured materials, with thousands of brownfield sites. This walk looks at the potential for greening brownfield sites to enhance our streetscapes. Between-Bricks.
Tube/Rail: Old Street, Shoreditch High Street; 55,149,243,242,8

Further beyond the Olympic Park – North to Walthamstow Wetlands (Sat), South to the Thames (Sun) ●
■ Meet: Sat/Sun 10.30am at Prince Edward Road by Hackney Pearl Cafe E9 5LX or Sat 2.30pm by Princess of Wales Pub, Lea Bridge Road E5 9RB or Sun 2.30pm outside House Mill, Three Mills E3 3DU. Pre-book ONLY by email on ralphward@blueyonder.co.uk. Duration approx 2hrs. Max 50 per walk. E A
Two walks Sat/Sun, morning and afternoon, exploring the historic hybrid landscape of the Lea Valley and the Thames. Ralph Ward, visiting Professor at UEL London East Research Institute, will be joined by William Mann, founder member of RIBA Stirling prize winners Witherford Watson Mann on Saturday and Michael Owens, former Chief Executive of the Leaside Regeneration Partnership and founder of London Urban Visits on Sunday. Route map, commentary and further information at www.londonurbanvisits.co.uk.
Rail: Hackney Wick (Sat/Sun am), Clapton (Sat pm), Bromley-by-Bow (Sun pm)

Clonbrock Road

Writer's Shed

Hackney's Timber Buildings – walking tour ●
■ Meet: Sat 10.30am at Murray Grove N1 7FB. First come basis. A G
Hackney has a cluster of three significant timber buildings just a short walk apart (Stadthaus, at 9 storeys is the world's tallest timber apartment block). This is an opportunity to view all three in the company of the architect Andrew Waugh. The tour will start at Murray Grove, go on to Bridport Place and end at Whitmore Road. Waugh Thistleton Architects.
Tube: Old Street

Woodberry Wetlands – Hidden Nature Reserve in Stoke Newington ●
■ Meet: East Reservoir Community Garden, 1 Newton Close N4 2RH. Sun tours at 1pm and 3pm, first come basis. Rare opportunity to visit the site before works begin including the New River, East Reservoir and the mid 19C Grade II* listed Gas House and the Ivy House Sluice. G T d
Important wildlife site closed to the public since construction in 1833. Woodbury Wetlands project will see the site enhanced to create a publicly accessible nature reserve, due to open in summer 2015. Allen Scott Associates and Kaner Ollette 1833/2015.
Tube: Manor House; Rail: Stamford Hill; 253,254,29,141,341

Supported by

⊕ **Hackney**

Key. A Architect on site **B** Bookshop **C** Childrens' activities **d** Some disabled access **D** Full wheelchair access **E** Engineer on site **G** Green Features **N** Normally open to the public **P** Parking **Q** Long queues envisaged **R** Refreshments **T** Toilets

Hammersmith & Fulham

See openhouselondon.org.uk/hammersmith
to find out more about this area

All Saints Church, Fulham Church Gate (by Putney Bridge) SW6 3LA

■ Sat 10am-4pm/Sun 1pm-5pm. N D T B P

15C tower, 19C nave and many fine monuments. Good Heaton, Butler & Bayne, William Wailes and Margaret Rope stained glass. Churchyard contains restored tomb of Granville Sharp, father of Abolitionist movement.
Tube: Putney Bridge; Rail: Putney; 14,22,39,74,85,220,270,430

BBC Television Centre Masterplan

Meet: Entrance to the BBC Television Centre, Wood Lane, Shepherd's Bush, W12 7RJ

■ Sat 10am-5pm. Architect led tours every 30mins. Pre-book ONLY on openhouse@ahmm.co.uk A

A rare chance to visit the iconic BBC Television Centre site as it prepares for a new chapter in its life and development, in which listed buildings will be retained and complemented by new architecture. Allford Hall Monaghan Morris 2014.
Tube: Wood Lane, White City; 72,95,220,228,272
www.ahmm.co.uk

Bush Theatre

7 Uxbridge Road W12 8LJ

■ Sat 10am-1pm. Regular tours, pre-book ONLY via Box Office on 020 8743 5050. Max 12 per tour. N R T B d

English Renaissance style by a prolific architect of public libraries prior to WW1. Recently redesigned to create beautiful contemporary theatre space. Maurice B. Adams/Haworth Tompkins (refurb) 1895/2011. Entry: library, theatre, studio.
Tube: Shepherd's Bush, Shepherd's Bush Market; 49,72,94,95,207

Charing Cross Hospital

Fulham Palace Road W6 8RF

■ Sat tour at 11am. Pre-book ONLY on 020 8383 5226 or email Julia Weiner on ajw65@aol.com. Max 20 on tour. D R T

Access to Riverside Wing (Ansell and Bailey 2006) with sculpture by David Mach, restored hospital chapel (Ralph Tubbs) and West London Mental Health Centre (Gibberd 2004) with sculpture and prints by Bill Woodrow.
Tube: Hammersmith; 190,211,220,295

Colet House

151 Talgarth Road W14 9DA

■ Sun 10am-4pm. First come basis. Last entry 3.45pm. T B d

Unique building for artists with three large studios, all with north light through expansive windows. Fairfax B Wade-Palmer 1885. Entry: top studio, 2 ground floor studios.
Tube: Barons Court; 9,10,27,190,211,295,391

Emery Walker's House

7 Hammersmith Terrace W6 9TS

■ Sun 11am-4pm. Regular tours. Max 8 at one time.

The home of Emery Walker, printer, antiquary and mentor to William Morris. A unique Arts and Crafts domestic interior. 1750. Entry: ground floor and garden only.
Tube: Stamford Brook; 27,190,267,391,H91

Fulham Palace

Bishop's Avenue SW6 6EA

■ Sun tours pre-book ONLY on 020 7736 3233 option 7. 10 & 11am tours of offices not normally open to the public.

2.30pm walking tour. First come basis, 12-3pm tours of ground floor public rooms. Restored vineries and walled garden open 10.15am to 4.15pm. N R T B P

Former residence of the Bishop of London. Tudor courtyard with Georgian additions (Stiff Leadbetter 1764-6 and Samuel Pepys Cockerell 1814) Butterfield Chapel (1867).
Tube: Putney Bridge; 14,74,220,414,430

Goldhawk Road Residence ●

179 Goldhawk Road W12 8EP

■ Sat/Sun 10am-1pm. First come basis, queuing outside if necessary. E A G d

A striking modern extension to a locally listed Victorian townhouse. Features an elegantly balanced all-timber structure with expansive glazed openings to maximise connectivity with the garden. Waind Gohil Architects 2012.
Tube: Goldhawk Rd, Shepherd's Bush; 94,237
www.waindgohil.co.uk

Greenside Primary School

Westville Road W12 9PT

■ Sat/Sun 1pm-5pm. Half-hourly tours, first come basis. Last entry 4.30pm. Max 50 at one time. D R T C P

One of only 2 schools designed using Goldfinger's school building system – precast reinforced concrete frame with brick infill. Fine, top-lit mural by Gordon Cullen. Grade II* listed. Ernö Goldfinger 1952. Entry: foyer, hall, one classroom.
Tube: Shepherd's Bush Market, Goldhawk Road, Ravenscourt Park; Tube/Rail: Shepherd's Bush; 94,237,283,260,207

LAMDA (London Academy of Music & Dramatic Art)

155 Talgarth Road W14 9DA

■ Sun 10am-4pm. Regular student-led tours and demonstrations. Last entry 3.30pm. Max 10 per tour. R T C d

Victorian building with recent extensions, including black box studio theatre and rehearsal rooms. Work begins on multimillion-pound redevelopment in 2014 to include rehearsal studios, Simon Sainsbury Theatre, Sackler Library and Study Centre. Niall McLaughlin Architects 1894/2003.
Tube: Barons Court, Hammersmith; 9,10,27,391

Larmenier & Sacred Heart Catholic Primary School ●

41A Brook Green W6 7BL

■ Sat 10am-4pm. Regular tours led by pupils, first come basis. Duration 20 mins. Last entry 4pm. Max 15 per tour. D T G

Extensive consultation with staff, parents and pupils inspired designs to create a school for young inquisitive minds. On its landlocked site, a 2-storey spiral building responds to environment, incorporating Fibonacci's 'golden mean' as a symbol for its young community. Studio E Architects 2006.
Tube: Hammersmith; 9,10,391,27

Maggie's Centre ● ●

Charing Cross Hospital, Fulham Palace Road W6 8RF

■ Sun 12pm-4pm. Last entry 3.30pm. R T d. Vocaleyes Audio Described Tours taking place, see p.14 for details.

A non-institutional 'open house', Maggie's is a flexible space designed to be welcoming, uplifting and thought-provoking. The raised roof allows natural light to enter the whole of the building. Partitions divide up the open structure, placing the kitchen at the heart of the building. RIBA Award Winner 2009. Rogers Stirk Harbour + Partners 2008.
Tube: Hammersmith, Barons Court; Rail: Putney; 190,211,220,295

Roca London Gallery

Station Court, Townmead Road SW6 2PY

■ Sat/Sun 11am-5pm. Architect-led tours Sat 12noon and 3pm, first come basis. Last entry 4.30pm. Max 30 per tour. N D T A

Inspired by various phases or states of water, offering a unique

visual and interactive experience with Roca, the leading global bathroom brand. Zaha Hadid Architects 2011.
Rail: Imperial Wharf; C3

Rogers Stirk Harbour + Partners

Thames Wharf Studios, Rainville Road W6 9HA

■ Sun 10am-4pm. Regular architect-led tours, first come basis. Last entry 3.45pm. Max 20 at one time. R T B Q C A d

RIBA award-winning architects' practice located in early 20C warehouses, overlooking the River Thames – formerly used to store oil tanks. A new spectacular two-storey lightweight roof was added in 1989. Richard Rogers Partnership 1984-7. Entry: reception and 3rd floor. Drawing and modelmaking activities.
Tube: Hammersmith; 74,190,211,220,295

St Andrew's Church and Star Community Centre

Greyhound Road W14 9SA

■ Sat/Sun 10am-4pm. Max 50 at one time. N D T

A striking and impeccable restoration and contemporary renewal of Victorian Arts & Crafts church. Newly commissioned artworks – beautiful hanging icon by Guido de Costanzo and limestone font by Anna Sikorska. Newman and Billing/Crowther Associates 1873/2012. Entry: church, centre.
Tube: Barons Court; 2,16,36,44

Temple Lodge

51 Queen Caroline Street W6 9QL

■ Sun 1pm-5pm. First come basis. T d R B A

Georgian listed building, once the studio of artist Sir Frank Brangwyn. Recently redeveloped into a church for the Christian community whilst retaining many of the original features. Nicolas Pople 2013. Entry: House and redeveloped church in former Brangwyn studio.
Tube: Hammersmith

The Hurlingham Club ● ●

Ranelagh Gardens SW6 3PR

■ Sat tours at 11am and 3pm only, first come basis, entry 15 mins prior to tour. No admittance at any other time. T d

Last of the grand 18C mansions which once fronted this part of the river, with magnificent interiors and extensive grounds. Dr William Cadogan/George Byfield 1760/1797-8.
Tube: Putney Bridge; 14,22,39,74,85,93,220,265,270,424

V&A Study Centre, Blythe House

23 Blythe Road

■ Sat/Sun 11am-5pm. Tours of the Clothworkers' Centre at 12noon, 2pm and 4pm. Pre-book ONLY on 0207 942 2211. Max 15 per tour. A

Victoria and Albert Museum's study centre at Blythe House, including new reception area by Haworth Tompkins and display of Eduardo Paolozzi's Krazy Kat Arkive of Twentieth-Century Popular Culture. Sir Henry Tanner/Haworth Tompkins 1899-1903/2013. Entry: Courtyard and reception areas.
Tube/Rail: Kensington (Olympia); 9,10,27,28

William Morris Society – Kelmscott House

26 Upper Mall W6 9TA

■ Sat/Sun 11am-4.30pm. Regular tours, first come basis. Max 40 at one time. N T B d

Residence of Sir Francis Ronalds, George MacDonald and (from 1878-96) William Morris (organised by William Morris Society). 18C. Entry: basement and coach house only.
Tube: Ravenscourt Park; 27,190,267,391,H91

Supported by

● AJ Library Building ● Green Exemplar ● Landscape/Public realm ● Infrastructure/Engineering
■ Open Saturday ■ Open Sunday ■ Open Saturday and Sunday

openhouselondon.org.uk | Hammersmith & Fulham | 39

Haringey

See **openhouselondon.org.uk/haringey**
to find out more about this area

13 Burgoyne Road
13 Burgoyne Road N4 1AA
- Sat 10am-5pm. First come basis, queuing outside if necessary. Last entry 4.50pm.

Remodelling and extension of a 3-storey Victorian terrace house, involving sensitive refurbishment of period features complemented by a rich and sophisticated material palette for the modern additions. Trevor Brown Architect 2014. Entry: Ground, first floor, garden.
Tube: Finsbury Park, Manor House 29,141,341, W5

24A Dorset Road ◐
24A Dorset Road, Alexandra Palace N22 7SL
- Sun 10am-5pm. First come basis. Last entry 4.30pm. A

A new build end of terrace Victorian cottage. Externally identical to the rest terrace, but with a modern interior including a lightwell above the stairs. Sam Tisdall 2013.
Tube: Wood Green; Rail: Alexandra Palace; 184, 221

66-68 Stapleton Hall Road ◐
68 Stapleton Hall Road N4 4QA
- Sat 1pm-5pm. Pre-book ONLY on openhouse2014@solidspace.co.uk. Last entry 4.45pm. A d R T

Modern take on the traditional Victorian terrace. These new houses are designed by Stephen Taylor in conjunction with Solidspace – the interiors are bold, light with character. Stephen Taylor Architects / Solidspace 2014.
Rail: Crouch Hill; Haringey; W3,210,W7,W5

639 Tottenham High Road
639 Tottenham High Road N17 8AA
- Sat 10am-1pm. First come basis. Last entry 1pm. N D T P

Grade II listed. Former gas showroom built in 1901 in attractive neo-Jacobean style, red brick with terracotta dressing and stone decoration. Elaborate gables and turrets at either end. Damaged during 2011 riots, now fully refurbished by GLA and managed by London Youth Support Trust as Enterprise Centre and support for local community. Sergison Bates 2012. Entry: ground floor, first and second floor hallways.
Tube/Rail: Seven Sisters; Rail: Bruce Grove; 149,259,279,349,476

Bruce Castle Museum
Lordship Lane N17 8NU
- Sat 1pm-5pm/Sun 2pm-5pm. Half-hourly tours. Trails and activity sheets for children. Medieval All Hallows Church open Sun 2-5pm. Last entry 4pm. Max 20 per tour. N D R T B C P

Tudor Manor House built for Sir William Compton in 1514, substantially altered in 17C and 18C. A museum since 1906 housing local history and exhibitions of Bruce Castle. 1514/17C. Entry: ground floor; other areas visited on tours.
Tube/Rail: Seven Sisters, Wood Green; Rail: Bruce Grove; 123,243

Clyde Road ◐
75 Clyde Road N22 7AD
- Sat/Sun 10am-5pm. Tours taking place, first come basis. Last entry 4.45pm.

A bold and innovative loft extension and whole house refurbishment to an Edwardian terraced house. Exploring the potential of an archetypal London terrace house under

24A Dorset Road

permitted development. Andrew Mulroy Architects Ltd 2012.
Tube: Bounds Green; Rail: Alexandra Palace; 102,299,184

Discover 150 years of Alexandra Park and Palace History
Alexandra Palace Way N22 7AY
- Sat/Sun 10am-4pm. Half-hourly tours of historic areas of Palace departing from the East Court (ice rink reception), pre-book ONLY. See www.alexandrapalace.com to book. Temporary exhibition about palace, grounds and park in WW1 in situ. Last tour 4pm. Max 20 per tour. R T d

One of the few grand 19C leisure buildings to survive to the present day. This 9.6 acre Grade II listed building has a rich modern-day entertainment history including a Victorian Theatre and the historic BBC Studios. Major refurbishment planned as part of HLF-funded project. BBC Studios will therefore not be open to the public however, tours will end in the Transmitter Hall where there will be a mock-up BBC studio. John Johnson & A Messon 1873. Entry: East Court, Theatre Foyer, Theatre, North Service Yard, Palm Court and the Transmitter Hall.
Tube: Wood Green; Rail: Alexandra Palace; W3

Hale Village ◒
Meet: Outside main entrance to Hale Village (nearest to Tottenham Hale station) N17 9LR
- Sat 10am-5pm. Hourly tours, except 1pm, first come basis. Last tour 4pm. Max 15 per tour. N G d

New high-density waterside development with green design features including biomass and green roofs. Includes residential for sale and rent, student accommodation and range of community facilities. BDP/KSS/RMA 2008/2012.
Tube/Rail: Tottenham Hale; 123

Highgate School Chapel & Big School
North Road N6 4AY
- Sat 10am-1pm. Regular tours. Max 20 at one time. R T

A programme of works restored and refurbished the Grade II listed Victorian Gothic School Chapel, and 'Big School' which was opened as the new library in 2013. The conversion of Big School into a library includes the provision of a new mezzanine floor. The Chapel interior has been completely renovated, including restoration of stone and brick surfaces, stained glass and ceiling paintings. F P Cockerell 1865/7/2014. Entry: school chapel, 'Big School'.
Tube: Highgate, Archway; 143,210,271

Highpoint
Highpoint, North Hill N6 4BA
- Sat 10am-5pm. Regular tours, pre-book ONLY at http://ohlhighpoint.eventbrite.co.uk from 1 Sep. Max 12 per tour. G

Grade I listed Modernist apartment blocks retaining many original features. Lubetkin & Tecton 1935/1938. Entry: (by accompanied tour only) common parts, including restored foyers and interior of a flat. NB. No photographs within the buildings or gardens permitted.
Tube: Highgate; 143,271,210,134,43

Hornsey Town Hall
The Broadway N8 9JJ
- Sat 9.30am-5pm. Regular tours. Last entry 3.30pm. Max 15 at one time. T d

Grade II* listed building, about to undergo a renovation, the quintessence of municipal modernity of the period. Notable Ashburton marble staircases, fine wood-panelled rooms and cork flooring. Marble & bronze foyers express the optimism of the period. Reginald H Uren 1934-5. Entry: most areas apart from council chamber and public halls.
Rail: Crouch Hill; 41,91,W5,W7

Light House
2a Fairfield Road N8 9HG
- Sat 1pm-5pm. First come basis, queuing if necessary. Last entry 4.45pm. Max 20 at one time. T Q A d

An award-winning new build home (Best Home Haringey Design Awards 2012) that makes maximum use of light and space on a tight urban site. Crawford Partnership 2012. Entry: whole house.
Tube: Highgate; Tube/Rail: Finsbury Park; Rail: Crouch Hill; W3,W7,41,91,W5

Markfield Beam Engine and House ●
Markfield Road N15 4RB
- Sat/Sun 11am-5pm. Engine steaming 12.30-1.15pm 2-2.45pm, 3.30-4.15pm. Sessions preceded by an introduction on the history of the site and engine. Display panels on development of sanitation in Victorian times and later and its effect on improving public health, particularly in densely populated urban areas. E N D R T B P

Grade II listed Victorian industrial building set within a park and next to the River Lea, with the original Wood Bros beam pumping engine in situ, as originally installed. Recently restored Engine and Engine House. 1886.
Tube/Rail: Tottenham Hale, Seven Sisters; Rail: South Tottenham; 41,76,123,149,243

Mayfield Road
19 Mayfield Road N8 9LL
- Sun 10am-5pm. Half-hourly architect-led talks, first come basis. Last entry 4.30pm. A

This project aims to open up the kitchen to the garden and create a seamless transition with minimum impact to enable increased use of the garden and bring natural daylight into

Key. A Architect on site **B** Bookshop **C** Childrens' activities **d** Some disabled access **D** Full wheelchair access **E** Engineer on site **G** Green Features
N Normally open to the public **P** Parking **Q** Long queues envisaged **R** Refreshments **T** Toilets

Clyde Road

the domestic space. Luis Trevino 2012. Entry: rear extension, kitchen, garden.
Tube/Rail: Finsbury Park; Rail: Harringay; W3

Music Studio
86a Florence Road N4 4DP
- ■ Sat 10am-5pm. First come basis, queuing outside if necessary. Music performance. Last entry 4.30pm. Max 25 at one time. E D T Q A

Music studio for chamber music practice and teaching, kitchen/dining extension in timber, zinc and glass plus Victorian house renovation/alterations. Chance de Silva 2013. Entry: music studio, ground floor extension.
Tube/Rail: Finsbury Park; 210, W3, W7, 29, 253

Muswell Hill Odeon
Fortis Green Road N10 3HP
- ■ Sat/Sun 10am-1pm. Last entry 12.45pm. Max 20 at one time. T d

Grade II* listed Art Deco cinema, converted to three screens in 1974 but retaining its fine original decor. This year celebrating its 78th year. George Coles 1936. Entry: foyer and large main auditorium.
Tube: Highgate, East Finchley; 43, 102, 134, 144, 234, W7

The Eco-Hub at Lordship Recreation Ground ● ●
Lordship Recreation Ground (near the pond), Lordship Lane N17 7QX
- ■ Sat 1pm-5pm. NB Lordship Rec Community festival will be taking place. Max 30 at one time. D R T A G

AECB silver standard strawbale and timber-frame construction with raised floor on timber piles. Part of regeneration of Lordship Recreation Ground. Clay boards and unfired clay blocks. Low energy consumption design with green roof. Anne Thorne Architects 2012. Entry: cafe, corridor, decking area, park.
Tube: Turnpike Lane; Rail: Bruce Grove; 123, 243, W4

The Old Schoolhouse
Hornsey Historical Society, 136 Tottenham Lane (corner Rokesly Avenue) N8 7EL
- ■ Sun 11am-4pm. Regular guided and self-guided tours. Special displays on houses and streets then and now, Victorian school built in 1848 and local architect John Farrer. Worksheets and plans of building for children. N D T B C P d

Small, early Victorian infant school, closed in 1934, and after conversion and some demolition reopened in 1981 as HQ of Society. John Henry Taylor/Marius Reynolds 1848/1981. Entry: main school room.
Tube/Rail: Finsbury Park; Rail: Hornsey, Harringay; 41, 91, W3, W5

Tottenham Town Hall
Town Hall, Approach Road N15 4RY
- ■ Sat 10am-4pm. Learn about the history of Tottenham in the Legacy Heritage Centre. D T

Complete external and internal refurbishment of Grade II listed Town Hall, rescued from English Heritage 'at risk' register, now returned to its former glory. Grand foyer and Moselle Room with its stunning Moorish-Jacobean style ceiling has been restored along with brickwork and repairs to the intricate Italian terrazzo mosaic floor. A salvage strategy was employed to recycle slate tiles, granite setts, bricks and stone window cills. AS Taylor & AR Jemmett/bptw partnership (refurb) 1904/2011. Entry: common areas, Moselle Room, Mayor's Parlour.
Tube: Seven Sisters; Rail: South Tottenham; 41, 476, 123, 73

Tower and Churchyard of St Mary's Hornsey
Hornsey High Street N8 7QB
- ■ Sun 2pm-5pm. Regular tours of tower. Max 15 at one time. Exhibition, self-guided churchyard trails, new planting and significant tombs. R P

Grade II* listed tower with restored chapel remaining from medieval parish church. Excellent views from top of tower. Organised by Friends of Hornsey Church Tower.
Tube: Turnpike Lane; Rail: Hornsey; 41, 144, W3

Weston Park Extension ●
11 Weston Park N8 9SY
- ■ Sat 10am-1pm. First come basis, queuing outside if necessary. Last entry 12.45pm. Max 20 at one time. A d

Full width family room rear extension, with a stealth-like folded rubber roof, asymmetrical rooflights, and 150 fibre optic lights in the ceiling. Knott Architects 2012. Entry: ground floor, rear extension, garden.
Tube/Rail: Finsbury Park; Rail: Crouch Hill, Hornsey, Harringay; W7, W3, 41, 91, W5

WALKS/TOURS

Cycle Tour: London's Other River – A Lea Valley Miscellany ● ●
- ■ Meet: Sun at 10am at Tottenham Hale Station N17 9LR First come basis. Duration 3 hours, finishes in Stratford Docklands. Max 20 at one time. E N G d W

The River Lee or Lea is the Thames's sleazy East End cousin, home to all manner of noisome industries and dubious activities – but recently smartened up to serve as the backdrop to the 2012 Olympic Games. This tour takes in some of the area's intriguing architectural oddments, from Victorian cultic temples to 21st-century urban villages. Tour led by David Garrard of English Heritage.
Tube/Rail: Tottenham Hale

Muswell Hill Walk
- ■ Meet: Sat 2pm beside Muswell Hill Library, Queen's Avenue N10 3PE. Duration approx 2½ hours. Talk and display at North Bank house at end of walk. Max 30 on tour. R P d

Tour takes in early and late Victorian, Edwardian and 1930s buildings, and gives an historical interpretation of how a rural enclave changed into a unique Edwardian suburb. Finishes at North Bank House, Pages Lane, one of the old Victorian villas. First visit to library accessible via stairs only. Walk is otherwise flat for duration. Organised by Hornsey Historical Society.
Tube: East Finchley, Highgate, Bounds Green; 43, 102, 134, 144, 234, W7

Tottenham Green conservation area architectural walk ●
- ■ Meet: Sat 11am outside Tottenham Town Hall, Town Hall Approach Road N15 4RY. Duration up to 2 hours with optional Turkish restaurant visit afterwards.

External guided tour around the buildings and public realm of Tottenham Green conservation area, which contains 17 nationally listed buildings and over 50 locally listed. Restored Town Hall will be open. Organised by Tottenham Civic Society.
Tube/Rail: Seven Sisters

Supported by

Haringey Council

Havering

See **openhouselondon.org.uk/havering**
to find out more about this area

Bower House
Orange Tree Hill, Havering-atte-Bower, Romford RM4 1PB
- Sat 10am-4pm. N R T B P d

Grade I listed mansion house commanding the most extensive southerly views over Essex. Leading landscape designer Charles Bridgeman and Sir James Thornhill (best known for his wall paintings at Blenheim Palace) involved with the design. Henry Flitcroft 1729. Entry: mansion house, grounds.
Rail: Romford; 375

CEME (Centre for Engineering and Manufacturing Excellence) ● ● ◍
Marsh Way, Rainham RM13 8EU
- Sat 9am-2pm. Regular tours. Video presentation in POD auditorium on building construction. Max 20 per tour. D T P

CEME is a dynamic hub of education, enterprise and manufacture for east London; a flagship project for the Thames Gateway regeneration. Its futuristic design alludes clearly to its role as a vehicle for innovation and growth. Sheppard Robson 2003. Entry: untenanted areas, grounds.
Tube: Dagenham Heathway; Rail: Rainham, Dagenham Dock; 171

Drapers' Academy
Settle Road, Harold Hill, RM3 9XR
- Sun 10am-1pm. First come basis. Tours at 11am and 12noon. Last entry 12.30pm. D R T A

Drapers' Academy is a new building for a new educational institution. It has been designed to provide first-class educational facilities for 900 pupils in years 7 to 11 and a 200-pupil sixth form. Feilden Clegg Bradley Studios 2014.
Rail: Harold Wood; 496

Elm Park Primary School
Elm Park, South End Road, Hornchurch RM12 5UA
- Sat/Sun 10am-3pm. N D R T G P

Bright, spacious award-winning school, providing flexible spaces. The two-storey building has a sedum grass roof with classroom spaces opening onto a double-height shared 'heart' space. Walters and Cohen 2011.
Tube: Elm Park; 165,252,365

Havering Museum
19-21 High Street RM1 1JU
- Sat/Sun 11am-5pm. First come basis. Last entry 4pm. Max 70 at one time. N D R T B

A flagship cultural centre for the borough, in a converted Romford brewery building near to the historic market place. Exhibition pieces have been carefully crafted into the existing structure to create a modern intervention that retains the historic value of the building. TTSP Architects (refurb) 2010.
Rail: Romford; 66,68,175,248,496

Havering Town Hall
Main Road, Romford RM1 3BD
- Sat 12pm-4pm. Regular tours, first come basis. Photographic exhibition of old photos of the town hall. D T

Grade II listed, result of an architectural competition won by Collins & Geens. Unique fittings using Bath stone, red cedar wood and Tasmanian oak, with full-height entrance hall and tall central staircase window and flagpoles. HR Collins & AEO

Geens 1935. Entry: ground and 1st floor.
Rail: Romford; 252,248,175,128,66

Langtons House ◍
Billet Lane, Hornchurch RM11 1XJ
- Sun 10am-5pm. Regular tours, first come basis. Exhibition of historic photographs. Last entry 4.45pm. Max 30 at one time. D T

Grade II listed neo-Georgian house with later additions. Landscaped garden with lake, orangery and gazebo. c1760. Entry: marriage rooms, orangery. Gardens open Sat and Sun.
Tube: Hornchurch; Rail: Emerson Park; 248,252,256,324,370

Myplace Centre ◍
Dagnam Park Drive, Harold Hill RM3 9EN
- Sat 9am-10pm/Sun 10am-6pm. Organic art exhibition. N D R T C G

New £4.7m youth centre with a range of facilities, and the borough's first zero carbon building – one of only a few in the UK. Sustainable features include high insulation, solar panels, sustainable timber construction. Jacobs Architects 2012.
Rail: Harold Wood; 174,674,294,256,499

Royal Liberty School (formerly Hare Hall)
Upper Brentwood Road, Gidea Park, Romford RM2 6HJ
- Sun 10am-5pm. Last entry 4.15pm. R T P

Grade II listed Palladian villa with west facing five-bay front of Portland stone with two wings. Interior contains original staircase. James Paine 1768. Entry: ground, 1st, 2nd floors.
Rail: Gidea Park; 496,674,294

Thames Chase Forest Centre
Broadfields, Pike Lane, Upminster RM14 3NS
- Sat/Sun 10am-5pm. Last entry 4.50pm. N D R T B C G

Award-winning visitor centre of modern timber construction forming an A-frame building roofed with cedar shingles, attached to 17C listed barn – one of the best preserved in London area. Sustainable features include timber construction, passive ventilation, underfloor heating, biomass boiler. Laurie Wood Architects 17C/2010.
Tube/Rail: Upminster; 347

The Queen's Theatre
Billet Lane, Hornchurch RM11 1QT
- Sat 10am-1pm. Backstage tours 10am, 11am, 12noon (may not be suitable for wheelchair users). Bookable in advance from Box Office on 01708 443333. Children's activities/ backstage treasure hunt running 10am & 12noon. Max 30 per tour. N R T C d

Opened by Sir Peter Hall, a robust example of 1970s civic architecture and a vibrant and successful producing theatre. Norman Brooks 1975. Entry: all front of house areas, and backstage with tour.
Tube: Hornchurch; 193,248,252,256,324

The Round House
Broxhill Road, Havering-atte-Bower, Romford RM4 1QH
- Sun tours at 10.30am, 12noon, 2pm, 3.30pm. Pre-book ONLY on michael@roundhouse38.fsnet.co.uk with name, tel numbers, mobile & landline and state preferred tour time required with alternatives. Max 4 per tour. T P

Grade II* listed late Georgian elliptical 3-storeyed stuccoed villa. Attributed John Plaw 1792-4.
Rail: Romford

Towers Junior School
Windsor Road, Hornchurch RM11 1PD
- Sat architect-led tour at 10am, first come basis. Duration 45 mins. D T A G

Towers Junior School has been refurbished and remodelled

---

on a limited budget, transforming almost every part of the building and responding to pupils' requests for their 'ideal school'. The same architects are now extending the school to allow an increase in pupil numbers from two forms of entry to three. Walters and Cohen 2010/2014. Entry: whole school.
Tube: Elm Park; Rail: Romford; 193,372,248,365

Upminster Old Chapel
70 St Mary's Lane, Upminster RM14 2QR
- Sat/Sun 2pm-5pm. Tours at 2.30pm, 3.30pm and 4.30pm. N D R T C P

Grade II timber-framed former Dissenters' Meeting House (1800) with pedimented facade. Two blank windows flank the Doric entrance porch. 1800. Fully refurbished, and re-opened to the public in 2013. Entry in the side foyer.
Tube: Upminster Bridge; Tube/Rail: Upminster; 248,348,370,373

Upminster Tithe Barn Museum
Hall Lane, Upminster RM14 1AU
- Sat/Sun 10.30am-4.30pm. Regular tours. Last entry 4.15pm. N P d

15C box-framed, 9-bay, aisled barn, weatherboarded with crown-post, collar-tie reed-thatched roof. Ancient monument.
Tube/Rail: Upminster; 248

Upminster Windmill
St Mary's Lane, Upminster RM14 2QH
- Sat/Sun 2pm-5pm. Regular tours. No children under five. Last tour 5pm. Max 10 per tour. N P

Fine Grade II* listed wooden smock windmill in use until 1934 and containing much original wooden machinery. (Organised by Friends of Upminster Windmill.) James Nokes 1803. Entry: mill interior.
Tube/Rail: Upminster; 248,370

WALKS/TOURS

Gidea Park Garden Suburb Walk
- Meet: Sat 10.15am at entrance to Balgores Square car park, (immediately north of Gidea Park Station) RM2 6AU For info call 01277 219 892. Max 40 per tour. Duration 2 hrs. T B d

The first Gidea Park Garden Suburb houses built as a result of open architectural competition. Further developments took place up until the mid-1930s. Tour takes in Gidea Park exhibition houses and Hare Street buildings. Interesting WW1 history with poets Wilfred Owen and Edward Thomas, and Noel Coward all connected with the site. 1911.
Rail: Gidea Park; 294,496

Rainham Hall and Marshes ◍
- Meet: Rainham Station, Ferry Lane, Rainham RM13 9YN Sat tours 10am, 1pm. Pre-book ONLY on 01708 525 579. Hard hat tours with LB Havering Regeneration team, Bakers of Danbury and members from National Trust. Over 18s only, limited facilities due to restoration work. Max 10 at a time.

Rainham Hall and Marshes is the site of an important new masterplan for London. The Hall is a fine example of a Queen Anne house. East/Alison Brooks Architects/Peter Beard and others, 1729. Entry: Gardens fully accessible, will also be open to visitors between 10am and 2pm.
Rail: Rainham; 103,287,165,372

Supported by

Key. A Architect on site **B** Bookshop **C** Childrens' activities **d** Some disabled access **D** Full wheelchair access **E** Engineer on site **G** Green Features
N Normally open to the public **P** Parking **Q** Long queues envisaged **R** Refreshments **T** Toilets

Hillingdon

See **openhouselondon.org.uk/hillingdon**
to find out more about this area

Cranford Stable Block & St Dunstan's Church
Cranford Park, The Parkway, Cranford TW5 9RZ
■ Sat 10.30am-4.30pm/Sun 12.30pm-6.30pm. Activities, refreshments, classic motorcycle meet, guided history walks. Max 20 at one time. R T B
Restored 18C stable block of now-demolished Cranford House, former seat of the Earl of Berkeley. The front has arches with stone keystones facing a cobbled yard. Entry to ground floor area (west stable). Also medieval St Dunstan's Church mentioned in the Domesday Book and famous for its early 14C wall paintings. Berkeley family tombs in cemetery.
Tube: Hatton Cross, Hounslow West; Rail: Hayes & Harlington; 105,111,81,222,498,E6,195

Manor Farm Site, Manor House
St Martins Approach, Ruislip HA4 8BD
■ Sat/Sun 11am-5pm. NB. Great Barn closed Sat & Sun. Site tours 11am, 2pm, first come basis. Meet at Manor Farm House. Last entry 4.30pm. Max 15 in Manor House at one time. N D R T
Oldest and largest heritage site in Hillingdon (Manor Farm has been occupied since 11C), was sympathetically refurbished in 2008, and is now home to a museum and interpretation centre in the 16C Manor House. Grade II listed Great Barn is the second largest in the country, with impressive sweeping tiled roof and weatherboarded walls. Entry: Manor House, Little Barn (Sat only), Norman Motte and Bailey, 22 acres of grounds.
Tube: Ruislip; Rail: West Ruislip; 331,H13,U10,U1,398,114

Old Water Tower
9 Watertower Close, Uxbridge UB8 1XS
■ Sat 10am-5pm. Tours every 20 mins, pre-book ONLY on 01895 253658. NB. head for heights essential. Not suitable for children under 10. Flat shoes and trousers suggested. Last tour 4.30pm. Max 12 per tour. R P
21m-high brick water tower, built 1905 in institutional Gothic style to improve the water supply to expanding Uxbridge following the arrival of the Metropolitan Railway. Converted to a residence in 1980. Access: Weather permitting by internal fixed safety ladder to tank and roof for views over London Basin. 1906.
Tube: Uxbridge; U1 (towards Ruislip)

St Martin's Church, Ruislip
High Street, Ruislip HA4 8DG
■ Sat/Sun 10am-5pm. First come basis. D T P
Church dates from 1250 with 15C additions and Victorian restorations. Grade II listed. Fine late Medieval wall paintings & funeral hatchments. Sir Gilbert Scott and Ewan Christian 13C/1870.
Tube: Ruislip; Rail: West Ruislip; 114, E7,331

St Martin's Parish Church, West Drayton
Church Road, West Drayton UB7 7PT
■ Sat 10am-4pm/Sun 12pm-4pm. First come basis. Max 6 in tower. N R T C
Unusually long 13C chancel, 15C nave and external flint work of 1852. Mentioned in the Domesday Book. 13C and 1852. Entry: all areas including tower (weather permitting) NB. no unaccompanied children allowed in tower, steps are very steep.

Old Water Tower

Tube: Uxbridge; Hounslow West; Rail: West Drayton; 222,U5,350,U3

St Mary's Church, Harefield
off Church Hill, Harefield UB9 6DU
■ Sat 10am-4pm/Sun 12pm-3pm. First come basis. N R T P d
Exceptionally fine 12C Medieval church, surrounded by large country churchyard, including Anzac Cemetery from WWI. Many notable monuments including Lady Spencer, Countess of Derby. Fine 18C 3-decker pulpit. Grade I listed. 12C. Entry: all areas except upper levels of the tower.
Tube: Uxbridge, Northwood then 331 or U9 bus; Rail: Denham (then 331)

St Mary the Virgin Church
High Street, Harmondsworth UB7 0AQ
■ Sat 10am-5pm/Sun 12pm-5pm. First come basis. N D R T
St Mary's Church has parts dating back to 11C, a fine Norman doorway and a Saxon sundial outside on the south wall. 12C.
Tube: Heathrow Central; Rail: West Drayton; U3,350 from Terminal 5 & West Drayton

St Peter & St Paul Harlington
St Peter's Way, High Street, Harlington UB3 5AB
■ Sat 10am-4pm/Sun 1pm-5pm. Regular tours. N T P d
Grade I listed church (16C) with Norman font and Norman stone arch carved with cats' heads. Interesting monuments including Easter sepulchre. Ancient yew tree in churchyard. Good restoration between 1830 and 1860. 12C.
Tube: Hatton Cross; Rail: Hayes & Harlington; 140,U4

Swakeleys House
Swakeleys Road, Ickenham (access from Milton Road) UB10 8LD
■ Sat 10am-4pm. Max 25 at one time, entry every 20-30 mins. P
By far the most important house in Ickenham and an outstanding example of a Jacobean country house built in the 1630s. Constructed of red brick, laid in English bond on an H plan. Great Hall includes the 1655 Harrington Screen, 18C marble fireplace and original panelling. 1638.
Entry: Great Hall, gardens.
Tube: Ickenham, Uxbridge; Rail: West Ruislip; U1,U2,U10

West Drayton Primary School

Uxbridge Lido
Hillingdon Sports and Leisure Complex, Gatting Way UB8 1ES
■ Sat 10am-1pm. First come basis, queuing outside if necessary. D T
This 1930's 'Moderne Art Deco' designed lido was refurbished in 2010 to include a £33m sports complex. It has closed down multiple times throughout its history but is currently enjoyed by the public. G. P Trentham 1935. Entry: lido, Clive Hamilton suite.
Tube: Uxbridge; U1,U2,U3,331

Uxbridge Quaker Meeting House
York Road Uxbridge UB8 1QW
■ Sat 12pm-4pm. First come basis Last entry 3.30pm. Max 20 at one time. T
Grade II listed typical Georgian Quaker meeting house, retaining its original features with an elders' gallery and full-size opening screens. 1818. Entry: large meeting house. Exhibition on 'Quakers and Uxbridge from 1658'.
Tube: Uxbridge; 222,331,427,607,U4

West Drayton Primary School ●
Kingston Lane, West Drayton, UB7 9EA
■ Sat 10am-5pm. First come basis. D T A
A new library, external canopy and playground for a book-loving school. The library is a miniature timber 'cathedral' inside a mysterious red box. The Architects Practice 2006. Entry: School library and early years playground.
Rail: West Drayton; U5,222,350

Whiteheath Infants & Nursery School ●
Ladygate Lane, Ruislip, HA4 7RF
■ Sat 1pm-5pm. First come basis. D T A
A single storey classroom extension to a much-loved local school. Three linked classrooms and a shared art zone provide a new base for Year 2. The Architects Practice 2011.
Tube: Ruislip; Rail: West Ruislip; 331,H13

Supported by

HILLINGDON
LONDON

Hounslow

See openhouselondon.org.uk/hounslow
to find out more about this area

Adobe Village Hounslow Heath Infant and Nursery School ●
Martindale Road TW4 7HE
■ Sat 10am-5pm. First come basis. Last entry 4.30pm. D R T C P
Unique playscape and adobe home structure that integrates outside learning with innovative earth forms. Construction is 'rammed' earth made from earth filled tubes. The children contributed to the scheme by sketching out their ideas for their eco-classroom. Small Earth 2011. Entry: adobe home, adobe village, large sandpit, moon gate.
Tube: Hounslow West; Rail: Hounslow; 237,117,235,116

Boston Manor House
Boston Manor Road, Brentford TW8 9JX
■ Sat/Sun 12pm-5pm. Tours 12.30pm, 2pm, 3.30pm, first come basis. Last tour 5pm. Max 30 per tour. T d
Jacobean Manor House set in parkland with lake and ancient trees. Richly decorated 17C plaster ceilings in State Rooms. Unknown/Donald Insall (restoration) 1623/1963. Entry: state room, dining room.
Tube: Boston Manor; Rail: Brentford; E8

Brentford & Isleworth Quaker Meeting House
Quaker Lane, Isleworth TW7 5AZ
■ Sat 10am-5pm. Last entry 4.30pm. R T B P d
Grade II* listed late-Georgian Quaker Meeting House set in garden with burial ground. Meeting room has wood panelling and elders' gallery. 1785. Entry: main meeting room, library, gallery, garden.
Tube: Hounslow East; Rail: Syon Lane; 110,235,H28,237,267

Gunnersbury Park & Museum ●
Gunnersbury Park Museum W3 8LQ
■ Sun 11.30am-5pm. Architect led tour at 11am with Rodney Melville Partners to explore the restoration project planned for 2015. Pre-book ONLY via gunnersbury@ealing.gov.uk. Regular tours of the well-preserved Victorian kitchens of the large mansion. Last tour 4pm. N R T C P d
Former home to the Rothschild family, now a local history museum set in beautiful 19C mansion on an elevated terrace overlooking lawns and parkland. Major restoration project is being planned. Alexander Copland/Sydney Smirke (extended) 1802/1835. Entry: Areas of Museum/house, 18C temple and bathhouse, usually closed to public.
Tube: Acton Town; E3

Hogarth's House
Hogarth Lane, Great West Road W4 2QN
■ Sat/Sun 1pm-5pm. Hourly tours of areas usually closed to the public, first come basis. Last tour 4pm, last entry 4.45pm. Max 6 per tour. N T B P d
Early 18C timber-framed, red brick home of artist William Hogarth extended significantly c1749-1764. Delightful walled garden containing famous ancient mulberry tree. A unique oasis in modern West London. c1715. Entry: attic, basement, store rooms, study rooms.
Tube: Turnham Green; Rail: Chiswick; 190

Kempton Great Engines Trust ●
Kempton Park Water Treatment Works, Snakey Lane, Hanworth TW13 7ND

Park Road, Chiswick

■ Sat/Sun 11am-4pm. First come basis. Last entry 3.30pm. E D R T B C P
Magnificent industrial cathedral (a National Monument) housing two triple expansion steam engines and two steam turbines. The engines were at the heart of the water treatment works supplying North London with drinking water taken from the Thames. 1928. Play packs, games, steam rail rides.
Rail: Kempton Park; 290,H25

Osterley Park House
Jersey Road, Isleworth TW7 4RB
■ Sat/Sun 11am-5pm. Timed tickets may apply. Last entry 4pm. Max 200 in house at one time. R T B d
One of Britain's most complete examples of Robert Adam's work. Set in over 350 acres of park, garden and farmland. Robert Adam 1761. Entry: house, park, garden.
Tube: Osterley; Rail: Isleworth; H28,H37,H91

Park Road, Chiswick ●
103 Park Road, Chiswick W4 3ER
■ Sat 10am-5pm. First come basis. Architect on site. Last entry 4.30pm A G
A striking re-modelling of a 1920s house with excellent environmental credentials, including a rear and side addition clad with glass reinforced concrete panels. Sam Tisdall Architects 2011.
Tube: Turnham Green, Gunnersbury; Rail: Chiswick; 272,190,E3

St Mary's Convent
10 The Butts, Brentford TW8 8BQ
■ Sat tours at 10am, 12noon, 3.00pm. Pre-book ONLY on 020 8568 7305. Duration approx 1 1/2 hrs. Max 8 per tour. T P d
Convent in 18C Grade II listed house with original features. Various additions including west wing (1913-15) and harmonious care home facilities and chapel by PRP Architects (1998-2001). 18C. Entry: lobby, community room, chapel, heritage room and Foundress' room (no wheelchair access to heritage & Foundress' rooms).
Tube: Boston Manor; Rail: Brentford; 235,237,267,E2,E8

West Thames College: New Campus
London Road, Isleworth TW7 4HS
■ Sat 10am-4pm. Regular tours. Last tour 3.30pm. Max 10 per tour. R T G P d
Modern, state-of-the-art college building with lots of natural light and vibrant, spacious interior. The building complements the Grade II listed Spring Grove House (see entry below). Sustainable features include rainwater harvesting and auto-sensor lighting. 2012 RIBA Award nominee. Mackenzie Wheeler 2011. Entry: tour takes in all facilities.
Tube: Osterley, Hounslow East; Rail: Isleworth; H37,235,237,H22

West Thames College : Spring Grove House
London Road, Isleworth TW7 4HS
■ Sat 10am-4pm. Regular tours. Last tour 3.30pm. Max 10 per tour. R T G P d
Remarkably intact prime example of late Victorian architecture, including stained glass windows and mosaics. Grade II listed with one remaining fine Georgian room. Restored and refurbished during 2011-12. Sir John Offley/various 1645 onwards. Entry: house and key rooms.
Tube: Osterley, Hounslow East; Rail: Isleworth; 117,H37,235,237,110
www.west-thames.ac.uk/en/events/open-house.cfm

WALKS/TOURS

Bedford Park
■ Meet: Sun 2.30pm at Victorian Society, 1 Priory Gardens W4 1TT. Duration approx 2hrs. P
Bedford Park was the first garden suburb. Some 400 homes, mostly in red brick with red tiled roofs, Dutch-style gables, balconies and artists' studios. Norman Shaw, EW Godwin, EJ May and Maurice B Adams 1875-1886.
Tube: Turnham Green; 94,E3

Brentford Walk ●
■ Meet: Sat 2.30pm at High Street & Half Acre Junction, Brentford TW8 0JG. Duration 1 1/2 hours.
Guided walk covering 300 years of architecture in Brentford starting on the route of the Roman Road and finishing at Jacobean Mansion.
Rail: Brentford; 195,235,237,267,E2,E8; parking in the Butts

Gunnersbury Park Landscape Tour ●
■ Meet: 2pm at entrance to Gunnersbury Park Museum, Gunnersbury Park W3 8LQ. Pre-book ONLY on gunnersbury@ealing.gov.uk, limited places.
Landscape architect tour of Gunnersbury Park to discuss the planned restoration of the park in 2015. The tour will give an insight into the future transformation of the heritage landscape which hosts over 20 listed features including an orangery, walled garden, bathhouse and the remnants of a horseshoe pond.
Tube: Acton Town; E3

Hounslow Open House Guided Cycle Tour
■ Meet: Sun 12.45pm Chiswick Station, car park W4 2DU Pre-book ONLY on www.hounslowtravelactive.co.uk Duration approx 2.5 hours.
Guided architectural bike tour led by the LB Hounslow transport project officers around Open House buildings.
Rail: Chiswick

Turnham Green Walk
■ Meet: Sun 2.30pm outside Chiswick Town Hall, Heathfield Terrace W4 4JN. Duration approx 1 hour.
Beginning at the Victorian/Edwardian Town Hall, this walk takes in the former Sanderson home (famous for their wallpapers), including the CFA Voysey industrial building, a statue of William Hogarth, a police station and the first fire station to be built with a hose tower.
Tube: Chiswick Park; Rail: Gunnersbury; 237,267,E3

Supported by

London Borough of Hounslow

Key. A Architect on site **B** Bookshop **C** Childrens' activities **d** Some disabled access **D** Full wheelchair access **E** Engineer on site **G** Green Features **N** Normally open to the public **P** Parking **Q** Long queues envisaged **R** Refreshments **T** Toilets

Islington

See **openhouselondon.org.uk/islington**
to find out more about this area

103 Copenhagen Street
103 Copenhagen Street N1 0FL
■ Sat 1pm-5pm. Tours at 1.15, 2.15, 3.15 and 4.15pm. Numbers limited, access only by tours. Max 20 per tour. D A G
Eight sustainable homes and office units, with generous social spaces, good daylight and attractive materials. Green design features include air-source heat pumps, green sedum roof and high level thermal insulation. Jake Ireland Architects 2013.
Tube: Angel; Rail: King's Cross St Pancras; Caledonian Road 17,91,153,259,274

72 Calabria Road
72 Calabria Road N5 1HU
■ Sun 10am-5pm. First come basis, queuing outside if necessary. Last entry 4.45pm.
Refurbishment and extension of a Victorian house featuring polished concrete cladding, double height spaces and landscaped garden. Architecture for London 2014. Entry: Ground floor and garden.
Tube/Rail: Highbury & Islington; 393,271,4,43,19

Angel Building ●○
407 St John Street EC1V 4AB
■ Sat 10am-5pm/Sun 1pm-5pm. Architect on site. First come basis, queuing outside if necessary. Last entry 4.15pm. Max 75 at one time. D T A G
Re-invention of an early 1980s office block with elegant and robust modern detailing, the existing concrete frame has been re-used and re-wrapped with a highly energy-efficient glazed skin. Striking Ian McChesney art piece in foyer and stunning London-wide views from terrace. RIBA and BCO Award Winner 2011 and Stirling Prize shortlist 2011. Allford Hall Monaghan Morris 2010. Entry: atrium, top floor terrace.
Tube: Angel; 19,38,341,73,214,30,205
www.derwentlondon.com | www.ahmm.co.uk

Bunhill Heat and Power Energy Centre ●
Central Street EC1V 3QB
■ Sat 9am-5pm. Regular tours, first come basis. Max 10 per tour. Last entry 4.30pm. G d
A ground-breaking decentralised energy scheme located in the south of the borough and part of Islington's wider strategy to reduce fuel poverty and yield financial and environmental benefits to the community. Tim Ronalds Architects 2012.
Tube/Rail: Old Street, Barbican

Caledonian Park Clocktower
Market Road N7 9PL
■ Sun 10am-1pm. Tours at 10am, 11am, 12noon. Pre-book ONLY at www.islington.gov.uk/caledonianpark Last entry 12noon. E N G d
Opened in 1855 as centrepiece of Metropolitan Cattle Market. The seven-storey clock tower offers magnificent views over London. The original working clock mechanism adds further interest. J.B. Bunning 1850-55. Entry: All levels.
Tube: Caledonian Road; Rail: Caledonian Road & Barnsbury, Kings Cross St Pancras; 274,390,17,91,259

Crossrail Farringdon Construction Sites ●
Site Office, Farringdon Road EC1M 3HN

■ Sat/Sun 9am-4.30pm. Hourly tours. Pre-book ONLY on www.crossrail.co.uk/openhouse. Max 15 per tour. E
View of worksites from a platform with experts onsite discussing the construction of the two eastern and western ticket halls. Aedas, PLP Architecture, John Robertson Architects. www.crossrail.co.uk/openhouse. www.mottmac.com. ice
Tube/Rail: Farringdon; 8,17,25,45,63

Cullinan Studio ●○
5 Baldwin Terrace N1 7RU
■ Sun 11am-1pm. Tours every 45 mins. Max 10 per tour. Display of recent work. Last entry 12.30pm. E D R T A G
Newly-retrofitted canal-side Victorian foundry building into BREEAM Excellent offices. Sustainable features include air-source heat pump, PV panels, recycled newspaper insulation. Cullinan Studio Architects 2012.
Tube: Angel, Old Street; 38,43,73,205,341
www.cullinanstudio.com

Finsbury Town Hall
Rosebery Avenue EC1R 4RP
■ Sun 10am-5pm. Regular tours. Last entry 4.45pm. Max 10 at one time. D T
Opened by Lord Rosebery, an ornate building with elegant decor influenced by the Art Nouveau movement. Several notable rooms including the Great Hall with unique stained glass, antique mirrors and Clerkenwell Angel statuettes. C. Evans Vaughan 1895. Entry: Great Hall, council chamber, marriage room, staircase.
Tube: Angel; Tube/Rail: Farringdon; 19,38,341

Graduate Centre – London Metropolitan University
166-220 Holloway Road N7 8DB
■ Sat 9.30am-1pm. Display of recently completed projects by Fraser Brown Mackenna, Architecture Research Unit, Molyneux Kerr. Last entry 12.30pm. Max 30 at one time. D T
Award-winning landmark building composed of three intersecting volumes which are clad entirely with embossed stainless steel panels creating a shining and ever-changing surface. Daniel Libeskind Studio 2004. Entry: lecture theatre, seminar rooms and postgraduate hub area.
Tube: Holloway Road; Tube/Rail: Highbury & Islington

Grenville Plug-in Allotment Garden ●
opposite 60 Grenville Road, corner Ormond Road N19 4EH
■ Sat/Sun 2pm-7pm. Architects/students on site. N A G P d
A project integrating a student design with community led bottom-up assembly. The garden consists of hovering planters at varied heights that plug into an elevated rain-water harvesting system. Each is built and stewarded by an individual family in the surrounding community. Students of Ittai Frank, AIU, London with Buro Happold 2012.
Rail: Crouch Hill; Tube/Rail: Finsbury Park; Tube: Archway

Highbury Grove School
8 Highbury Grove N5 2EQ
■ Sat 10am-2pm. First come basis. D T A G
Flat slab concrete frame construction built around existing buildings on site and generating 20% of its energy from on-site renewable energy installations. Highly commended in the Most Sustainable School Design category of Excellence in BSF 2008 Awards. BDP 2010. Entry: all areas.
Tube/Rail: Canonbury, Highbury & Islington; 236,393,4,19

Impact Hub King's Cross ●
Impact Hub King's Cross, 34B York Way, London N1 9AB
■ Sat 10am-5pm. Hourly tours, first come basis. Last entry 4.45pm. Max 20 per tour. D R T G
Innovative workspace for social entrepreneurs with recycled fittings and furniture. Housed within Grade II listed building.

Meeting rooms contain hanging glass and writable glass walls. 00:/ 2008.
Tube: King's Cross St Pancras; 10,17,30,45,59,63,91,205,259,390

Imperial Hall / Leysian Mission
104-122 City Road EC1V 2NR
■ Sat 10am-1pm. First come basis.
Previously known as the Leysian Mission, the Grade II listed structure was built in 1904 and operated until 1983 as a Methodist mission, after which it was converted to 63 high-end residential flats. J.J. Bradshaw & Gass 1904.
Tube: Old Street; 214,205,43,55,243

Ironmonger Row Baths
1 Norman Street EC1V 3AA
■ Sat/Sun 9am-6pm. Regular tours, first come basis. Free parking on Sunday. Last entry 5.30pm. N R T d
Grade II listed building, original features, Turkish baths, laundry, swimming pool. Historical details of 1931 bath, maps and photos in purpose built history room. AWS & KMB Cross/ Tim Ronalds Architects 1930s/2012.
Tube/Rail: Old Street; 55,43,205,214,243

John Jones Arts Building
Finsbury Park N4 3JG
■ Sat 10am-3pm. Tours taking place, pre-book ONLY on marketing@johnjones.co.uk. Max 15 per tour. D T
Inspired by 1930s New York office buildings and industrial Clerkenwell warehouses, The Arts Building's six storeys feature raw concrete floors, full height windows and incredible views across London's skyline. David Gallagher Associates 2014. Entry: Project space, design, conservation fitting studios.
Tube/Rail: Finsbury Park; 4,19,29,106,153

Kings Place
90 York Way N1 9AG
■ Sat tours at 10am, 11.15am & 1.15pm / Sun tours at 10am and 1.15pm. First come basis. Max 20 per tour. 1 hr. N D R T C
Iconic mixed-use building with glass and limestone facades comprising of three basic components: a smaller scale block on Battlebridge Basin; The Rotunda and a street-like atrium. Advanced acoustic design with interior veneer carved from single oak tree. RIBA Award Winner 2009. Dixon Jones 2008.
Tube/Rail: King's Cross St Pancras; 10,17,91,214,390,259

Lockwood Residence
2 Bevan Street N1 7DY
■ Sat 11am-4pm. Closed between 1-2pm. First come basis.
Sited in a conservation area, this narrow terraced house was transformed by a new storey in the butterfly roof structure creating open plan living space. Diamond Architects 2013.
Tube: Angel; 341,73,476,38,56

London Canal Museum
12-13 New Wharf Road N1 9RT
■ Sat 10.30am-4.30pm. Regular tours and talks on the history of the building. N R T B C G
Canalside building built 1862 as an ice warehouse for Carlo Gatti. The unique ice wells may still be seen. 1862.
Tube/Rail: King's Cross St Pancras; 10,17,91,259,390,476

Marx Memorial Library
37a Clerkenwell Green EC1R 0DU
■ Sun 11am-4pm. Regular tours and talks. Last entry 3.30pm. Max 50 at one time. R T B d
Grade II listed, a library since 1933. Lenin worked here 1902-03 and his office is preserved. Fresco on 1st floor. Late 15C tunnels. Sir James Steere 1737. Entry: Lenin Room, lecture hall, reading room, basement tunnels. www.marx-memorial-library.org
Tube/Rail: Farringdon, King's Cross St Pancras; 55,63,243

Morelands (AHMM offices)

Morelands 5-12 Old Street EC1V 9HL

■ Sat 1pm-5pm. Architect led tours at 2pm, 3pm, 4pm. T R A

Home to a variety of creative industries and the office of AHMM since 1995, the Morelands interventions stitch together a convoluted tangle of disparate warehouse blocks, alleys and entrances; the most recent refurbishment has achieved BREEAM Outstanding. 5th floor completed in 2013. Allford Hall Monaghan Morris 2013.
Tube: Old Street, Barbican; Rail: Farringdon; 4,55,56,243
www.ahmm.co.uk

Museum of the Order of St John

St John's Gate EC1M 4DA

■ Sun 10am-5pm. Design activities and hide and seek trails for children (4yrs+) Last entry 4.30pm. N T B C

Building dates from 1504 with 19C and early 20C additions by Richard Norman Shaw and John Oldrid Scott. Crypt of the priory church was begun in the 1140s.
Tube/Rail: Farringdon, Old Street; 63,55,243
www.museumstjohn.org.uk

New House, Elfort Road

58A Elfort Road N5 1AZ

■ Sat/Sun 1pm-5pm. First come basis. D A

New single storey house on a corner site. The irregular shaped building sits between the gable ends of two terraces. Studio 54 Architecture 2014.
Tube: Arsenal

Oak Rooms, New River Head ●

New River Head, 173 Rosebery Avenue EC1R 4UL

■ Sat/Sun 10am-4pm. Hourly tours. Pre-book ONLY on londonopenhouse@thameswater.co.uk, subject line: 'Oak Rooms – Open House'. Max 16 per tour.

Formerly the boardroom of the 17C water house the Oak Room is a fine late Renaissance room demonstrating the New River Company's wealth. Fine 1697 carved oak interior, attributed to Grinling Gibbons. Austen Hall (refurbished) 1696/1914-20. Entry: Oak Room & Oak Room approaches.
Tube: Angel; Tube/Rail: Farringdon; 19,38,153,341

Ott's Yard ● ②

Southcote Road N19 5FB

■ Sat 10am-5pm. Half-hourly tours, first come basis. Last entry 4.30pm. d A G

Award-winning residential development replacing derelict joinery workshop with two new green-roofed houses. The plans relate to existing triangular geometry of courtyard site. Gardens and green roofs by Arabella Lennox-Boyd. vPPR Architects 2012.
Tube: Tufnell Park; Rail: Gospel Oak; 390,4,134

Park Theatre ●

Clifton Terrace N4 3JP

■ Sat tours at 10am, 11.15am, 12.15pm. Max 20 per tour. N D R T

A £2.6m conversion of office block into state-of-the-art theatre with two auditoriums, cafe bar and education studio. Together Park Theatre and John Jones Arts Building are two of the major driving forces around the exciting new regeneration programme in Finsbury Park. David Hughes Architects 2012.
Tube/Rail: Finsbury Park; 4,19,29,253

Penthouse flat, The Print House

32 Aylesbury Street EC1R 0ET

■ Sat 10am-5pm. Regular tours. Last tour 4.15pm. Max 15 per tour. A G

Penthouse apartment over 2 floors of converted and extended former print works with large open-plan living/dining/

cooking space featuring helical stair within top-lit polished plaster drum. Winner 'Best Apartment' Evening Standard New Homes Awards 2013. FORM Design Architecture 2012. Entry: flat interior at 4th & 5th floors, terrace.
Tube/Rail: Farringdon; 55,243,153,63
www.form-architecture.co.uk

Pollard Thomas Edwards

Diespeker Wharf, 38 Graham Street N1 8JX

■ Sat 10am-5pm. Regular architect-led tours. Last entry 4.30pm. Max 20 per tour. R T C A

Conversion of a canalside Victorian warehouse, formerly a timberyard, into spacious offices, garden and glazed extension with one of the best waterside views in London. Visit award-winning project Angel Waterside apartments. Sculptor/metalsmith on site, exhibition and hosting workshops. Pollard Thomas Edwards 1990s/2003. Entry: upper & lower ground floors, courtyard and neighbouring Angel Waterside.
Tube: Angel, Old Street; 38,43,73,214
www.pollardthomasedwards.co.uk

Priory Green ●

Hugh Cubitt House, 48 Collier Street N1 9QZ

■ Sat 10am-5pm. Last entry 4.30pm. Max 10 at one time. D

Modern movement estate, received Conservation Area status after extensive refurbishment by Peabody. Pioneering use of concrete and sculptural stairways. Includes 4 blocks, Old Laundry building and landscaped areas. Tecton & Lubetkin 1957. Entry: external areas, internal access to Old Laundry building. NB. no entry to flats.
Tube: Angel; Tube/Rail: King's Cross St Pancras; 73

Richard Desmond Children's Eye Centre at Moorfields Eye Hospital

3 Peerless Street EC1V 9EZ

■ Sun 11am-1pm. Half-hourly tours, first come basis. Last entry 12.30pm. Max 10 per tour. D R T

A world-class, contemporary healthcare building, dedicated to the treatment of children's eye conditions. Functional excellence with an award-winning and non-institutional design. Penoyre & Prasad 2007. Entry: all public areas.
Tube/Rail: Old Street; 43,135,205,214

Sadler's Wells Theatre

Rosebery Avenue EC1R 4TN

■ Sat 10am-11am. Tour at 10am. Max 20 per tour. T B d

A theatre has stood on site for 300 years. 20C design has full-height glazed screen façade. Auditorium lined with metal gauze panels that take dramatically transforming light and image projection. FGM Chancellor/RHWL and Nicholas Hare Architects 1931/1998.
Tube: Angel; Tube/Rail: Farringdon, King's Cross St Pancras; 73,43,341,19,38

St Mary, Islington

Upper Street N1 2TX

■ Sat 10am-5pm/Sun 1pm-5pm. Tower tours Sat. Max 8 per tour. D R T C G

One of the oldest parishes in the UK with layers of history, including what has been suggested as a Norman stone in the crypt, an 18C tower and a grand, open worship space, rebuilt after bombing. Sustainable features include the largest solar panels on a church in London. 18C/1959.
Tube: Angel; Tube/Rail: Highbury & Islington; 4,19,30,43

St Paul Street ●

74 St Paul Street N1 7DA

■ Sun 1pm-5pm. Pre-book ONLY on mail@studiocma.co.uk. Architects Daniela Ciarcelluti and Greg Mathers and

Engineer Robbie Belmore onsite. N d A E

Alterations and extension to a typical Victorian terrace creating an open plan ground floor with strong connection to the garden. The design also includes fitted joinery and kitchen. Ciarcelluti Mathers Architecture 2013.
Tube: Angel, Old Street; 21,141,271,76,38

The Goldsmiths' Centre ●

42 Britton Street, EC1M 5AD

■ Sat 10am-5pm. Tours 10.30am, 12noon, 2pm, 4pm. First come basis. Last entry 4.30pm. Max 15 per tour. N D R T G

RIBA award-winning centre for the training and advancement of the goldsmith's craft combining early Grade II listed Victorian board school and modern 4-storey block clad in York stone and brass. Lyall, Bills and Young 2012. Entry: Cafe, atrium, exhibition space, 4th floor conference rooms and terrace, training workshops and studios in old school building.
Tube/Rail: Farringdon; 63,45,17,243,55
www.goldsmiths-centre.org

The Small House

90A Richmond Avenue N1 0NA

■ Sat/Sun 10am-5pm. First come basis, queuing outside if necessary. Last entry 4.45pm.

Grade II listed former flower shop rebuilt into one of London's smallest self-contained dwellings. Built from pre-fabricated timber with furniture dressed in cedar, leather and felt. Result is diminutive pied-a-terre – also spacious and enjoyable existenzminimum. Dyvik Kahlen Architects 2013.
Tube: Angel, Caledonian Road; 153,274,38,19,17
www.dyvikkahlen.com

Union Chapel

Compton Terrace N1 2XD

■ Sat 10am-4pm/Sun 1pm-4pm. Regular tours. Sat 12noon-4pm performances. N T B d

Octagonal Grade I listed Congregational chapel, containing vast and theatrically balconied interior. Now a concert space, as well as church and day centre. James Cubitt 1877. Entry: main auditorium, chapel, ancillary rooms.
Tube/Rail: Highbury & Islington; 4,19,30,43,271

W. Plumb Family Butchers

493 Hornsey Road N19 3QL

■ Sat 10am-7pm/Sun 10am-5pm. First come basis, queuing outside if necessary. Max 25 at one time. D R

Grade II listed, ornate former Victorian butcher's shop c1900 with art nouveau wall tiling, geometric tiled floor, scrolled meat rails and mahogany cashier's booth with etched and brilliant cut glass. Well preserved. c1900. Entry: butcher's shop.
Tube: Archway; Rail: Upper Holloway; 41,91,210

Wesley's Chapel and House

49 City Road EC1Y 1AU

■ Sat 10am-4pm/Sun 12.30pm-2pm. Regular tours. Groups over 6 people should book in advance on 020 7253 2262. Last entry Sat 3.30pm/Sun 1.30pm. Max 50 at one time (15 in Wesley's house). N T B C d

Fine Georgian complex built by John Wesley as his London base. George Dance the Younger 1778. Entry: chapel, museum, John Wesley's house, gardens.
Tube: Moorgate, Old Street; Tube/Rail: Liverpool Street; 21,43,76

Supported by

🛡 ISLINGTON

Kensington & Chelsea

See openhouselondon.org.uk/kensington
to find out more about this area

3floor-in2 Apartment
17 Elgin Crescent W11 2JD
■ Sun 3pm-6pm. Tours every 20mins, first come basis,
queuing outside if necessary. Shoes off. Max 20 per tour. A P
This project unites two old flats with the insertion of
dramatic full-height vertical space: a stair rises through three
new minor levels that shape this new tall atrium and link into
the two main previous floor levels. Sunlight beams into the
lower, previously shaded north spaces. The variations in
height and depth simultaneously animate private and more
playful spaces. Andrew Pilkington Architects/Elliott Wood
Partnership 2013.
*Tube: Notting Hill Gate, Ladbroke Grove, Westbourne Park;
23,52,452,328,316,70*
www.elliottwood.co.uk

18 Stafford Terrace – The Sambourne Family Home
18 Stafford Terrace W8 7BH
■ Sat 10.30am-5pm. First come basis. Entry at set intervals –
cards will be given out with entrance time. Last entry 4pm.
Max 15 at one time. T B Q
From 1875, the home of the Punch cartoonist Edward Linley
Sambourne, his wife Marion, their two children and their live-
in servants. Today, the house is recognised as the best surviving
example of a late Victorian middle-class home in the UK. It
is remarkably well-preserved and complete with its original
interior decoration and contents. Joseph Gordon Davis 1871.
Entry: ground floor and basement only.
*Tube: High Street Kensington; Tube/Rail: Kensington (Olympia);
9,10,27,28,49,328*

264 Westbourne Park Road
264 Westbourne Park Road W11 1EJ
■ Sat 10am-12pm/Sun 3pm-5pm. First come basis, queuing
outside if necessary. Shoes to be removed before entry. Last
entry 15 mins before closing times. Max 6 per tour. Q A G
New building as an urban accent, consisting of two
independent houses placed on top of each other. While
contemporary in design the building draws from the tectonic
composition of the adjacent Victorian houses with their
clearly expressed bases. Features rain water harvesting,
extensive roof garden, solar water heating and heat recovery.
Studio Bednarski 2011.
*Tube: Ladbroke Grove, Westbourne Park; Tube/Rail: Paddington;
7,70,452,52,23*

Blechynden Studios
54 Blechynden Street W10 6RJ
■ Sat/Sun 12pm-6pm. Last entry 5.30pm. Max 100 at one
time. D T G P
Striking deck architecture with walkways opening onto
individual artists' studios with wall to ceiling Reglit double
glazed panels, galvanised and silver-anodised finishes,
concrete and white painted walls. Orefelt Associates 1999.
Entry: 23 artists' studios.
Tube: Latimer Road; 295,316

Brompton Cemetery Chapel, Colonnades and Memorials
Old Brompton Road SW5 or Fulham Road SW10 9UG

Chelsea Academy

■ Sat/Sun 1pm-5pm. Tour at 2pm starting at the Cemetery
Chapel. For info on tours ring 020 7351 1689. Max 35 at one
time. R T B d
London's finest Grade I listed Victorian cemetery of 40 acres
with many memorials, designed by architect who had
previously worked on rebuilding of Windsor Castle. Benjamin
Baud 1840. Entry: chapel, cemetery grounds.
Tube/Rail: West Brompton; 14,74,190,211,328,C3,414

Chelsea Academy ● ◎
Lots Road SW10 0AB
■ Sat 10.30am-3.30pm. Hourly tours only, first come basis.
Last tour 3.30pm. Max 12 per tour. D T A G
One of a new generation of schools on a very tight urban
space. The architectural language is classical, formal and
restrained recalling the local terraces, but enlivened with
subtle variations. Numerous energy-saving measures are
incorporated. RIBA Award Winner 2011. Feilden Clegg Bradley
2010. Entry: classrooms, theatre, sports hall, climbing wall, roof
terraces, chapel.
Tube: Fulham Broadway; Rail: Imperial Wharf; 11,22,C3

Embassy of the Czech Republic
26 Kensington Palace Gardens W8 4QY
■ Sat/Sun 10am-5pm. First come basis, queuing if necessary.
Exhibition on War Photographers 1914-1918. Last entry
4.45pm. D R T
Unlike so many examples of precast concrete buildings which
are weathering badly, this is a refined example of its kind,
skilfully detailed technically and aesthetically. RIBA Award
Winner 1971. Jan Bocan, Jan Sramek and Karel Stepansky 1970.
Entry: Parts of the interior of the embassy and the garden.
Tube: Notting Hill Gate; 94,148,52,390,328

The Yellow Building

Embassy of the Kingdom of The Netherlands
38 Hyde Park Gate SW7 5DP
■ Sat 10am-5pm. Regular tours, first come basis. British Sign
Language (BSL) tours at 11am and 2pm – contact lon-ppc@
minbuza.nl if you have any access or communications
requirements. Last entry 4.30pm. D R T
The administrative and public building of the Dutch
diplomatic mission in London. Red brick with stone dressings.
Entry: dining room, atrium, public areas on first 3 floors.
Tube: Gloucester Road, High Street Kensington; 52,452,70,9,10

Embassy of the Slovak Republic
25 Kensington Palace Gardens W8 4QY
■ Sat/Sun 10am-5pm. Last entry 4.30pm. d
Modern Brutalist-style by Jan Bocan, Jan Srámek and Karel
Stepansky. The building is made out of reinforced concrete
panels, long glass rows of window with wooden partitions
separating the interior spaces. The first phase of planning the
former Czechoslovak embassy started in 1965. Jan Bocan, Jan
Srámek and Karel Stepansky 1970. Entry: Ground and First floor.
Tube: Kensington High Street, Notting Hill Gate; 27,28,52,70,94

Hidden House ● ◎
39 Russell Garden Mews W14 8EU
■ Sun 10am-6pm. Regular tours, first come basis, shoes off.
Last tour 5.45pm. Max 20 per tour. R Q A G
A new build 2600 sq ft mews house as featured on Grand
Designs. Four floors with a large basement living space and
night club dance floor wrapped around a courtyard with a
pond and waterfall. The house achieved BREEAM 'Excellent'
home rating. Sustainable features include air-source heat
pump, photovoltaics, super-insulation and water recycling.
Hogarth Architects 2011. Entry: all areas.
Tube/Rail: Kensington (Olympia), Shepherd's Bush; 49,C1,27,9,28

● AJ Library Building   ● Green Exemplar   ● Landscape/Public realm   ● Infrastructure/Engineering
■ Open Saturday   ■ Open Sunday   ■ Open Saturday and Sunday

openhouselondon.org.uk | Kensington & Chelsea | 47

...all at Olympia London

The Ismaili Centre

Institut francais du Royaume-Uni
17 Queensberry Place SW7 2DT
■ Sat/Sun 12pm-7pm. Regular tours for adults and kids of the Institute and newly renovated Reading Room. Historical documentary screenings. Presentation of future library after renovation. Max 15 at one time. N R T B d
1939 Art Deco listed building refurbished in 1950, then restructured and modernised. Contains an authentically classic cinema, private salons, multimedia library and bistro. Patrice Bonnet/Jean-Francois Darin/Stefanie Fisher/ Bisset Adams 1939/1996/2010/2013. Entry: library, hall, photography exhibition.
Tube: South Kensington; 14,49,70,74,345,C1

Leighton House
12 Holland Park Road W14 8LZ
■ Sat/Sun 10am-5.30pm. Last entry 5pm. T B Q
Originally home and studio of Lord Leighton, President of the Royal Academy, the house is one of the most remarkable buildings of 19C. Extraordinary Arab hall with fountains and tiling; superb staircase. Recently the subject of a £1.6m refurbishment project, the work involved extensive repairs to the original fabric of the house as well as the redecoration of the interiors. RIBA Award Winner 2011. George Aitchison/ Purcell Miller Tritton (refurb) 1865-79/2010.
Tube: High Street Kensington; Tube/Rail: Kensington (Olympia); 9,10,27,28,49

Pillar Hall at Olympia London
Olympia Way W14 8UX
■ Sat 10am-2pm. First come basis. T
A columned hall in a rich, eclectic classical style. Its upper floors house a decommissioned cinema space, gallery and projector room. The exterior façade has a palazzo front with red brick and stone dressings. Henry Coe 1885.
Tube: Kensington (Olympia) 9,10,27,28,49,391
www.olympia.co.uk/organising/olympia-venues/pillar-hall

Royal Danish Embassy
55 Sloane Street SW1X 9SR
■ Sat 11am-3pm. Tours at 11am, 1pm and 3pm. Pre-book ONLY at www.denmark.org.uk – please bring photo ID. Tours led by Dr Peter Thule Kristensen, Arch Phd, Head of Royal Danish Academy, School of Architecture. Max 60 per tour. T A
Only example in London of work by Denmark's best-known architect. After his death in 1971 the detailed design was completed by his successors Dissing and Weitling. Arne Jacobsen 1977. Entry: reception, canteen, office area, courtyard.
Tube: Knightsbridge, Sloane Square; Tube/Rail: Victoria; 19,22,137,C1

Saatchi Gallery
Duke of York's HQ, King's Road SW3 4RY
■ Sat/Sun 10am-6pm. First come basis. Last entry 5.30pm. N D R T B
Gallery within the listed walls of a former drill hall known as the Duke of York's HQ. The building was stripped back to its shell and a new entrance sequence locates 15 inter-connected galleries on three levels, exploiting the elegance of the large, well-proportioned rooms. Allford Hall Monaghan Morris 2008.
Tube: Sloane Square; Tube/Rail: Victoria; 11,22,137,319,211
www.ahmm.co.uk

Serpentine Sackler Gallery ● ●
West Carriage Drive, Kensington Gardens W2 2AR
■ Sat/Sun 10am-6pm. First come basis, queuing outside if neccessary. N D R T B
Grade II* listed former gunpowder store converted into the new Serpentine Sackler Gallery by Zaha Hadid. With 900 square metres of gallery, restaurant and social space, the Serpentine's second space in Kensington Gardens is a new cultural destination in the heart of London. Zaha Hadid 2013.
Tube: Lancaster Gate, Marble Arch; 148,274,390,94

St Columba's Church of Scotland
Pont Street SW1X 0BD
■ Sat 10am-5pm/Sun 2pm-5pm. First come basis, tours of some areas. Last entry 4.30pm. R T B d
Distinctive listed white building replacing earlier Victorian building destroyed in WWII. Sanctuary retains sense of modernity. Sir Edward Maufe 1955. Entry: sanctuary, chapel, library, Kirk Session room, lower hall, Columbarium, tower.
Tube: Knightsbridge, South Kensington, Sloane Square; 137,19,22,452,C1

St Cuthbert's Church
50 Philbeach Gardens SW5 9EB
■ Sat 10am-5pm/Sun 1pm-5pm. N
Spectacular late Victorian high church. Features arts and crafts furnishings with metalwork by W Bainbridge Reynolds. H R Gough 1887.
Tube: Earls Court; Tube/Rail: West Brompton; 31,74,C1,C3

St John's Notting Hill
St John's Church, Lansdowne Cresent, Notting Hill W11 2NN
■ Sat 1pm-7pm. Informal tours taking place. Access to organ project and bell tower. 3-5pm talks and activities. Free concert at 7pm. Max 5 inside clock/bell tower, 1 inside organ. R T d A E
Built on the former site of a hippodrome and designed in the Early English style (1843-5). Major engineering works in 1994. Current restoration of organ funded by the Heritage Lottery Fund. Excellent views of the surrounding area from disused bell tower. John Hargrave Stevens/Simon Ablett 1845.
Tube: Holland Park, Notting Hill Gate, Ladbroke Grove; 228
www.stjohnsorganproject.com

The Ismaili Centre
1-7 Cromwell Gardens SW7 2SL
■ Sun 10am-4pm. Regular tours. Last tour 4pm. Max 100 at one time. T d. Audio Described Tours taking place as part of our VocalEyes partnership, see p.14 for details.
Part of an international family of Ismaili Centres, this is the first religious, cultural and social space for the Shia Ismaili Muslim community in the West. From the serenity of the entrance fountain to the remarkable roof garden, it draws upon Muslim traditions in architecture and design while remaining conscious of its context. A sanctuary of calm amidst the bustle of the city. Casson Conder Partnership 1983.
Tube: South Kensington; 14,70,74,345,414,C1

The Yellow Building
1 Nicholas Road W11 4AN
■ Sun 10am-1pm. First come basis, queuing outside if necessary. T A
The Yellow Building is the 15,000m2 landmark headquarters for fashion company Monsoon Accessorize. Intended to read as a creative powerhouse, the building has a dramatic top-lit atrium with a stunning open staircase running from top to bottom. Allford Hall Monaghan Morris 2008. Entry: all external areas, ground floor atria, internal main staircase to 5th floor – no access onto floors.
Tube: Latimer Road; 316,295
www.ahmm.co.uk

Victoria and Albert Museum
Cromwell Road SW7 2RL
■ Sat 11am-5pm. Tours at 11am, 2pm, 4pm, pre-book ONLY on 020 7942 2211. Max 20 per tour. N R T B
Introducing the rich and varied architecture of the V&A Museum, allowing access to some areas usually closed to the public. V&A and RIBA Architecture Gallery, ongoing restoration of historic interiors, and the latest gallery projects including furniture gallery by NORD Architecture. Francis Fowke/ Sir Aston Webb and others 1856 onwards.
Tube: South Kensington; C1,14,74,414

WALKS/TOURS

World's End Estate walk
■ Meet: Sun 2.30pm, 4.30pm at 16 Blantyre Street SW10 0DS Duration 2 hours. T
Designed by Eric Lyons and constructed in the mid-70s, the World's End Estate is a deliberate architectural attempt to not only overcome many of the issues of previous high-rise developments, but also to eliminate monotonous and bland facades through the use of alternative designs and materials. Eric Lyons (Principal) 1969-76.
Tube: Sloane Square, Earls Court; Rail: Imperial Wharf; 11,22,19,49,328

Supported by

THE ROYAL BOROUGH OF
KENSINGTON AND CHELSEA

Key A Architect on site **B** Bookshop **C** Childrens' activities **d** Some disabled access **D** Full wheelchair access **E** Engineer on site **G** Green Features **N** Normally open to the public **P** Parking **Q** Long queues envisaged **R** Refreshments **T** Toilets

Lambeth

See openhouselondon.org.uk/lambeth
to find out more about this area

West Norwood Health and Leisure Centre

54 Cambria Road ●
54 Cambria Road SE5 9AS
■ Sat 10am-5pm. Informal discussion around eco conversion of 19C housing stock. Building bird houses for children. Last entry 5pm. Max 15 at one time. E R T C A G P d
Self build conversion of 19C terrace: reorganised living spaces, reclaimed materials, natural insulation, solar thermal and PV, biofuel heating, vegetable growing, bees, hens. Baraitser Smith (conversion) 19C/2008. Entry: house and garden.
Tube/Rail: Brixton; Rail: Loughborough Junction; P4,35,45,176,345

Akerman Health Centre ●
60 Patmos Street SW9 6AF
■ Sat 1pm-4pm. Architect-led half-hourly tours, first come basis. Last tour 3.30pm. Max 10 per tour. N D T A
White brick structure mimics a cathedral, creating a late 'monument' to the NHS. It incorporates artworks by Daniel Sturgis (outside) and Paul Morrison (inside). BREEAM Excellent. RIBA Award Winner 2013. Henley Halebrown Rorrison 2012.
Tube: Oval; 185,436,36,P5

Arts Lav
180 Kennington Lane SE11 4UZ
■ Sat/Sun 10am-5pm. First come basis, queuing outside if necessary. Last entry 4.45pm.
Once a Victorian Gentleman's lavatory, ArtsLav is now a thriving arts hub in a listed and semi-restored Kennington landmark. Original features include marble urinals, glass water tank, mosaic floor, ventilator shaft and horse trough. 1898/2013. Entry: all areas.
Tube: Kennington; Rail: Elephant & Castle; 3,59,159,196,360

Bateman Mews ●
3 Bateman Mews SW4 8AS
■ Sat 12pm-4pm. First come basis, queuing outside if necessary. Last entry 3.45pm. Max 7 at one time. Q A G d
Five houses for a wooded backland site were designed as 'huts in the garden' of the large surrounding villas, of well-insulated FSC timber frame construction, shingle clad, with green roofs and a large shared garden. RIBA Award Winner 2010. Anne Thorne Architects Partnership 2009. Entry: tours inside one house, shared front entrance and garden.
Tube: Clapham North; Rail: Clapham High Street; 137,417,355

Beaconsfield
Lambeth Ragged School, 22 Newport Street SE11 6AY
■ Sat/Sun 11am-5pm. First come basis. Exhibition by John Timberlake 'We Are History'. Max 200 at one time. N R T G d
The remaining girls' wing of the former Lambeth Ragged School built 1851 by local philanthropist Lord Beaufoy – now a unique space for contemporary art. Living roof structure in yard. 1851. Entry: all areas.
Tube: Lambeth North; Tube/Rail: Vauxhall, Waterloo; 77,344,360

BFI IMAX
Waterloo Roundabout SE1 8XR
■ Sat/Sun 11am-4pm. Regular tours of projection booth, pre-book ONLY by email on imax.education@odeonuk.com. R T D

Multi-storey, glass-enclosed cylinder, illuminated by coloured lighting at night, with most sophisticated motion-picture projection system in the world. Avery Associates Architects 1999. Entry: ground and 1st floor foyers.
Tube/Rail: Waterloo; 1,4,26,59,68,76,77,168,171,176,188,211,243, 341,381

Brockwell Lido, Brockwell Park
Dulwich Road SE24 0PA
■ Sat 9am-1pm. Regular tours, first come basis. (Pool open at normal charge). Max 8 per tour. R T d
Classic 1930s open air swimming-pool restored to former glory with the addition of a single storey extension replicating the original design. H A Rowbotham & T L Smithson/Pollard Thomas Edwards (refurb) 1937/2007. Entry: lido pool side, reception.
Tube/Rail: Brixton; Rail: Herne Hill; 3,37,68,196,322,468

Christ Church, Streatham
3 Christchurch Road SW2 3ET
■ Sat 10am-5pm/Sun 1pm-4pm. Photos of restoration work and self-guided tours. R T C P d
Grade I listed pioneering brick polychromy. Designed with early Christian, Italian, Ottoman, Alhambran, Mamluk, Sevillian and Ancient Egyptian influences with fine mosaics and stained glass by Walter Crane, J F Bentley and John Hayward. James Wild and Owen Jones 1841. Entry: all except bell tower.
Tube/Rail: Brixton; Rail: Streatham Hill, Tulse Hill; 50,59,109,250,133

City Heights E-ACT Academy ● ●
33 Abbots Park SW2 3PW
■ Sat 10am-1pm. Tours taking place, pre-book ONLY on admin@chea.org.uk. Last entry 12.30pm. D R T A E G
Situated on two sites, the academy combines the rebuilding of Fenstanton Primary School for 638 children, and the creation of a new 1100-place Academy. The academy specialises in language skills and is partnered with Dulwich College. Shared facilities including sports pitches and a pavilion will be located on a second site close by. Green design features include solar panels and passive ventilation. Jestico + Whiles 2014.
Tube: Brixton; Rail: Tulse Hill; 2,68,196,201,322

Clapham Library ●
Mary Seacole Centre, 91 Clapham High Street SW4 7DB
■ Sat 10am-5pm/Sun 1pm-5pm. Last entry 4.30pm. Max 5 at one time. N D T
The building is based around a spiral theme that allows a building of multiple uses to feel like one space to reinforce a sense of community spirit. Studio Egret West 2012.
Tube: Clapham Common, Clapham North; 35,37,88,137,155

Clapham Manor Primary School ●
Belmont Road SW4 0BZ
■ Sat 10am-1pm. First come basis, queuing outside if necessary. Practice Director Philip Marsh on site. Last entry 12.30pm. Max 20 at one time. D R T
A polychromatic extension inserted into a tight urban context offering this DCSF outstanding school a new identity with much-needed new learning spaces and an organisational hub, whilst maintaining external play space. RIBA Award Winner 2010. de Rijke Marsh Morgan (dRMM) 2008.
Tube: Clapham Common; Rail: Clapham High Street; 35,37,417,137,345

Cressingham Gardens
Cressingham Gardens Rotunda, Tulse Hill SW2 2QN
■ Sat/Sun 10am-5pm. Regular tours, first come basis. Exhibition in Rotunda. R T P C
Low-rise leafy estate located next to beautiful Brockwell Park noted for its innovative design, incorporating pioneering architectural elements and echoing the natural topography. Ted Hollamby 1967-78. Entry: Rotunda, private homes.
Tube/Rail: Brixton; Rail: Herne Hill; 415,432,2

EDF Energy London Eye ●
County Hall, Belvedere Road SE1 7PB
■ Sun 9am-10.30am. Lecture with Director David Marks or Julia Barfield including a 15 minute Q&A followed by a rotation on the London Eye. By ballot through Open House ONLY. Please see p.16 for more info. 100 tickets maximum allocation. NB. Over 12 years only. D T B A
The world's tallest cantilevered observation wheel which has rapidly become a much-loved symbol of modern Britain. RIBA Award Winner. Marks Barfield Architects 1999.
Tube: Westminster; Tube/Rail: Waterloo; RV1,211,24,11

Lambeth Palace

Foxley Road
19 Foxley Road SW9 6ET
■ Sat/Sun 1pm-5pm. First come basis, queuing outside if necessary. Architects Gavin & Shigemi Challand on site. T A
Refurbishment of a one-bedroom garden apartment in a listed Georgian house. The interiors combine ingenious and space-saving design solutions with bold and theatrical use of materials. N.P. Rothery / Catfish Studio Ltd (refurb) 1824/2014. Entry: Private apartment, garden.
Tube: Oval; 3,36,59,133,159,185,415,436
www.catfishstudio.demon.co.uk/foxleyroad

H10 London Waterloo ⊕
284-302 Waterloo Road SE1 8RQ
■ Sat/Sun 1pm-5pm. First come basis. Last entry 5pm. Max 5 at one time. D T
Newly-built 13-storey 4-star hotel with striking civic composition, clearly defining the base, middle and top of the building. A ground level cut-back provides a generous pedestrian path and the resulting overhang shelters the glazed entrance foyer. Variegated brickwork provides solidity and permanence, alternating on the south facade where large flush openings and deep brick reveals dynamic patterns. Maccreanor Lavington 2010. Entry: public areas, bedrooms.
Tube: Lambeth; Tube/Rail: Waterloo

Jubiloo
Queen's Walk, Jubilee Gardens SE1 7PB
■ Sat 1pm-5pm. Tours on the hour with practice director, first come basis. T A d
The pavilion's dramatic canopy is like a vessel moored downstream of the EDF Energy London Eye. Commissioned following a South Bank competition, this extraordinary building was shortlisted for BCI and NLA awards. Sustainable

features include rain-water harvesting, and modular construction. Mark Power Architect 2012. Entry: WC Pavilion.
Tube/Rail: Waterloo, Charing Cross; Tube: Embankment; 77,139,168,211,341

Lambeth Palace
Lambeth Palace Road SE1 7JU
■ Sat 10am-4pm. Tours every 15 mins, duration 1 hour. Pre-book ONLY on www.archbishopofcanterbury.org.uk. Last tour 3pm. Max 25 per tour. T d
Archbishop of Canterbury's London home, dating from 13C; 19C work by Blore, and crypt vestibule opened 2000. 13C onwards. Entry: chapel and crypt courtyard, guardroom, picture gallery. NB. Limited toilets available.
Tube: Lambeth North; Tube/Rail: Waterloo; Vauxhall; 3,77,344,507,C10

Lambourn Road
1 Lambourn Road SW4 0LY
■ Sat 10am-5pm. Regular architect-led tours, first come basis. Last entry 4.30pm. Max 15 per tour. A G d
Architect-owned Victorian house, substantially extended and remodelled to create a contemporary new home. Includes a range of retrofit features. Granit Architects 2013.
Tube: Clapham Common; Rail: Wandsworth Road; 77,452

London's Engineering Heritage: ICE boat tours ⊕
■ Departs: Sat 11am & 1pm from Festival Pier SE1 8XZ. First come basis. Max 100 per tour. Arrive in good time to board, departures are prompt. Bar onboard MV Kingwood selling light refreshments. Bring rainwear if you wish to sit on open deck. Duration 1 1/2 hours. E D R T Q
The capital's inspirational engineering with live commentary from London's leading engineers on aspects including Bazalgette's legacy, flood risk management, current and future engineering landmarks and London's historical structures. Organised by the Institution of Civil Engineers. **ice**
Tube/Rail: Waterloo; 211,24,11

Morley College
61 Westminster Bridge Road SE1 7HT
■ Sun 1pm-4.30pm. Half-hourly tours from 1.30pm. First come basis. Last tour and entry 4pm. Max 15 per tour. Max 120 at one time. R T d
Morley was extensively damaged during WWII, though its 1937 extension by Edward Brantwood Maufe survives. Rebuilt by John Brandon-Jones in 1958, a J Winter extension was added in 1973. Extensive murals from the 1960s by Edward Bawden and Justin Todd in the refectory. Morley College celebrates its 125th anniversary in September 2014. Edward Maufe/John Brandon-Jones/John Winter 1924-1973. Entry: main building, refectory, Holst room, library.
Tube: Lambeth North; Tube/Rail: Waterloo, Elephant & Castle; 12,3,453,159,C10

Pullman Court
Streatham Hill SW2 4SZ
■ Sun 11am-5pm. Display of site-specific art works 'A Happier alternative to What's going on' – and a photographic exhibition of Venezuelan mid 20th Century architecture: 'Modernism+Caracas' Max 10 at one time in flats. D
Grade II* listed Modern Movement building, with balcony walkways and period internal features. Frederick Gibberd 1936. Entry: flats (differing types), common parts, gardens.
Tube/Rail: Brixton; Rail: Streatham Hill; 159,137,133,109,250,45, 201,417,319,57,118

Rambert
99 Upper Ground, SE1 9PP
■ Sat 10am-5pm. First come basis, tours on the hour. Last entry 4pm. Max 15 per tour. D T
Rambert's award-winning new home provides the company with state of the art facilities for the creation of new choreography and music for dance. It also enables the company to unlock the riches of the Rambert archive – one of the oldest and most complete dance archives in the world. Allies and Morrison 2013. Entry: Studios, workshops, wardrobe and offices covered as part of tour.
Tube/Rail: Waterloo; RV1

Roots & Shoots
Walnut Tree Walk SE11 6DN
■ Sat 10am-5pm. Tours at 1.30pm, 2.30pm, 3.30pm. Exhibition and displays. Max 50 per tour. N D R T G
Training centre providing environmental education for all, built on an inner-city site. Large photovoltaic roof, solar water heating, three planted roofs and a rubble roof. Paul Notley/CPP Architects 2008. Entry: plant nursery, wild garden.
Tube: Lambeth North; Rail: Waterloo; 159,59,3,360

Royal Festival Hall ⊕
Belvedere Road SE1 8XX
■ Sat/Sun 10am-11pm. Behind the scenes tours at 10.30am, 12.30pm, 2.30pm, first come basis, duration 1 hour. NB. Due to nature of areas covered, no children under 16 and unsuitable for those with vertigo or special access requirements. No high heels or big bags. N D R T B
The major refurbishment of Royal Festival Hall has enhanced the acoustics and comfort to world class standards, increased audience facilities and accessibility, and created an entirely new education and learning centre. RIBA Award Winner 2008. LCC Architects Department/Allies and Morrison (refurb) 1951/2007.
Tube: Embankment; Tube/Rail: Charing Cross, Waterloo; 172,181, 176,26,188,RV1,68,76,77,168,171,341

South London Botanical Institute
323 Norwood Road SE24 9AQ
■ Sun 1pm-5pm. Regular tours, first come basis. Small plant sale, botanical activities. Last entry 4.30pm. N R T C P d
Brick-built Victorian villa c1876 set back from road with sweeping drive. Few interior changes since 1910 when retired Indian government administrator Alan Octavian Hume founded the Institute. c.1876. Entry: herbarium, botanical library, garden with wide variety of plants.
Rail: Tulse Hill; 68,196,322,2,P13,201,468,415,432

South London Theatre
The Old Fire Station, 2a Norwood High Street SE27 9NS
■ Sat/Sun 1pm-5pm. Regular guided architectural and theatrical tours with opportunities to view play rehearsals, 2 theatres and wardrobe rooms. R T
Grade II listed 1881 former fire station with prominent watch tower and original fire doors. Owen Luder (conversion) 1881/1967. Entry: all areas except watch tower and roof.
Rail: West Norwood, Tulse Hill; 2,68,196,315,322,432,468

The Brix at St Matthews, Brixton
Brixton Hill SW2 1JF
■ Sat 10am-5pm. First come basis. Tours at 15mins past the hour. Last entry 4pm. Max 14 per tour. N R T d
A classical church in the Greek style extensively modified internally to provide six floors of accommodation for a variety of uses including performance space, hall, offices, hot-desking, worship and leisure. 1824.
Tube/Rail: Brixton; 2,3,35,37,45,59,159

Bateman Mews

London's Engineering Heritage: ICE boat tours

Clapham Manor Primary School

The Cinema Museum ●
The Master's House, 2 Dugard Way (off Renfrew Road) SE11 4TH
■ Sun 10am-5pm. Regular tours, first come basis. SE1 Picture Palaces and Cinema Uniform exhibitions on site. Last tour 3.30pm, last entry 4pm. Max 15 per tour. E D R T B P
The Master's House of the Lambeth Workhouse is ornate Victorian Gothic with polychrome brickwork, contrasting stone and narrow horizontal terracotta panels in dog-tooth pattern. R Parris and TW Aldwinkle 1871.
Tube: Kennington; Tube/Rail: Elephant & Castle; 3,59,133,156,196

The Clock House: 5 Chestnut Road
5 Chestnut Road SE27 9EZ
■ Sun 10am-4pm. Tours at 10am, 12noon, 2pm, 4pm, first come basis. T A P d
Victorian house extended with large contemporary, highly colourful living space. Pre-patinated copper roof, large areas of glass, Douglas Fir detail. Glass floor/ceiling between living areas. See also The Clockworks. Michael Crowley Architect 2001. Entry: lower 2 floors.
Rail: West Norwood; 2,432,196,68,468

The Clockworks
6 Nettlefold Place SE27 0JW
■ Sun 11am-4.30pm. Tours at 11am, 1pm, 3pm, 4.30pm. Last entry 4.30pm. Max 50 at one time. E D T P
Internationally pre-eminent museum and integral workshops devoted to electrical timekeeping and the distribution of accurate time (1840-1970). Practical education and conservation in action. See also The Clock House entry. Michael Crowley Architect 2012. Entry: gallery, workshops, library.
Rail: West Norwood; 2,432,196,68,468

The Livity School
Adare Walk SW16 2PW
■ Sat 10am-4pm. Hourly tours, first come basis. Last entry 3pm. Max 20 per tour. D T A
A special educational needs primary school for children with autistic spectrum disorders and profound learning difficulties. Design includes slender dark brick and timber curtain walling and a ribbon of folded perforated anodised aluminium reflecting the leafy surroundings. Haverstock 2012.
Rail: Streatham Hill; 118,133

The Mulberry Centre (One O'Clock Club)
Myatt's Fields Park, adjacent to Calais Street (entrance through Park) SE5 9LP
■ Sat 10am-1pm. First come basis, queuing outside if necessary. Max 20 at one time. N D T A G
The Mulberry Centre is a children's building in the refurbished Myatt's Fields Park. As well as being a social and play club for parents and toddlers (One O'Clock Club), facilities are provided for parenting classes and staff training. Sustainable features include rainwater harvesting and air-source heat pump. Knox Bhavan Architects LLP 2010.
Tube: Oval; Rail: Loughborough Junction, Denmark Hill; 36,436,185,P5

West Norwood Cemetery & Greek Chapel
■ Meet: Sun at 2pm, 2.30pm, 3pm inside main cemetery gate, Norwood Road SE27 9JU. Duration 90 mins. Cemetery grounds open at all times. Max 35 per tour. T B P
Opened 1837, with monuments to famous Victorians. 69 Grade II/II* listed structures, including Greek Chapel c1872, architect uncertain, mausolea by EM Barry and GE Street and entrance arch by W Tite. 1837.
Tube/Rail: Brixton; Rail: West Norwood, Tulse Hill; 2,68,196,322,432,468

West Norwood Health and Leisure Centre
25 Devane Way, West Norwood SE27 0DF
■ Sat/Sun 10am-5pm. Architect led tours at 11am, first come basis. T Y A
Innovative new centre providing a mix of community and health facilities to promote well-being, including a 25m swimming pool, health and fitness suite and gym, dance studio, community meeting rooms, and GP and dental surgeries. Allford Hall Monaghan Morris 2013.
Rail: West Norwood; 2,68,196,315,432,468
www.ahmm.co.uk

Young Vic ●
66 The Cut SE1 8LZ
■ Sun 10am-5pm. Tours on Sunday at 10.30am, 11.30am, 2pm, 3pm and 4pm. Pre-book ONLY on 020 7922 2922. T d
A major £12.5 million rebuilding theatre project. Main auditorium retained with extra height and with 2 newly-built smaller, naturally-lit studios. Foyer has double-height mezzanine. Exterior includes mesh facade and painted screen by artist Clem Crosby. RIBA Award Winner 2007 and shortlisted for the RIBA Stirling Prize 2007. Haworth Tompkins 2007. Entry: front of house, some theatrical spaces.
Tube/Rail: Waterloo; Tube: Southwark; Rail: Waterloo East

WALKS/TOURS

Clapham Old Town and Venn Street ●
■ Meet: Sun 2pm by the Clock Tower next to Clapham Common tube SW4 0BD. Walk with landscape architect, first come basis. Duration 2 hours. Max 20 on tour.
Once dominated by parked cars and fast moving through-traffic, Venn Street is now Clapham Old Town's destination for alfresco dining, following a radical redesign using the principles of 'shared space' and 'naked streets'. It now also hosts a food market. The same principles have been employed to redesign the rest of Old Town, including the introduction of 'Copenhagen' style side road crossings. Urban Movement + LB Lambeth 2011.
Tube: Clapham Common

Supported by

Lambeth

Lewisham

See openhouselondon.org.uk/lewisham
to find out more about this area

Blackheath Quaker Meeting House
Lawn Terrace, Blackheath SE3 9LL
■ Sat 10am-5pm. Regular tours, first come basis. Last entry 4.45pm. Max 25 at one time. D R T B
A calm space for Quakers and others in octagonal meeting room lit naturally from high central roof lantern and side 'turrets'. Civic Trust Award 1973. Concrete Society Commendation 1974. Trevor Dannatt 1972. Entry: all areas.
Rail: Blackheath; 54,89,108,202,380,386

Boone's Chapel
Lee High Road SE13 5PH
■ Sat/Sun 12pm-5pm. First come basis. Exhibition material on the social history of the building. Max 30 at one time. N D A
Grade I listed former almshouse chapel restored in 2008 as an architect's studio and exhibition space. Brick and Portland stone chapel (1682) with contemporary service building and small garden in grounds of the Merchant Taylors' Almshouses. Green features include recycled materials, sheep's wool insulation and lime plaster. 1682/2008. Entry: chapel.
Rail: Blackheath, Lewisham, Hither Green; 321,178,261,122

Cutting House
Circus Street, SE10 8SG
■ Sun 10am-5pm. First come basis. Last entry 4.30pm. A
One bedroom house arranged around a full height glazed courtyard. Built on an infill plot on the site of a derelict brick cobbler's workshop. Pre-fabricated timber frame with natural fibre insulation. High-quality hard finishes throughout. Architect on site: Sam Cooper. E2 Architecture 2014.
Rail: Greenwich

Deptford Green School ●
Deptford Green, Edward Street, New Cross SE14 6AN
■ Sat 11am-1pm. Tours every 15 minutes from 11am to 12.30pm with students. Crafts for children to enjoy. Last entry 12.30pm. N T C A G
Winner of LABP best educational building award in 2013. The design of the building reflects the importance of the student voice and wider community access. The design provides an impressive new street frontage whilst minimising the building's footprint and maximising available external space for both learning and social use. Highly sustainable design and rated BREEAM Excellent. Watkins Gray International 2012. Entry: Roof top classrooms, conference hall and tours of classrooms.
Overground/Rail: New Cross, New Cross Gate; 171,172,225,436,453

Deptford Lounge
9 Giffin Street, Giffin Square SE8 4RJ
■ Sun 10am-5pm. Regular tours, first come basis. Last tour 4pm. Max 15 per tour. N R T C G
Part of a visionary concept that combines a replacement primary school with the Deptford Lounge – a new state-of-the-art district library that also provides new community facilities. Sustainable features include 10% renewable energy through Biomass CHP and BREEAM Very Good rating. Pollard Thomas Edwards 2012. Entry: Rooftop Ball Court, Deptford Lounge, shared areas between the Lounge and Tidemill School.

Spring Gardens

DLR: Deptford Bridge; Rail: Deptford; 1,47,188,199,453
www.deptfordlounge.org.uk

End House
87a Manwood Road SE4 1SA
■ Sun 9.30am-12.30pm. First come basis, queuing outside if necessary. Last entry 12.15pm. Max 10 at one time. G d
A fresh, contemporary end of terrace house that makes clever use of a small site by using a simple form to offer privacy combined with open plan living. Sustainable features include recycled newspaper insulation and breathable walls. Edgley Design 2010.
Rail: Ladywell, Crofton Park, Honor Oak Park; 284,P4,171,172,122

Explorer House
Sydenham Road SE26 5EN
■ Sat 10am-1pm. Tours taking place, first come basis. Last entry 12.45pm. G P
Development of 17 flats and houses on a tight infill site. Contemporary design to address the adjacent period terraces constructed in brick clad timberframe. Green features include PVs and biodiverse roof. Baily Garner/Amicus Horizon 2014. Entry: Communal Garden, internal corridors.
Overground: Sydenham

Fairlawn Primary School
Honor Oak Road, London SE23 3SB
■ Sat 10am-5pm. Half-hourly tours, first come basis. Max 10 per tour.
Grade II listed building designed by the associate architect for the Royal Festival Hall. The school also features works by the artist and architect Victor Pasmore. Peter Moro/Michael Mellish 1957.
Rail: Honor Oak Park; P4,185

Forest Hill Pools
Dartmouth Road SE23 3HZ
■ Sat 1pm-5pm. Last entry 4.30pm. N D R T
New facility providing community pools, fitness, café and meeting rooms whilst retaining the original Victorian pool superintendent's building. Roberts Limbrick Architects (redevelopment) 1885/2012. Entry: reception, cafe.
Rail: Forest Hill; 185,197,176,122,356

Forest Mews
Rockbourne Mews SE23 2AT
■ Sat 10am-4.30pm. Tours every 45 minutes. Pre-book ONLY on jessica@stolon.co.uk – Dispays on sustainable design features including drainage and flood mitigation. Last entry 4pm. T A G
Three bespoke houses, each with a studio and courtyard, set around a communal courtyard. Each courtyard of the house

Surrey Canal Roof Top Box

forms the centre of the open plan ground floor, with living on one side and studio on the other, inspired by views of ivy growing over trees in wintertime – all three houses are to be clad with striking green walls, trained to a geometric pattern. Robert and Jessica Barker 2014.
Rail: Forest Hill; 185,197

Glass Mill Leisure Centre
41 Loampit Vale SE13 7FT
■ Sat/Sun 1pm-5pm. Last entry 4.30pm. N D R T C G
Glass Mill has superb environmental credentials and offers a range of the most up-to-date facilities including a regional competition-standard 8-lane swimming pool with seating for 300 spectators, a 100-station gym and a climbing wall. The centre has a creche, 2 aerobics studios and a cafe. LA Architects 2013.
DLR/Rail: Lewisham; 21,47,136,321,436

Horniman Museum and Gardens ●
100 London Road SE23 3PQ
■ Sat/Sun 10.30am-5.30pm. Sat behind the scenes tours at 2pm & 4pm, pre-book ONLY via Horniman website. Duration 45 mins. Last entry 5.20pm. Max 25 per tour. N D R T B C
A landmark building – Charles Harrison Townsend's original arts and crafts building (1901) and his ideas on the arts and crafts aesthetic. The 16.5 acre gardens have re-opened after major redevelopment by Land Use Consultants (2012) including a Pavilion by Walters + Cohen plus a bandstand terrace with views over London. C H Townsend/Land Use Consultants/Elliott Wood Partnership 1901/2012.
Rail: Forest Hill; 176,185,363,P4,356
www.elliottwood.co.uk

Lewisham Arthouse/Deptford Library
140 Lewisham Way SE14 6PD
■ Sun 1pm-5pm. Tours every 15-20 mins. Small historical display and video screening. Art and drawing workshops related to the details of the building for children. Last tour 4.45pm. Max 10 per tour. T C P d
Former library, converted to studios. Grade II listed building in classical Renaissance style with curved glass vaulted roof. A Brumwell Thomas 1914. Entry: all main parts of building although restricted access to studios.
Tube/Rail: New Cross, New Cross Gate; DLR/Rail: Lewisham; Rail: Deptford; 21,136,321,436,171,172,53,453

Prefab Museum
17 Meliot Road, Catford SE6 1RY
■ Sat/Sun 10am-5pm. First come basis, queuing outside if necessary. Tours of the Prefab Estate at 2.30pm on both days. Last entry 4.45pm. Max 30 per tour.

Key. A Architect on site **B** Bookshop **C** Childrens' activities **d** Some disabled access **D** Full wheelchair access **E** Engineer on site **G** Green Features **N** Normally open to the public **P** Parking **Q** Long queues envisaged **R** Refreshments **T** Toilets

The Green Man (Phoenix Community Housing)

The Prefab Museum is a living museum in a post-war prefab on the Excalibar Estate in Catford. It celebrates prefab life by showing the work of 15 artists and by re-creating a post-war atmosphere. Engineering Company Ltd 1945. Entry: Prefab and garden.
Rail: Catford, Catford Bridge; 124

Richard Hoggart Building, Goldsmiths, University of London
Lewisham Way, SE14 6NW
■ Sat 11am-4pm. Tours on the hour, sign in for a tour on arrival. Last tour at 3.00pm. Max 20 per tour.
Built in 1843 and used as a Royal Naval School until 1891 when Worshipful Company of Goldsmiths acquired the building. Further acquisition by the University of London re-established the building as Goldsmiths College in 1904. In 2012 the College began ongoing renovation work on the building and exterior landscaping. John Shaw Jr/Dannatt Johnson Architects 1843/2014.
Rail: New Cross, New Cross Gate; 21,36,136,171,177,321,343,436,453

Spring Gardens
Ennersdale Road SE13 6JQ
■ Sat 1pm-4.30pm. No visitors under the age of 18. Last entry 4.30pm. Max 20 at one time. R T G d
The first purpose-built hostel for homeless people, offering high-quality accommodation for 85 residents in buildings arranged around a beautiful garden with existing mature trees. Kitchen garden, with chickens. Light, open and airy and with additional training spaces. Sustainable features including solar panels and grey water system. Peter Barber Architects/Buller Welsh Architects 2010. Entry: communal areas, activity rooms.
Rail: Hither Green; 181,273

Surrey Canal Roof Top Box ● ●
Roof Top, Guild House, Rollins Street SE15 1EP
■ Sat/Sun 10am-5pm. First come basis. Hourly presentations on the half hour. Children's activities include Skyline Bingo and Big City Masterplanning for kids. Last entry 4.30pm. C
Surrey Canal is Renewal's consented masterplan for the 30-acre area south of South Bermondsey Station. Studio Egret West's masterplan will create a new neighbourhood in London including a new overground station, London's largest indoor sports centre for community use and 2,500 new homes. Work is due to start in late 2015. Studio Egret West 2014-2025. Entry: Roof Top Box is a temporary onsite office designed by Studio Egret West with Petroschka Architects as exclusive architects.
Rail: Queen's Road Peckham, South Bermondsey; P12

The Green Man (Phoenix Community Housing) ● ●
355 Bromley Road SE6 2RP
■ Sat 11am-3.30pm. Tours at 11am, 12.30pm, 2pm and 3pm. Pre-book ONLY on openhouse@black-architecture.com – max 20-25 per tour.
Two contemporary timber-framed buildings set around new public open space. Rated BREEAM Excellent, the spaces house a market hall, community cafe, credit union and training kitchen. Numerous sustainable features including low energy light fittings, radiant sail cooling system, wild flower green roof and structural insulated panel construction. Shortlisted for 2014 building awards. Black Architecture 2013.
Rail: Beckenham Hill, Bellingham; 54,136,181,227,320

The Master Shipwright's House
Watergate Street SE8 3JF
■ Sat 10am-5pm. First come basis, queuing outside if necessary. Max 25 at one time. R
The oldest upstanding building – the home and office of the master shipwright since 1513 – remodelled in early 18C. Exhibition of Dockyard, plans and images. "Hidden London at its delightful best" – The Telegraph, 1708. Entry: selected rooms, garden.
Rail: New Cross, Deptford; DLR: Deptford Bridge, Greenwich; 188,36,47,177

The Pavilion
The Pavilion, Pagoda Gardens, Blackheath, SE3 0UZ
■ Sat 10am-5pm. First come basis. Last entry 4.30pm.
Voted UK's Top Eco Home on the Guardian online, this is an uncompromisingly modern house in the Blackheath Conservation area adjacent to Grade II* listed Pagoda. Features include Code Level 5, full home automation, verdant gardens and open plan living flooded with natural light. E2 Architecture 2014.
Rail: Lewisham, Blackheath

The Seager Distillery Tower
4-12 Deptford Bridge SE8 4HH
■ Sat 10am-5pm/Sun 10am-1pm. Tours on the hour, first come basis. Last tour Sat 4pm, Sun 12noon. Max 20 per tour. D Q
Part of a regeneration project by Galliard Homes on site of former Seager distillery, which includes refurb of a 19C warehouse, conversion of former 19C Holland House, a new crescent building, office pavilion and 27-storey residential tower with viewing gallery. John McAslan & Partners/BUJ Architects 1999/2012. Entry: 27th floor viewing gallery.
DLR: Deptford Bridge; Rail: Deptford

The Stephen Lawrence Charitable Trust
39 Brookmill Road SE8 4HU
■ Sat 11am-1pm. Tours at 11am, 1pm, first come basis, duration approx 1 hr. Max 15 per tour. D T
Community centre in honour of Stephen Lawrence, the architectural student murdered in 1993. Angled facade with expanded aluminium cladding. The position and form of the building is a response to the constraints of the site, triangular in form. Adjaye Associates 2008. Entry: centre.
DLR: Deptford Bridge; Rail: St John's; 47,225

TNG Wells Park Youth Venue
111 Wells Park Road SE26 6AD
■ Sat/Sun 10am-5pm. Hourly tours, first come basis. Last entry 4pm. Max 20 people per tour. N D T A G
TNG is a new-build venue designed by RCKa working closely with Lewisham Council, its partners and the local community. The project provides a range of vocational, leisure and support services for the young people of Lewisham. Opened by the Mayor in 2013, TNG has been heralded as a beacon of youth service provision across the region. It received a Commendation in the Civic Trust Awards in 2014 and is a 2014 RIBA Regional London award winner. RCKa 2013. Entry: all except offices.
Rail: Sydenham, Sydenham Hill

Trinity Laban Conservatoire of Music and Dance ●
Creekside SE8 3DZ
■ Sat tours at 3pm and 4pm only. Sun tours at 1pm, 2pm only. Duration 45mins. D R T B G
The largest purpose-built contemporary dance centre in the world. A gently curving facade with richly coloured plastic cladding by architects of Tate Modern leads into spaces filled with vivid colour and dynamic form created through collaboration with artist Michael Craig-Martin. 2003 Stirling Prize winner. Herzog & de Meuron 2003. Entry: dance spaces.
DLR: Cutty Sark, Deptford Bridge; Rail: New Cross, Greenwich, Deptford; 188,47,199

Walter Segal self-build houses ● ●
8 & 10 Walters Way, Honor Oak Park SE23 3LH
■ Sun 1pm-6pm. Regular tours, first come basis. Videos of Segal buildings and self-build. Last entry 5.45pm. Max 20 at one time. R T d
A close of 13 self-built houses. Each house is unique, many extended and built using a method developed by Walter Segal, who led the project in the 1980s. Both houses have benefited from extensions and renovations. Sustainable features include solar electric, water and space heating. Walter Segal 1987. Note: Two steps to each house
Rail: Honor Oak Park; P4,P12,171,63

WALKS/TOURS

Fordham Park ●
■ Meet: Sun 11am at corner of Douglas Way and Amersham Vale, New Cross SE14 6LE. First come basis, tour led by Alastair Ferrer. Duration approx 1 hour.
Fordham Park and Walpole Road underpass in New Cross forms part of one of the Mayor's Great Spaces. Its recent £1.8m regeneration has helped reconnect communities in an urban area fragmented by barriers of roads and railways and created a public space that is memorable, well-used and much-loved. The park is part of the North Lewisham Links programme and won the Landscape Institute Award in 2012. The Landscape Partnership 2012.
DLR: Deptford Bridge; Rail: New Cross; 21,36,136,171,172,177,225,321

Supported by

Lewisham

Merton

See **openhouselondon.org.uk/merton**
to find out more about this area

15 Edge Hill ◉
15 Edge Hill SW19 4LR
■ Sat 10am-5pm. Owner/architect-led regular tours, first
come basis. Last tour 4.30pm. Max 15 per tour. T A d
New build rear extension to Victorian house, entailing
extensive remodelling of ground floor to create a large open
plan flow-through living, dining and kitchen space. Close
integration with the garden is achieved by careful design of
levels and paving surfaces. Asif Malik 1870s/2011. Entry: ground
floor, garden.
Tube/Rail: Wimbledon; 57,131,200

31b St Mary's Road
31b St Mary's Road SW19 7BP
■ Sat 10am-4pm. Closed 12-2pm. Half-hourly tours, pre-book
ONLY on jaci2000@fastmail.co.uk – last tour 3pm.
One of a small number of Peter Foggo, single-storey, flat-
roofed houses inspired by the US Case Study Houses scheme
and Mies van der Rohe's Farnsworth House, with skylights,
two wings, mahogany panelling and floor-to-ceiling windows.
A large open-plan living room looks out onto a landscaped
garden. Peter Foggo & David Thomas 1965. Entry: all except
1 bedroom.
Tube/Rail: Wimbledon; 493,93,200

40a Dawlish Avenue ◉
40a Dawlish Avenue SW18 4RW
■ Sat 10am-5pm. Regular tours, first come basis. Max 12 per
tour. A G
Award-winning sustainable private house designed by
architect-owner. Lacey and Saltykov 2012.
Tube: Wimbledon Park; Rail: Earlsfield; 270,44,77

9 Parkside Avenue
9 Parkside Avenue SW19 5ES
■ Sun 12pm-4pm. Architect-led regular tours, first come basis,
queuing if necessary. A
Complex series of interlocking spaces within a simple overall
volume, the house has references to the dramatic and hidden
sources for lighting spaces seen in Baroque churches and the
work of Sir John Soane. Sustainable features include solar
panels. Holden Harper 1999. Entry: house, garden.
Tube/Rail: Wimbledon

Baitul Futuh Mosque
Ahmadiyya Muslim Association, 181 London Road, Morden
SM4 5PT
■ Sat/Sun 10am-5pm. Regular talks and tours, pre-book ONLY
on 020 8648 5255. Talks given in Urdu, Arabic, German and
English. N D R T B G P
Purpose-built mosque (2003) and the largest in Europe,
with 15m diameter dome and minarets 36m and 23m high,
accommodating 13,000 worshippers. The building is a blend
of Islamic and modern British architecture and incorporates
much of the structure of an old dairy site. Facilities include
halls, library, creche, studios. Voted one of top 50 buildings in
the world by Independent Magazine. Sutton Griffin Architects
2003. Entry: all areas.
Tube: Morden; Rail: Morden South; 93,154,213,80

40a Dawlish Avenue

Buddhapadipa Temple
14 Calonne Road SW19 5HJ
■ Sun 9am-4pm. Regular 10-minute tours. Last entry 3pm.
Max 30 per tour. N R T P
Complex of buildings on 4 acres of land with Buddhist
Theravada Temple in Thai style – one of only two outside Asia.
Interior walls with excellent mural paintings by Thai artists,
depicting aspects of the Buddha's life. Praves Limparangsri
Architect with Sidney Kaye Firmin Partnership 1980.
Entry: temple, gardens.
Tube/Rail: Wimbledon; 93

Elliott Wood
241 The Broadway SW19 1SD
■ Sun 10am-4pm. Max 20 at one time. E R T G
A Victorian villa with impressive 2-storey vaulted steel and
glass office space with mezzanine for structural engineers
Elliott Wood. Civic Trust Commendation 2006. Sustainably
refurbished in 2012 with Alex Ferguson architects with natural
ventilation, cooling from ground pipes and solar panels.
Richard Paxton Architects (original refurbishment) 2004.
Tube: South Wimbledon; Tube/Rail: Wimbledon
163,164,93,57,131,219
www.elliottwood.co.uk

Hollymount School
Cambridge Road SW20 0SQ
■ Sat 10am-4pm. Hourly tours, first come basis. Last entry
3pm. Max 20 per tour. D T A
Extension of an existing primary school on a constrained site
in Wimbledon with new double-height top-lit gallery space
to create a new heart for the school. BREEAM rated Very Good.
Haverstock 2012.
Rail: Raynes Park; 200

Mitcham Cricket Club Pavilion
4 Cricket Green, Mitcham CR4 4LA
■ Sat 10am-4.30pm. Players on hand. T
The building is locally listed and has been the club's pavilion
for over 100 years, whilst Mitcham Cricket Green has had
cricket played on its pitch for over 300 years. 1904.
Tube: Colliers Wood; Tram: Mitcham; Rail: Mitcham Junction,
Mitcham Eastfields; 200,127,118

Morden Hall Park, Stable Yard ◉
Morden Hall Road, Morden SM4 5JD
■ Sat/Sun 11am-3pm. 1 ½ hour behind the scenes history
tours at 11am and 1.30pm including access to Morden
cottage and Morden Hall and regular short tours of
stableyard and turbine. Last tour and entry 2.30pm.
Max 20 per tour. N D T B G P

Award winning Stable Yard, part of the original Morden Hall
estate – an oasis in suburbia. Stable Yard renovated using
renewable technologies, including the first Archimedes Screw
hydroelectric turbine in London. RICS award winner. Cowper
Griffith (refurb) 2011.
Tube: Morden; Tram: Phipps Bridge; 93,157,154,164,293

St Mary's Church, Merton Park
Church Path, Merton Park SW19 3HJ
■ Sun 12pm-5pm. Tours 2pm, 3pm plus short talk on history
of church. N D R T P
Grade II listed gem of a country church built in 1115, now in
the heart of a suburban conservation area. Norman features,
William Morris glass and associations with famous people
including Nelson. 1115.
Tramlink: Merton Park; Tube: South Wimbledon; Tube/Rail:
Wimbledon; 163,164,152

The Chapter House, Merton Priory
Merton Abbey Mills, Merantun Way SW19 2RD
■ Sat/Sun 10am-5pm. The remains lie under the A24
Merantun Way, between Merton Abbey Mills and
Sainsbury's. Adjacent Merton Abbey Mills market will be
open. Archaeologist David Saxby on site. Archaeology for
kids and fabric block printing demonstration. Max 50 at
one time. N D B C P
Fascinating excavated foundations of the Chapter House of
Merton Priory c1100-1200, one of the most important of all
Augustinian monasteries prior to its destruction in 1538 by
Henry VIII. c1100-1200. Entry: Chapter House archaeological site.
Tube: Colliers Wood; Tube/Rail: Wimbledon; 57,131,152,200,219,470

The Wheelhouse
Merton Abbey Mills, Merantun Way, Wimbledon SW19 2RD
■ Sat/Sun 10am-5pm. N D R T B P
Precious listed building (c1820) with unique 7-spoke Victorian
waterwheel, the only daily working example in South London,
originally used by Liberty's for rinsing printed silk, and now the
home of a craft pottery. c1820.
Tube: Colliers Wood; Tube/Rail: Wimbledon; 57,131,152,200,219

Wimbledon Windmill
Windmill Road SW19 5NR
■ Sat 10am-5pm. Regular tours, first come basis. Architect
for restoration and curator on site. Hands-on models and
equipment for children. Max 50 at one time. D R T B C A P
Rare example of a hollow post mill (1817). Grade II* listed, it now
contains a museum depicting the history and development
of windmills in Britain. Many working models, windmill
machinery, equipment and tools. 1817.
Tube/Rail: Wimbledon; 93

WALKS/TOURS

Mitcham Cricket Green Community and Heritage
■ Meet: Sat 2.30pm at Mitcham Cricket Club Pavilion, Cricket
Green, Mitcham CR4 4LA. First come basis. Max 30 on tour.
Duration 1 hour.
Heritage walk taking in the diverse buildings within the
conservation area including Canons grounds, Cranmer Gree,
Three Kings Piece, monuments and historic cricket grounds.
Tube: Colliers Wood; Tram: Mitcham; Rail: Mitcham Junction,
Mitcham Eastfields; 200,127,118

Supported by

merton

Key: A Architect on site **B** Bookshop **C** Childrens' activities **d** Some disabled access **D** Full wheelchair access **E** Engineer on site **G** Green Features
N Normally open to the public **P** Parking **Q** Long queues envisaged **R** Refreshments **T** Toilets

Newham

See **openhouselondon.org.uk/newham**
to find out more about this area

Chobham Academy

Abbey Mills Pumping Station ●
Abbey Lane E15 2RW
- Sat & Sun tours at 10am, 11am, 12noon, 1pm, 2pm & 3pm.
  Pre-book ONLY on londonopenhouse@thameswater.co.uk
  – clearly marking the subject – ABBEY MILLS: Open House –
  Please do not turn up on the day without pre-booking.
  Max 20 per tour. E T P
View the Abbey Mills pumping station A, built by engineer
Joseph Bazalgette, Edmund Cooper and architect Charles
Driver. Built between 1865 and 1868 it has been described as
the cathedral of sewage. 1997.
Tube: Bromley-by-Bow, Bow Road; DLR: Pudding Mill Lane; 25,86

Canning Town Caravanserai: Collecting 100 Caravanserai Stories
Canning Town Caravanserai, Silvertown Way E16 1EA
- Sat/Sun 9am-8pm. A weekend of story telling, music and
  film-making. Workshops start at 10am, 1pm and 4pm to
  help tell traveller's tales. Performances from 6pm. Site will
  be open for informal architectural tours by the architects
  and Caravanserai team. Last entry 7.30pm. Max 100 at one
  time. N T C A G d
The new trading post in East London is an intelligent shanty
town for mixing up all kinds of production and consumption.
Not an 'amenity space', but a palatial space for doing stuff
where enough always feels like a feast. Ash Sakula Architects
2011 ongoing.
Tube/DLR: Canning Town; 474,541

Carpenters Estate
Dennison Point, E15 2LY
- Sat 1pm-5pm. First come basis, tours on the hour.
  Information about the estate and history of the area will be
  on display. Last entry 4pm. Max 30 per tour.
Stunning views across the Olympic site and the city from the
22nd floor of the 1960s tower block Dennison Point on the
Carpenters Estate. Thomas North and Kenneth Lund / What if:
projects Ltd 1967.
Tube/Rail/DLR: Stratford; 108,425,D8,276,25

Chobham Academy ●
40 Cheering Lane, Stratford E20 1BD
- Sat/Sun 10am-1pm. Architect led tours at 10am and 12noon.
  D T A
A new all-ages school in the East Village, close to the Queen
Elizabeth Olympic Park. A powerful drum form centres three
connected buildings, defining space on a campus that is open,
attractive, economical and sustainable. Allford Hall Monaghan
Morris 2011.
Tube: Stratford; Rail/DLR: Stratford International; 97,308
www.ahmm.co.uk

Cody Dock ●
11c South Crescent, Canning Town E16 4TL
- Sat 10am-10pm/Sun 10am-5pm. First come basis. Sat/
  Sun 2pm 1½ hour guided tour of Cody Dock and Imperial
  Gaswork site. Evening bat walk starting from Cody Dock
  6.30pm Sat. R T C G P d
Now being transformed into one of East London's most
exciting Arts and Heritage spaces by the Charity G.D.P.

Cody Dock's new gardens and paths provide the gateway
to exploring the Lower Lea Valley. Constructed for Harper
Twelvetrees as part of Imperial Chemical Works 1871. Entry:
community gardens, riverside walks and the River Princess bar
and gallery space.
DLR: Star Lane

Connaught Tunnel ●
445 North Woolwich Road, Silvertown E16 2DA
- Sat 10am-2pm. Tours at 10am, 12noon and 2pm only.
  Pre-book ONLY through janine.mars@taylorwoodrow.com
  (Max 2 places per booking). Max 10 per tour.
Connaught Tunnel, originally built in 1878 forms part of
the Crossrail Project. By combining the refurbishment and
redevelopment of this Victorian brick arched tunnel underneath
the Royal Docks, its life is renewed for another 120 years. **ice**
DLR: Pontoon Dock; 474,473

House Mill ●
Three Mills Lane E3 3DU
- Sat/Sun 11am-4pm. Regular tours. Last tour 3.30pm. Max 18
  per tour. R T B P d
The UK's oldest and largest tidal mill. 5-storey, timber-framed,
brick-clad watermill with four waterwheels, originally built
1776 to mill grain for distillery trade. Operational until 1940.
(Organised by River Lea Tidal Mill Trust.) Entry: ground, 1st
floors of mill and rebuilt house.
Tube: Bromley-by-Bow; DLR: Devons Road; 25,108,D8,S2

Lee Tunnel & Beckton Sludge Power Generator ●
Thames Water Beckton, Jenkins Lane, Barking IG11 0AD
- Sat/Sun 10am-4pm. Hourly tours, pre-book ONLY by email
  to louisa.fala@leetunnel.co.uk – tour duration 2 hours.
  Minimum age 16. Last tour 3pm. Max 30 per tour. E T P
The biggest sewage treatment works in the UK and one
of the largest in Europe is undergoing a major expansion
programme. From 2010 to 2015, around £1billion will be
invested in the site to increase capacity, reduce odour and
boost renewable energy at Beckton. This investment includes
four key improvement projects: the sewage works upgrade
(including wind turbine), odour control project, the Lee Tunnel,
and the Thermal Hydrolysis Plant (THP). The Lee Tunnel is the
deepest tunnel in London and will prevent an average of 16m
tonnes of sewage mixed with rainwater from overflowing into
the River Lee, a tributary of the River Thames.
DLR: Gallions Reach; 325,366

Lee Valley Hockey and Tennis Centre ● ●
Eton Manor, Leadmill Lane, Queen Elizabeth Olympic Park E20
3AD
- Sat 2pm-4pm. First come basis, queuing if necessary. Hourly
  tours. Max 25 per tour.
Final stage of transformation of the Eton Manor site, from
its use as a 2012 Olympic and Paralympic Games venue into
a legacy sports facility. A 'build it once' concept took legacy as
the starting point of design, enabling minimal transformation
with a distinct architectural identity at each phase. Stanton
Williams/Arup 2014.
*Tube: Stratford, Leyton; Rail/DLR: Stratford International;
308,388,W15*

London Regatta Centre
1012 Dockside Road E16 2QT
- Sat/Sun 7am-5pm. First come basis. N T P
Robust and sharply angular boathouse. A 2-storey building
with glass facade overlooking the Royal Dock, containing a
gym, indoor rowing tank, restaurant and accommodation.
Ian Ritchie Architects 1999.
DLR: Royal Albert

Old Ford Water Recycling Plant ● ●
Dace Road E3 2NW site can be accessed from the Greenway.
- Sat 9am-5pm. Hourly tours, pre-book ONLY on christopher.
  james@thameswater.co.uk – last tour 4pm. Max 12 per
  tour. T G d
The largest community-scale wastewater recycling facility in
the UK using membrane technology to convert raw sewage
to non-potable water to supply Olympic Park venues. Clad
in timber, gabion baskets and corten steel to blend within
the Old Ford Nature Reserve (a site of SWCI Conservation
Importance). Sustainable features include sedum roofs. Lyall
Bills and Young Architects 2012. Entry: Old Ford Island and
treatment building. **ice**
*Rail: Hackney Wick; DLR: Pudding Mill Lane; Tube/Rail: Stratford;
276,388*

Lee Valley Hockey and Tennis Centre

Portability: Art on the Move
Queen Elizabeth Olympic Park, E20 2ST
- ■ Sat/Sun 10am-5pm. First come basis. Art works on display.

Queen Elizabeth Olympic Park is hosting a celebration of ingenious and extraordinary mobile art vehicles from across the country. From the smallest portable theatre, to fully functioning mobile studios, this unique event explores what it means for art to be mobile.
Tube/Rail/DLR: Hackney Wick, Stratford; 388,308,339,25,69

Stratford Circus
Theatre Square E15 1BX
- ■ Sun 9.30am-6.30pm. Tours at 10am, 12noon, 1pm of theatre spaces, technical booths. Max 10 per tour. N T d

Space, light, inspiration – a contemporary building achieves the original vision to create a modern user-friendly facility with multi-functional spaces. Levitt Bernstein 2001. Entry: foyer, cafe, theatres.
Tube/DLR/Rail: Stratford; 25,69,108,473

Stratford Picture House
Gerry Raffles Square, Salway Road E15 1BN
- ■ Sat/Sun 12pm-4pm. Tours on the hour, first come basis. Last tour 4pm. Max 10 per tour. D R T

Contemporary cinema in the heart of Stratford, a linear east-west glass and steel building, dramatically revealing its structure and functions to the passer-by. Four screens with state-of-the-art sound. Burrell Foley Fischer Architects 1997.
DLR/Tube/Rail: Stratford; 25,69,86,104,108,158,238,241,257, 262,276,308,473

Sugarhouse Studios
107 High Street Stratford, E15 2QQ
- ■ Sat 10am-10pm/Sun 10am-5pm. First come basis, tours on the hour until 5pm. Open studios from tenants all day. Max 20 per group.

Sugarhouse Studios is a small complex of work, event and workshop space studios, including wood, metal, model and casting rooms, open-plan event and exhibition space, 14 new build artists in a purpose built structure, Yardhouse, a micro-brewery and Assemble's shared studio. Assemble/Lewis Jones 2014. Special event: Visit the production line and launch of multiple pop-up books by artist Hilary Powell.
Tube: Bow Road; DLR: Bow Church, Tube/Rail: Stratford; 8,25,108,276,455

The City of London Cemetery and Crematorium at Aldersbrook
Aldersbrook Road E12 5DQ
- ■ Sat tours 10am & 1pm and Sun 10am. Max 20 per tour. Duration approx 2 hours. Talk from Superintendent on the history/heritage of site. N R T P d

A stunning Grade I listed 200 acre landscape designed and landscaped in 1856 to deal with the environmental/health/space issues of London's cramped and over-used churchyards. Rich in architecture from the Victorian era. William Haywood & William Davidson/Edwin George Chandler 1855-56/1974. Entry on tour: chapels, monuments, archives.
Rail: Manor Park; 101

The Crystal – A Sustainable Cities Initiative by Siemens ● ● Ⓐ
One Siemens Brothers Way, Royal Victoria Docks E16 1GB
- ■ Sat/Sun 10am-7pm. Regular tours, first come basis. Last entry 6.30pm. E D R T B C G P

London's newest landmark building and the world's first centre dedicated to improving our knowledge of urban sustainability through its programme of exhibitions and lectures. One of the most sustainable buildings in the world. Wilkinson Eyre Architects 2012. Entry: ground floor. ice
Tube: Canning Town; DLR: Royal Victoria; Emirates Cable Car

Theatre Royal Stratford East
Gerry Raffles Square E15 1BN
- ■ Sun tour at 12noon, first come basis. N D R T

Built as a playhouse and entertaining audiences for over 100 years. Having undergone £7.5million refurbishment it now has the best of both worlds: an original Victorian auditorium with beautiful Frank Matcham interior; and state-of-the-art backstage and front of house facilities. Grade II* listed. JG Buckle, Frank Matcham 1884. Entry: theatre, backstage areas.
DLR/Tube/Rail: Stratford; 25,108,69

Three Mills Lock ● ●
Prescott Channel, Three Mills Island, Bromley-by-Bow E3 3DU
- ■ Sat 11am-4pm. Regular tours, first come basis. Last entry 3.45pm. E N G

This state-of-the-art structure is the first lock to be built in London for over 20 years. Positioned at the mouth of the Olympic site, the mechanism offered a sustainable transport link for the 2012 Games. The dock, weir, fish belly gates and fish pass opened in 2009 to control the water level in the Bow back rivers. VolkerStevin 2009. Entry: lock area and lock control room.
Tube: Bromley-by-Bow; DLR: Bow Church; 488,D8,108

Timber Lodge and Tumbling Bay Playground ●
- ■ Meet: 12.30am on Sat at Queen Elizabeth II Olympic Park outside the Timber Lodge Café E20. Architect-led tour, Pre-book ONLY on http://bit.ly/10Wu64b. Max 40 per tour. A

Set to be one of the most innovative play spaces in London, this award winning highly naturalistic yet playful design aims to complement and tell the story of the wider riverine landscape of the park. The timber-clad building integrates seamlessly into the landscape providing a cafe and community space. Erect Architecture Ltd and LUC Landscape Architects 2013.
Tube/Rail/DLR: Stratford

Waterside Park
North Woolwich Road, Royal Docks, E16 2HP
- ■ Sat 10am-4pm. Tours at 10am, 11.30am, 2pm and 3pm. Pre-book ONLY on rsvp@alliesandmorrison.com – max 15 per tour. A

Part of a wider regeneration of disused land to the north of the Thames Barrier, Waterside Park for Barratt London provides 780 dwellings, retail and community, assembly and leisure uses, in a series of urban courtyard blocks set around a new urban park. Allies and Morrison/Maccreanor Lavington 2014. Entry: external public areas: internal access to residential courtyards. NB no entry to flats.
DLR: King George V; Woolwich Ferry; 473,474

WALKS/TOURS

ICE Engineering Highlights Cycle Tour of the Queen Elizabeth Olympic Park ●
- ■ Meet: Sun at 2pm outside the Timber Lodge Café, Honour Lea Avenue, Queen Elizabeth Olympic Park E20 3BB

Join leading engineer Andrew Weir, Director, Expedition Engineering and architect Kay Hughes, Director, Khaa on a cycle tour. Bikes not provided – come on your own bike wearing appropriate clothing. Barclays Cycle Hire at Stratford and Stratford International. Duration 2 hours. E A
Tour will explore the Olympic Park's enabling works and the construction of the venues, through to the utilities and their supporting infrastructure. Organised by the Institution of Civil Engineers. ice
Tube: Stratford, Leyton; Rail/DLR: Stratford International

Walk in the Olympic Park: Function and Beauty in Landscape
- ■ Meet: Sun 1pm at the Timber Lodge Cafe, 1A Honour Lea Avenue, Queen Elizabeth Olympic Park E20 3BB. Walk led by Dr Phil Askew, Project Sponsor Parklands and Public Realm.

Opportunity to tour the new Queen Elizabeth Olympic Park. Discover how the river and canals were moved, deculverted and managed to make the site what it is and the key role that sustainable drainage played in designing and protecting the site.
Tube: Stratford; Rail/DLR: Stratford International; 25,69,86,97,104,108,158,308,473

Supported by

Newham London

Key. A Architect on site **B** Bookshop **C** Childrens' activities **d** Some disabled access **D** Full wheelchair access **E** Engineer on site **G** Green Features **N** Normally open to the public **P** Parking **Q** Long queues envisaged **R** Refreshments **T** Toilets

Redbridge

See **openhouselondon.org.uk/redbridge**
to find out more about this area

Bancroft's School
611 High Road, Woodford Green IG8 0RF
■ Sat 10am-2pm. Last entry 2pm. T P d
A dignified and impressive design with later additions. Spiral staircase leads to the top of the tower, giving excellent views of East London. Formerly a Drapers' Company charitable school in Mile End Road, Bancroft's moved to its present site in 1889. Sir Arthur Blomfield 1889. Entry: chapel, great hall, library, dining hall, tower, grounds.
Tube: Woodford; Rail: Chingford; 20,179, W13

Christ Church
Wanstead Place E11 2SW
■ Sat 10am-5pm/Sun 12pm-5pm. Contemporary artworks. DT
Grade II* listed church with ragstone tower, spire, good stained glass by Kempe and newly restored William Hill organ. A characteristic work of Scott. Sir George Gilbert Scott 1861.
Tube: Wanstead, Snaresbrook; 66,101,145,308, W13, W14

Fullwell Cross Library
140 High Street, Barkingside, Ilford IG6 2EA
■ Sat 9.30am-4pm. Talk 2pm 'Every Town Needs A Crown: Frederick Gibberd and Fullwell Cross'. Last entry 3.30pm. N DT
The library was built together with the swimming baths on an open site in Barkingside High Street. The circular library design copies the nearby roundabout. The complex is set back from the pavement and was intended to form a new local civic centre with a public space. Refurbished in 1990 and 2011. Frederick Gibberd/Coombes & Partners/H C Connell 1958-68.
Tube: Barkingside, Fairlop; 128,150,167,169,247,275,462

Gurdwara Karamsar
400 High Road, Ilford IG1 1WT
■ Sat/Sun 1pm-5pm. Regular tours, first come basis. Respectful dress please including head cover. Shoes must be removed in foyer. Last entry 4.45pm. Max 30 on tours. N D T P
Sikh temple of sandstone shipped from Rajasthan, beautifully and intricately handcarved by Rajasthani stoneworkers. Domes on top and gold insignia with contemporary finishes inside. Narinder Singh Assi (Agenda 21) 2005. Entry: all areas.
Rail: Ilford, Seven Kings; 86

Ilford War Memorial Hall
Ilford War Memorial Gardens, Eastern Avenue, Newbury Park IG2 7RJ
■ Sat/Sun 11am-4.30pm. D
Grade II listed memorial hall situated within the War Memorial Gardens. Panels inside the building record the names of the Ilford men killed during WWI. The Hall was designed to serve as the entrance to the now demolished children's ward of the Ilford Emergency Hospital. C J Dawson & Allardyce 1927.
Tube: Newbury Park; 66,169

Quaker Meeting House, Wanstead
Bush Road E11 3AU
■ Sun 1pm-5pm. Last entry 5.15pm. N R T P d
Modernist building based on four hexagons within an Epping Forest setting. Contains a sunny meeting room for Quaker worship facing onto a wooded burial ground of simple headstones, including that of Elizabeth Fry. Norman Frith 1968. Entry: foyer, meeting room, social room, kitchen, grounds, wildflower meadow.
Tube: Leytonstone; 101,308

Redbridge Town Hall, Council Chamber
128-142 High Road, Ilford IG1 1DD
■ Sat 10am-5pm. Tours on the hour 11am to 2pm, first come basis. Tour by council's constitutional expert including council chamber. Max 15 per tour. D T
Built in 3 stages consisting of the Old Town Hall (1901) with facade in free classic style and some original decorations, library (1927) and additional buildings (1933). B Woolard 1901. Entry: ground and 1st floors.
Tube: Gants Hill; Rail: Ilford; 25,86,123,128,129,145,147,150,167, 169,179,296,364

The Hospital Chapel of St Mary & St Thomas
48 Ilford Hill, Ilford IG1 2AT
■ Sat 10am-4pm/Sun 1pm-5pm. Regular tours. Last entry half hour before close. N D R T B
Founded c1145 by the Abbess of Barking as a hospice for 13 old and infirm men, the present building is 12C and 19C. Grade II* listed with many interesting monuments, including Burne-Jones windows. (Organised by Friends of the Hospital Chapel.) 12C/19C.
Tube: Gants Hill; Rail: Ilford; 25,86,123,150,179,EL1,EL2

The Temple
Wanstead Park E11 2LT
■ Sat/Sun 12pm-5pm. Last entry 4.45pm. N R T B C d
18C garden building in style of a Doric temple, one of the last remaining structures surviving from Wanstead Park's days of grandeur. 18C statuary fragments and Roman finds on display. Display of prints of Wanstead House, plus a decoupage craft activity using these iconic images. Entry: ground and first floor.
Tube: Wanstead; 66,101,145,308, W13, W14, W19

Uphall Primary School Nursery
Uphall Road, Ilford IG1 2JD
■ Sat/Sun 9am-1pm. Max 10 at one time. T P d
Unusual 1930s ship-shaped school building, converted to nursery. Dropped ceilings and child-height porthole windows give suitable scale of space whilst complementing external elevations. Grade II listed. Civic Trust commendation 2000. Artist Sally Labern of the drawing shed worked with the school's children to create a neon artwork around the Olympic principles of inclusiveness using the original 1930s clear red neon – viewable until after dusk. Tooley and Foster c1937. Entry: nursery, playground.
Tube: Barking; Rail: Ilford; EL1,EL2,169

Valentines Mansion
Emerson Road, Ilford IG1 4XA
■ Sun 11am-5pm. Last entry 4pm. N D R T B C G
Large, late 17C Grade II* listed house with fine staircase and Venetian window and with Georgian additions, used as a family dwelling until the early 1900s. Reopened to the public in Feb 2009 following extensive restoration works of period furnished rooms, Victorian kitchen and pantry, temporary exhibition gallery. Richard Griffiths Architects 2009. Entry: Ground, 1st & 2nd floors. Vintage Wedding Fair 11am-3pm.
Tube: Gants Hill; Rail: Ilford; 128,296,150,396,167

Valentines Mansion

Woodford County High School for Girls
High Road, Woodford Green IG8 9LA
■ Sun 1pm-5pm. Half-hourly tours, first come basis. Last entry 4.30pm. N R d
Formerly Highams Manor, an elegant Georgian manor house built for the Warner family with grounds by Repton. William Newton 1768. Entry: house, grounds (ground floor only for those in wheelchairs)
Tube: Woodford; 20,179,275, W13

WALKS/TOURS

Fullwell Cross Library and the Better Barkingside scheme ●
■ Meet: Sat 1pm-5pm. Fullwell Cross Library, 140 High Street, Barkingside IG6 2AE. Tour of the library at 12.30pm, tour of Better Barkingside at 4.00pm. David Knight, Better Barkingside architect is giving a talk on Sir Frederick Gibberd at 2pm at the library. N D T B C A
Fullwell Cross Library and Leisure Centre designed by Sir Frederick Gibberd and Partners used the circular shape of the adjacent roundabout and rectilinear form to provide an ensemble of modernist civic buildings, now the backdrop to the Better Barkingside project.
Tube: Fairlop, Barkingside; 128,150,167,169,275

Wanstead Heritage Walk ●
■ Meet: Sun 10am outside Wanstead Station, 21 The Green, Wanstead E11 2NT. Duration 2 hours.
A guided walk from Wanstead Station to The Temple, Wanstead Park, highlighting the ancient chestnuts, St Mary's Church, a view of the Basin and Stable Block and other historical remnants of the Grade II listed historical landscape that formed the grounds of Wanstead House. Finishes at The Temple where walkers can find out more about the history of the rise and fall of this important Palladian mansion.
Tube: Wanstead; 66,101,145,308, W13, W14

> **Revealing Better Barkingside**
> The launch of Better Barkingside is being planned for Saturday 27 September. Find out more about this important public realm project by visiting
> **www.redbridge.gov.uk/betterbarkingside**

Supported by

London Borough of
Redbridge

Richmond

See **openhouselondon.org.uk/richmond** to find out more about this area

52 Pensford Avenue, Kew

■ Sun 10am-5pm. First come basis, queuing outside if necessary. Last entry 4.45pm. d A

Radical refurbishment of a 1930s house in Kew, involving complete demolition and rebuilding behind the existing frontage and adding a new basement. The house retains the 1930s style of the neighbouring properties whilst the extension and basement offer sleek and contemporary design fitted with modern products. 3s architects & designers 1930/2013.
Tube/Rail: Kew Gardens, North Sheen; 391,65,R68

Garden Room House

Address to be given on booking

■ Sat 1pm-5pm. Architect-led tours on the hour, pre-book ONLY on events@paulmcaneary.com D T B A G P

This innovative, warm minimalist project expands the family's living spaces by exploring the garden as a transformable glass framed room, whilst maximising storage and natural light. Paul McAneary Architects Ltd 2014. Entry: ground floor.
Tube/Rail: Kew Gardens; 65,391,237,267

Garrick's Temple to Shakespeare, Hampton

Garrick's Lawn, Hampton Court Road, Hampton TW12 2EN

■ Sun 2pm-5pm. Design activities for children. Garrick/ Shakespeare exhibition includes replica Roubiliac statue. Last entry 4.45pm. Max 30 at one time. N D R T C

Georgian garden building (1756). Tribute to Shakespeare built in the Ionic style by actor David Garrick. Arcadian Thames side setting in restored 18C gardens by Capability Brown. Civic Trust Award commendation and Green Heritage site award. 1756.
Ferry: Hampton pedestrian ferry from Molesey; Rail: Hampton, Hampton Court; 111,216,R68
www.garrickstemple.org.uk

Grove Gardens Chapel

Richmond Cemetery, Grove Gardens, off Lower Grove Road (entrance opposite Greville Road) TW10 6HP

■ Sun 1pm-5pm. First come basis. Max 30 at one time. D T A

Small, charming Gothic chapel of imaginative design with plate tracery and mosaic triptych. Former cemetery chapel, now restored for mixed community use. Thomas Hardy was apprenticed to the architect. Sir Arthur Blomfield c1873.
Tube/Rail: Richmond; 371

Ham House and Garden

Ham Street, Ham TW10 7RS

■ Sat 12pm-4pm. Regular short talks. Gardens also open 10am-5pm. Art activities and trail for children. Last entry to house 3.30pm. R T B C P d

Built in 1610 for a Knight Marshall of James I, Ham House was greatly extended in the 1670s. One of a series of grand houses and palaces built along the Thames, Ham House and Garden is an unusual complete 17C survival. Fine interiors and historic gardens. 1610/1670. Entry: areas of house, garden, outbuildings.
Tube/Rail: Richmond; Rail: Kingston; 371,65

Hampton Court Palace – The Georgian House

Hampton Court Palace, East Molesey KT8 9AU

■ Sat/Sun 10.30am-4pm. Regular tours, first come basis. R T B

Richmond Theatre

Explore The Georgian House, the Landmark Trust holiday apartment adjoining Hampton Court Palace, built to cater to the Hanoverian King George I. Join us as we reveal the 'German Kitchen' behind the modern residence. 18C-20C. Entry: First and second floors only, no step-free access.
Rail: Hampton Court; 111,216,411,R68

JMW Turner's House, Sandycombe Lodge

40 Sandycoombe Road, St Margarets, Twickenham TW1 2LR

■ Sat/Sun 10am-3pm. Regular short tours, first come basis. T B d

Small rustic villa built to Turner's own design, with inspiration from John Soane, for his own use as a rural retreat. JMW Turner 1812. Entry: ground floor, basement, garden.
Tube/Rail: Richmond; Rail: St Margarets; H37,R70,R68,H22,33

Kew House

10 Cambridge Road, Kew TW9 3JB

■ Sat/Sun 10am-5pm. First come basis. Please remove shoes on entry. Last entry 4.30pm. E R T A

A contemporary family home formed of 2 weathering steel volumes inserted behind the retained facade of a 19C brick stables, set within a conservation area on the doorstep of Kew Gardens. Piercy & Company 2013.
Tube/Rail: Kew Gardens; Rail: Kew Bridge; 391,65

Kilmorey Mausoleum

275 St Margarets Road (opposite Ailsa Tavern) TW1 1NJ

■ Sun 1pm-5pm. Max 5 inside mausoleum. R d

Egyptian-style, pink and grey mausoleum for the second Earl of Kilmorey. The form relates to the shrines at the heart of Egyptian Temples. HE Kendall 19C. Entry: mausoleum, main grounds, wildlife garden.
Tube/Rail: Richmond; Rail: St Margarets; H37

Kneller Hall

33 Royal Military School of Music, Kneller Road TW2 7DU

■ Sat/Sun 10am-4pm. Regular tours. Live music throughout the day. R T B P d

Grade II listed, site of house designed by Wren for court portrait painter Sir Godfrey Kneller. Rebuilt 1848 in stately neo-Jacobean style. Army's Royal Military School of Music since 1857. Sir Christopher Wren (attributed) 1709. Entry: chapel,

museum, bandstand, practice room, grounds.
Tube: Hounslow East; Rail: Twickenham, Whitton; H22,281,481

Langdon Down Centre

2a Langdon Park TW11 9PS

■ Sun 12pm-4pm. Tours at 12.30pm, 1.30pm, 2.30pm. Displays of community aspect. Last entry 3.45pm. N D R T B C P

Grade II* listed Normansfield Theatre and Langdon Down Museum of Learning Disability. Gothic proscenium arch and elaborate stage and scenery. Originally built as part of the Normansfield Hospital for patients/students with learning disabilities. Rowland Plumbe 1877. Entry: theatre, basement.
Rail: Hampton Wick; 281,285

Langham House Close

Langham House Close, Ham Common TW10 7JE

■ Sat 10am-5pm. First come basis, queuing if necessary. Last entry 5pm. Max 20 inside flats at one time. Q d

A landmark in 'Brutalism'. Exposed shuttered concrete and brick construction with iconic oversized concrete 'gargoyles' and geometric fenestration. Interior features exposed brick chimney/mantle/squint and architect-designed cupboards. Stirling and Gowan 1958. Entry: entrance hall to flats 25-30, interior of flat 7.
Tube/Rail: Richmond; Rail: Kingston; then 65 bus to Ham Common

Orleans House Gallery, Octagon Room and New Arts Education Centre

Riverside TW13DJ

■ Sun 2pm-5pm. Family activities 2-4pm. Max 60 at one time. N R T B C P d

Louis Philippe, Duc d'Orleans, lived here between 1815-17. Gibbs' Octagon room and adjoining gallery/stable block are remaining parts of Orleans House. Coach house education centre opened 2006. Further developments 2007-08 including cafe. John James/James Gibbs/Patel Taylor (new centre) 1710/1720/2006/2008. Entry: Octagon Room, main gallery, stables gallery.
Tube/Rail: Richmond; Rail: St Margarets, Twickenham; 33,490,H22,R68,R70

Parish Church of St Anne

Kew Green TW9 3AA

■ Sat 9.30am-1pm. N R T P d

Grade II* listed, originally built as a chapel under the patronage of Queen Anne in 1714 and subsequently enlarged. Many notable memorials including to scientist William Jackson Hooker and tombs of Thomas Gainsborough and Johan Zoffany. Joshua Kirby/Robert Browne 1714/1770/1805.
Tube/Rail: Kew Gardens; Rail: Kew Bridge; 65,391

Pope's Grotto and Radnor House School

Radnor House School, Pope's Villa, Cross Deep TW1 4QG

■ Sat tours at 10am, 11am, 12noon. Pre-book ONLY on hdolan@radnorhouse.org – max 25 at one time. R T P

Grotto with mineral decoration is last remaining part of Alexander Pope's villa built 1720, demolished 1808 and replaced and redeveloped many times in following years. Alexander Pope 1720. Entry: grotto, school.
Rail: Twickenham, Strawberry Hill; 33,R68,R70,H22,267

Richmond Lock Building (Surrey Side)

The Towpath, Richmond TW9 2QJ

■ Sun 10am-4pm. Regular talks by lock keeper. Last entry 3.30pm. Max 30 at one time. N T G P d

Example of good-quality late-Victorian functional design. 1894. Entry: lock cottage and lock side.
Tube/Rail: Richmond; Rail: St Margarets; 33,65,490,H22,R68,R70

Key. A Architect on site **B** Bookshop **C** Childrens' activities **d** Some disabled access **D** Full wheelchair access **E** Engineer on site **G** Green Features **N** Normally open to the public **P** Parking **Q** Long queues envisaged **R** Refreshments **T** Toilets

Style Council

Kew House

The American International University in London, Richmond
Richmond Hill Campus, Queen's Road TW10 6JP
■ Sat 10.30am-4pm/Sun 11am-3.30pm. First come basis. Hourly tours. Last entry 3pm. N R T P d
An Impressive neo-Gothic building set in 5 acres. Originally home of the Wesley Theological Institution and now Richmond University, built of Bath stone with facade largely unchanged. Grounds contain many rare specimens of plants and trees. Andrew Trimen 1843. Entry: main building, grounds.
Tube/Rail: Richmond; 371

Richmond Theatre
The Green, Richmond TW9 1QJ
■ Sat tours at 10.15am and 11.45am, pre-book ONLY on 08448 717 651. Max 20 per tour. Architecture-inspired treasure trails and art activities for children aged 4+. R T C
A typical Matcham design, this beautiful 840-seat theatre was exhaustively researched and then restored in 1989 to a fabulous crimson, cream and gold. All original mouldings restored and renewed. Frank Matcham 1899. Entry: auditorium, backstage, foyers.
Tube/Rail: Richmond; 65,371,419,493

Sir Richard Burton's Mausoleum
St Mary Magdalen's RC Church, 61 North Worple Way, Mortlake SW14 8PR
■ Sun 1pm-5pm. Last entry 4.30pm.
Recently restored Grade II* listed mausoleum in the form of an Arab tent with ripples in the stone imitating canvas. Interior is embellished with oriental lamps, devotional paintings and strings of camel bells. Isabel Arundell Burton 1890. Entry: exterior only, interior views through panel in roof via step ladder.
Tube/Rail: Richmond; Rail: Mortlake; 209,33,337,493,485

St Mary Magdalene
Paradise Road, Richmond TW9 1SN
■ Sat 10am-5pm/Sun 8am-8pm. Tours of the tower and monuments taking place. Refreshments at 10.30am on Sun with 6.30pm evensong. N D R T A
A historic living parish church, progressively shaped from the Tudor to the Edwardian period. Newly restored windows recapture the original airiness of the eighteenth-century nave. A.W.Blomfield/G.F. Bodley 1506.
Tube/Rail: Richmond

St Mary the Virgin, Twickenham
Church Street, Twickenham TW1 3NJ
■ Sat 10am-4.30pm. Tours at 10am/11am/12noon/3pm/4pm. Max 10 per tour. N d
Beautiful riverside church, a building of remarkable contrasts: a 15C ragstone tower and a red-brick Queen Anne nave and chancel, the previous nave having collapsed in 1713. Godfrey Kneller and Alexander Pope buried here. John James 14C/1714-15.
Tube/Rail: Richmond then H22 bus; Rail: Twickenham, St Margarets; 267,281,H22

Style Council
46 Barnes Avenue SW13 9AB
■ Sat 10am-5pm. Half-hourly tours. Last entry 4.30pm.
'Style Council' is the transformation of a former post WW1 Council house into a stylish, modern, energy efficient home. Located on a large south facing corner plot, the house has been extended in every direction possible, with the interiors completely re-planned as light filled open plan spaces for multi-generational family living. Features include bamboo sliding screens, modern 'peek-a-boo' bay windows, a suspended 'musical' staircase, granny lift, dynamic furniture and private courtyard connected to new garden studio.

KSKa Architects 2014. Entry: Ground floor, garden.
Tube: Hammersmith; Rail: Barnes Bridge; 33,72,485
www.kska.co.uk

The Cedars (Span House) ●
2 The Cedars, Teddington TW11 0AX
■ Sat 10am-4.30pm. First come basis, queuing outside if necessary. Max 15 at one time. Q G P d
Example of a T2 house by Span Developments with Eric Lyons, famous for forward-looking housing of the '50s and typified by modernist lines, good internal planning and communal gardens. Recent ground floor extension and refurbishment with 'Mondrian' primary colour scheme, plus many sustainable features including solar PV cells, solar heating of water, and wood burning stove. Eric Lyons/KMK Architects 1958/2011.
Rail: Teddington; 33,R68,281,285

The Old Town Hall, Richmond
Whittaker Avenue, Richmond TW9 1TP
■ Sat 10am-4pm. Tours at 10am, 12noon, 2.30pm. N T d
Red brick and Bath stone grand 'Elizabethan Renaissance' style building altered by war, political changes and reflecting Richmond's history. Overlooking the war memorial and the Thames. W J Ancell 1893.
Tube/Rail: Richmond; 65,33,H37,H22,R70

Twickenham Museum
25 The Embankment, Twickenham TW1 3DU
■ Sat/Sun 11am-5pm. Last entry 4.30pm. Max 25 at one time. N T B P
Grade II listed former waterman's cottage c1720. Restored and converted into a museum celebrating the rich history of Twickenham, Whitton, Teddington and the Hamptons. Anthony Beckles Willson (restoration & conversion) 1720/2000.
Tube/Rail: Richmond; Rail: Twickenham; H22,R68,R70,290,490

White Lodge
Richmond Park (nearest gate Sheen Gate) TW10 5HR
■ Sat/Sun 10am-12.30pm. First come basis, queuing outside if necessary. N T P d
Commissioned as a royal hunting residence, a Grade I listed English Palladian villa, inspired by the high renaissance design principles of Palladio and the neo-classical interiors of Inigo Jones. The Museum explores the principles of classicism, embodied by the building of White Lodge and fundamental to the training undertaken within by students of The Royal Ballet School. Roger Morris 1727-30. Entry: selected rooms on ground floor of main villa, White Lodge Museum, view of west front from gardens.
Tube/Rail: Richmond; Rail: Mortlake

WALKS/TOURS

Richmond Park walk ●
■ Meet: Outside Information Centre at Pembroke Lodge in Richmond Park TW10 5HX. Sat tours at 10am, 12noon and 2pm. Max 20 per tour. N R T P d
Park walk showcasing the landscape of London's largest royal park and the largest enclosed urban park in Europe. It has 130,000 trees including over 1,300 veteran trees over 300 years old, and impressive vistas over London.
Tube/Rail: Richmond; 371

Supported by

LONDON BOROUGH OF RICHMOND UPON THAMES

Southwark

See **openhouselondon.org.uk/southwark**
to find out more about this area

80 Great Suffolk Street
80 Great Suffolk Street SE1 0BE
■ Sat/Sun 1pm-5pm. First come basis. T d A
TDO Architecture studio is a stunning plywood office suspended from a grid of red steelwork in a renovated arch under the railway on Great Suffolk Street. TDO Architecture 2013.
Tube: Southwark, Borough; Tube/Rail: London Bridge, Waterloo

95 Choumert Road
95 Choumert Road SE15 4AP
■ Sat 10am-5pm. Tours on the hour, pre-book ONLY on chris.newman@parityprojects.com. Last entry 4pm. Max 10 per tour. A G P
A 1874 townhouse that underwent a deep energy retrofit resulting in 90% CO2 savings and negative energy bills. Cost effectiveness was the driving philosophy. Parity Projects, 2013/1874.
Rail: Peckham Rye; 176,185,37,12,P12

240 Blackfriars
240 Blackfriars Road, SE1 8NV
■ Sat 10am-1pm. Architect-led talk and tours at 10am, 11am and 12noon. Pre-book ONLY on openhouse@ahmm.co.uk. Max 25 per tour.
New 89m tall, 220,000sqft office and retail building with adjoining residential development at the south end of Blackfriars Bridge. The building's crystalline form is wrapped in a fluid 'pinstripe' glass skin. Allford Hall Monaghan Morris 2014.
Tube: Southwark; 63,59
www.ahmm.co.uk

Allies and Morrison
85 Southwark Street SE1 0HX
■ Sat 10am-1pm. Regular tours, first come basis. Max 8 at one time. D T A
For Allies and Morrison's 30th Anniversary year there will be a retrospective exhibition and the opportunity to take a tour of the studio designed by the practice for its own use in 2004 and extended in the last year with 2 new buildings. RIBA Award Winner 2004. Allies and Morrison 2004/2013.
Tube/Rail: London Bridge, Blackfriars; Tube: Southwark; 381,RV1

ARK All Saints Academy and Highshore School
140 Wyndham Road SE5 0UB
■ Sat 1pm-5pm. First come basis. Architect-led tours of the schools and church. T A
Two co-located schools adjoining the new brick chapel and tower of St Michael and All Angels Church. Central streets linked to a series of courtyards animate the schools' three prefabricated pavilions with movement and natural light. Allford Hall Monaghan Morris 2013.
Tube: Oval; 36,185,436
www.ahmm.co.uk

Brunel Museum ●
Railway Avenue SE16 4LF
■ Sat/Sun 10am-5pm. First come basis, queuing outside if necessary. Guided descents of underground chamber half the size of Shakespeare's globe. Trains to view Thames Tunnel portico, one time shopping arcade, banquet hall and fairground. Bring travel ticket valid for zone 2. Award-winning river gardens. Sat 5- 11pm 'Liquid engineering', cocktails with the Midnight Apothecary in the roof gardens above the Thames Tunnel. R T B C P
The Brunel Museum is housed in the Brunel Engine House. The Engine House was designed by Sir Marc Isambard Brunel to be part of the infrastructure of the Thames Tunnel. Sir Marc Brunel 1842.
Rail: Rotherhithe; 1,188,381

Canada Water Library
21 Surrey Quays Road SE16 7AR
■ Sat 11am-4pm/Sun 12noon-4pm. Tours Sat 10am, 11am, 3pm, Sun 1pm. Max 20 per tour. N D T
A civic centrepiece for the regeneration of the area around Canada Water. Its inverted pyramid form is an innovative response to providing an efficient single large library floor on a smaller footprint site. CZWG 2011. Entry: entrance area, main library level, mezzanine level, roof.
Tube: Canada Water; 1,47,188,199,225,381,P12

Caroline Gardens Chapel
Asylum Road SE15 2SQ
■ Sat 9am-6pm. First come basis. N D T P
An extraordinary centrepiece of a large almshouse complex, the chapel was originally intended for retired publicans and brewers. It was severely damaged in WWII, but a collection of funerary monuments and painted glass windows survived. Sealed up until recently it is now an arts centre. Henry Rose 1827-33. Entry: chapel, general estate.
Rail: Queens Road Peckham; P12

Cathedral ●
St Thomas's Church, St Thomas Street SE1 9RY
■ Sun 12pm-4pm. Architect led tours, first come basis. T A
Refurbishment of a Grade II listed church on English Heritage's 'at risk' register to create a headquarters for the developer Cathedral. New and old have been carefully integrated to create flexible and reconfigurable working environments. Allford Hall Monaghan Morris 2008.
Tube/Rail: London Bridge; 43,47,RV1,383
www.ahmm.co.uk

City Hall ●
The Queen's Walk, More London (from Tower Hill, walk across Tower Bridge) SE1 2AA
■ Sat 9am-6pm. City of a 1000 Architects kids activity 11am-3pm. Last entry 5.30pm. N D R T Q C G
Home of the Mayor of London and London Assembly, an environmentally-aware building with innovative spiral ramp and fine views across London. Special Event for OHL weekend: City of a Thousand Architects junior activity in London's Living Room. Foster + Partners 2002. Entry: London's Living Room, spiral ramp, chamber.
Tube: Tower Hill; Tube/Rail: London Bridge; 47,42,78,381,RV1

Coach House12
11a Sydenham Hill SE26 6SH
■ Sat 10am-5pm. First come basis, queuing if necessary. Last entry 4.30pm. Max 15 at one time. A
Combining a rich palette of traditional and vernacular materials with a contemporary understanding of detail and space, this house proposes a new vision of domesticity based on craft, tactility and light. John Smart Architects 2013.
Rail: Crystal Palace, Sydenham, Gipsy Hill; 3,122,202,363,450

Courtyard House
35 Dovedale Road SE22 0NF
■ Sun 10.30am-5.30pm. First come basis, queuing outside if necessary. Last entry 4.30pm. Max 8 at one time. D A G P

Southwark Integrated Waste Management Facility

Single-storey courtyard house on constrained site, built out to the perimeter whilst providing light and private views to the habitable rooms and avoiding overlooking of the surrounding properties. Bathrooms are located along the street facade with opaque glass windows to provide a buffer zone between the living space and the pavement. Design-Cubed 2012.
Rail: Honor Oak Park; 63,363

Crystal Palace Subway
Crystal Palace Parade SE19 1LG
■ Sat/Sun 10am-5pm. Regular tours. Pre-book ONLY by email on events@cpsubway.org.uk or 020 8133 0973, for ticket ballot. Please specify number of places required and Sat/ Sun preference. Under 18s must be accompanied by an adult. No wheelchair access. Last entry 4.30pm.
Magnificent subway under Crystal Palace Parade resembling a vaulted crypt. The subway connected the High Level Station (E M Barry 1865; demolished 1961) to the Crystal Palace (Joseph Paxton 1854; burnt down 1936). 1865.
Rail: Crystal Palace; 3,202,322,410,450

Dilston Grove
Southwest corner of Southwark Park SE16 2DD
■ Sat/Sun 11am-4pm. First come basis. N D T
A former Clare College mission church, now contemporary art gallery and recently renovated, was the first concrete-poured building in England, now Grade II listed. 2010 renovation by Walter Menteth & Sherry Bates. Sir John Simpson & Maxwell Ayrton/Walter Menteth & Sherry Bates (renovation) 1911/2010. Entry: lobby and main space.
Tube/Rail: Canada Water; Rail: Surrey Quays; 1,47,188,199,225

Elmwood Road
33 Elmwood Road, SE24 9NS
■ Sat 10am-5pm. First come basis. Last entry 4.30pm. A
One of a pair of new-build terraced houses which replace a 1960s building which occupied a gap in the existing Victorian terraces. The houses restore the rhythm of the street with a contemporary take on their neighbours. Knox Bhavan Architects LLP 2014. Entry: House and garden.
Rail: North Dulwich, Herne Hill; 37,68,42,468,P4

Employment Academy
29 Peckham Road SE5 8UA
■ Sat 10am-5pm. Half-hourly tours. R T d A E G
The Employment Academy is a Grade II Listed, late Victorian 'Baroque' building that has now become a local asset to the Southwark community. Edwin Thomas Hall/Peter Barber Architects 1904/2013.
Rail: Peckham Rye, Denmark Hill; 171,436,36,12,345

Key. A Architect on site **B** Bookshop **C** Childrens' activities **d** Some disabled access **D** Full wheelchair access **E** Engineer on site **G** Green Features
N Normally open to the public **P** Parking **Q** Long queues envisaged **R** Refreshments **T** Toilets

Friendship House (LHA) ●

Belvedere Place, off Borough Road SE1 0AD

■ Sat 9.30am-4.30pm. Half-hourly tours. Last tour 4.30pm. Max 10 per tour. D T G

Angular walls of dramatic zinc tiles and bright render enclosing a quiet courtyard with reflective pool as modern self-catered accommodation for 179 residents. RIBA Award Winner 2005. MacCormac Jamieson Prichard 2003. Entry: common rooms, dining areas, bedsits, garden.

Tube: Borough, Southwark; Tube/Rail: Elephant & Castle, London Bridge; 344,35,40,133

Friern Road, East Dulwich

190A Friern Road SE22 0BA

■ Sat 10am-5pm. Hourly tours 11-4pm, first come basis. Last entry 4.30pm. A G d

Contemporary self-build architect's house designed around a 100-year old pear tree, constructed of board marked concrete and timber cladding featuring onsite crafted joinery and light fittings. Edgley Design 2014. Entry: whole house.

Rail: Peckham Rye; 12,197,176,185,363

Jerwood Space

171 Union Street SE1 0LN

■ Sat/Sun tours at 2.30pm, 4.30pm. Portable loop system available for hard-of-hearing (please pre-book on 0207 654 0171). N R T P d

Former Victorian school converted in contemporary idiom (Paxton Locher Architects 1998) to provide theatre/dance rehearsal facilities, plus striking gallery alongside a cafe and glazed courtyard (the Glasshouse – Satellite Architects 2003). New studios and meeting rooms (Munkenbeck & Partners 2007) on the restored top floor (lost to wartime bombing). Sustainable features include sedum roof. Paxton Locher/ Satellite Architects/Munkenbeck and Partners/Elliott Wood Partners 1998/2003/2007. www.elliottwood.co.uk

Tube: Southwark; Tube/Rail: London Bridge; 40,45,63,344,RV1

Kirkaldy Testing Works

99 Southwark Street SE1 0JF

■ Sat 10am-4.30pm. Regular tours, first come basis. Last entry 4pm. Max 20 at one time. T d

Grade II* listed industrial building, purpose-built to house D Kirkaldy's unique materials testing machine, now restored. T Roger Smith 1873. Entry: ground floor, basement.

Tube: Southwark; Tube/Rail: London Bridge; 45,63,100,381

Laundry Houses

21-22 Albert Way, Peckham SE15 1DG

■ Sat 12pm-5pm. First come basis. Last entry 4.30pm.

One of two new build 4-bedroom houses constructed in cross-laminated timber panels. Designed and developed by Quay 2c Architects. Short films will be shown by artist Julia Manheim. Quay 2c 2014.

Rail: Queens Road Peckham; 436,36,53,P12,453

London Fire Brigade Museum, Winchester House

94 Southwark Bridge Road SE1 0EG

■ Sat 10am-4pm. Tours at 11am and 2pm exploring how the building has evolved. Last entry 3.30pm. Max 150 at one time. N T B

Georgian Mansion built as two houses in 1820, converted in 1878 into one large residence for the Chief Officer of the LFB. Grade II listed, retaining many original features including an exquisite mosaic entrance. 1820. Entry: Winchester House and LFB Museum.

Tube: Borough, Southwark; Tube/Rail: London Bridge, Blackfriars; 344,40,35,133,343

City Hall

London Southbank University (CEREB) ●●

CEREB, 8th Floor, K2 Building, Keyworth Street SE1 0AA

■ Sat 11am-5pm. Hourly tours. Last tour 4pm. Max 15 per tour. T d

The Centre for Efficient and Renewable Energy in Buildings is a teaching, research and public demonstration facility in the K2 building with a stunning atrium. Shepheard Epstein Hunter 2009.

Tube/Rail: Elephant & Castle; 12,148,171,172

LSBU Clarence Centre of Enterprise and Innovation

6 St George's Circus SE1 6FE

■ Sat 10am-4pm. Regular tours, first come basis. Last entry 3pm. D R T A G

Office space and support for start-up businesses at London South Bank University, incorporated into two Grade II listed Georgian terraces and a former pub. A careful juxtaposition of new and old. Rivington Street Studio 2013.

Tube/Rail: Elephant & Castle; 1,45,63,68,148,172

Mobile Gardeners Planting Station ●

137-149 Walworth Road SE17 1JZ

■ Sat/Sun 1pm-9pm. Talks and gardening workshops throughout the day. N D R T C G

Explore London's only mobile community garden, parked Autumn 2014 in a pop-up site on a former petrol station forecourt. Activities include harvest festival, food and drink, disco and soul, pumpkins and sunflowers. 2012.

Tube/Rail: Elephant & Castle; 35,40,68,148,171

Nunhead Cemetery ●

Linden Grove SE15 3LP

■ Sat/Sun 1pm-5pm. Tours at 2pm, 3pm of the cemetery and chapel. N T B G P d

Magnificent Victorian cemetery with Gothic chapel and ruined lodge. One of London's wildest and most overgrown cemeteries, a square mile of inner city forest. Restored with the help of a lottery grant. Unique in London – 50 acres of wilderness, complete with bats, owls, foxes and squirrels. Thomas Little & JJ Bunning 1840. Entry: cemetery, chapel.

Rail: Nunhead; 484,P3,P12

Old Operating Theatre Museum & Herb Garret

9a St Thomas Street SE1 9RY

■ Sun 10.30am-5pm. Access via 32 step bell tower spiral staircase. Last entry 4.45pm. Max 60 at one time. B

St Thomas' Church attic (1703) once part of old St Thomas' Hospital, houses the Herb Garret and Britain's only surviving 19C operating theatre. Thomas Cartwright 1703.

Tube/Rail: London Bridge; 21,35,40,43,47,48,133,149

ORTUS

82-96 Grove Lane, Denmark Hill SE5 8SN

■ Sat 10am-5pm. Hourly tours, first come basis. Last entry 4.40pm. N D R T A G

A new 1550sqm pavilion housing learning and events facilities, cafe and exhibition spaces. The central focus of this unique project, initially coined 'Project Learning Potential', is to create a totally immersive learning environment generating a series of interconnecting spaces to encourage intuitive learning activities. Duggan Morris Architects/Elliott Wood Partnership/ Skelly & Couch 2014.

Rail: Denmark Hill; 40,42,68,176,185,468,484
www.elliottwood.co.uk

Passmore Edwards Library and Bath House

Wells Way SE5 0RN

■ Sat 1pm-5pm. First come basis, queuing outside if necessary. R T

The old library is adjacent to the bathhouse which is used by well-known boxing club Lynn AC. Main entrance porch is flanked by 2 Ionic columns, decorative carvings and relief work. On the side of the building the Camberwell Beauty butterfly is rendered in ceramic tiles. 1902.

Tube/Rail: Elephant and Castle; 42,343,136

Peckham Library ●

122 Peckham Hill Street SE15 5JR

■ Sat 10am-5pm/Sun 12pm-4pm. Sat 11am, 2pm & Sun 2pm tours to non-public areas. Max 25 per tour. N D T G

A dramatic design resembling an upside-down 'L' of coloured glass and green copper. A pure 21C building. RIBA Award Winner. Alsop and Stormer 2000.

Tube/Rail: Elephant and Castle (then bus 12,63,171,343); Rail: Peckham Rye

Peckham Platform ●

89 Peckham High Street SE15 5RS

■ Sat/Sun 10am-5pm. First come basis. Exhibition of new work by Eileen Perrier. Last entry 3.45pm. Max 60 at one time. N D T C

This striking green and white timber building is a highly sustainable design with clean, dynamic lines, dramatic unsupported overhangs and great use of natural light. Sustainable features include marine ply build. Penson 2010. Entry: main project/exhibition space.

Tube: Oval; Rail: Peckham Rye, Queens Road Peckham; 343,12,171,36,436

Perronet House

48, 74 & 79 Perronet House, Princess Street (buzz flat 74 to enter) SE1 6JS

■ Sat 1pm-5pm. First come basis. Last entry 4.45pm. R T

Purpose-built council block with scissor construction flats with spectacular views of Elephant & Castle roundabout. Commended in 1971 Good Design in Housing Awards. Detailed historical notes and images shown. One flat significantly remodelled in 2012. Sir Roger Walters 1970. Entry: 3 homes.

Tube/Rail: Elephant & Castle; 12,176,63,344,188

Quay House ●

2C Kings Grove (Queens Road end) SE15 2NB

■ Sat 12pm-5pm. First come basis, queuing if necessary. Tea and cakes served. Quay 2C practice work on display. Last entry 4.30pm. R T B A G P d

As seen on BBC4 & Channel 5's 'I Own Britain's Best Home', conversion of 1930s milk depot into architect's office, sculpture studio and home with new-build development of three flats above. Exhibition in m2 gallery at the front of the building by video artist Nic Sandiland. Sustainable features include re-use

of existing derelict building with recycling of materials. Quay 2C 2001. Entry: ground floor house, office, studio.
Rail: Queens Road Peckham; 436,171,12,63, P12

Regeneration at Heart of Community – Camberwell Residential
149 Southampton Way, Camberwell SE5 7EW
■ Sat/Sun 11am-5pm. Half-hourly tours, first come basis. Queuing in cafe at ground floor if necessary. Max 4 per tour.
Reconstruction of a building derelict for more than 40 years and transformation into a modern residential property over a community restaurant/bar, including a striking two-storey glass roof extension. Twist In Architecture 2012. Entry: All areas.
Tube: Oval, Kennington; Tube/Rail: Elephant & Castle; Rail: Denmark Hill; 343,136

Royal Road
Enter using courtyard gate on Otto Street SE17 3NR
■ Sat 10am-1pm/Sun 1pm-5pm. First come basis. Tours taking place. Small exhibition with scale model. Last entry 30mins before closing. Max 10 per tour. D A G
A new development with heights varying from four to nine storeys provides 100% affordable housing. All homes are spacious with two or three aspects focused around a central communal garden. Retaining most of the healthy mature trees, the development blends into the streetscape.
Panter Hudspith Architects 2013. Central courtyard and communal areas.
Tube: Kennington, Oval; Tube/Rail: Vauxhall, Elephant & Castle; 133,155,333,415, P5

Sands Films Studios & Rotherhithe Picture Research Library
82 St Marychurch Street SE16 4HZ
■ Sat/Sun 10am-5pm. Hourly tours, first come basis. Last entry 5pm. R T B P d
Grade II listed riparian granary built with reclaimed timbers felled in 1700s. Converted in 1970s to picture library, film studios, prop and costume workshops. Oscar-winning international costume house for film, TV, theatre, opera, ballet. 1770s-1940s. Entry: picture research library, film studio, cinema, costume and prop workshops, canteen.
Tube: Bermondsey, Canada Water, Rail: Rotherhithe; 47,188,381,C10,P12

Siobhan Davies Studios ●
85 St Georges Road SE1 6ER
■ Sat 2pm-6pm. First come basis. Last chance to see Daniell Lobb riparian landscape installation in the building. Last entry 5.30pm. Max 150 at one time. N D T
A landmark home for dance. A daring design with 2-storey atrium and undulating ribbon roof that breathes life into an old school building. RIBA Award Winner 2006. Many sustainable features. Sarah Wigglesworth Architects 2006.
Tube: Lambeth North; Tube/Rail: Elephant & Castle, Waterloo; 12,53,148,344,360,453
www.siobhandavies.com

Solidspace Connect ●
100 Union Street SE1 0NL
■ Sat 10am-5pm/Sun 10am-1pm. First come basis. T d G
A publicly-accessible garden and temporary concrete frame – a prototype for two split level apartment units. The two year project will provide an opportunity to research technical and experiential data. Solidspace Ltd with EXYZT 2014.
Tube: Southwark, Borough, London Bridge; 48,149,43,141

Southwark Integrated Waste Management Facility ●●
43 Devon Street, off Old Kent Road SE15 1JR
■ Sat 10am-4pm. Half hourly tours, first come basis. No heels or open toe shoes can be worn on the tours. Last tour 3.30pm. Max 20 per tour. E R T C G d
One of Europe's most advanced recycling facilities, comprising many sustainable features including grey water, solar panels and green roof. Designed for the purpose of turning waste into a resource. Thorpe Wheatley 2012.
Tube/Rail: Elephant and Castle; Rail: Queens Road Peckham; 453,53,21,172
www.veolia.co.uk

Springbank
Springbank, 81A Grove Park SE5 8LE
■ Sat/Sun 10am-5pm. First come basis, queuing outside if necessary. Last entry 4.30pm. T d A E G P
One of a pair of modern houses on a sensitive site in a conservation area. A staircase atrium runs the full height, and ground floor areas open onto courtyard gardens on three sides. SE5 Architects 2013. Entry: all areas.
Rail: Denmark Hill, Peckham Rye; 176,185,40,63,12

The Exchange – Bermondsey Spa Gardens
17 Spa Road, Bermondsey, SE16 3SA
■ Sat/Sun tours at 11.30am and 1pm. First come basis.
The Exchange is a new mixed-tenure housing development, designed as an urban village for modern living for Notting Hill Housing. PCKO Architects 2014.
Tube: Bermondsey; 1,78,188,42,47

The Old Mortuary
St Marychurch Street SE16 4J E
■ Sat/Sun 10am-5pm. Regular tours and special display of features of local history. Last entry 4pm. Max 10 per tour, max 25 at one time. D R T P
Erected in 1895 and situated in Rotherhithe Conservation Area. Retains many original features including a vaulted ceiling in Russell Hall, original doors, lantern skylight and iron girder in Varney Room (formerly post-mortem room), wooden panelling in chapel. Now community centre with local history group (Time and Talents Association). 1895. Entry: former mortuary, post mortem room, chapel.
Tube: Bermondsey, Canada Water; Rail: London Bridge, Rotherhithe; 47,188,381,C10,P12

The Pioneer Health Centre
St Mary's Road SE15 2EE
■ Sun 11am-2pm. Hourly tours, first come basis. Photographic display of building's former use. Last tour 1pm. Max 50 at one time. E R P
Grade II* listed Modernist building, famously described by Walter Gropius as "an oasis of glass in a desert of brick". Originally built to house 'The Peckham Experiment': an innovative health centre in the 30s. It was converted to private dwellings in 2000, retaining the original indoor pool. Sir E Owen Williams 1935.
Rail: New Cross Gate, Queens Road Peckham; 36,78,136,436,171,177,P12,P13

Unicorn Theatre
147 Tooley Street SE1 2HZ
■ Sat 10am-5pm. Hourly tours, first come basis. First tour 10am and no tour between 1pm and 2pm. Performances running throughout day. Last tour 4pm. Max 18 per tour. N D R T B C
The first professional, purpose-built theatre for young audiences in UK. Described as an asymmetric pavilion, the

building has transparent elevations revealing its core, and was designed in consultation with young people. RIBA Award Winner 2006. Keith Williams Architects 2005. Entry: theatre, foyer, some backstage areas.
Tube/Rail: London Bridge; 47,RV1,381,17,21,35

Weston Williamson Architects Offices
12 Valentine Place SE1 8QH
■ Sat 1pm-5pm. First come basis. T A d
Architects' studio within a 19C warehouse building in the Valentine Place conservation area. Many original features have been restored, celebrated and coupled with contemporary fittings and furniture. Weston Williamson 2013. Entry: all areas.
Tube/Rail: Waterloo, Southwark; 45,63,100

William Booth College
Champion Park SE5 8BQ
■ Sat 9am-5pm. Half hourly tours. Entry to tower 9am-4pm. Talk on building in assembly hall 10am, 11am 2pm, 3pm. R T G
This monumental Grade II listed college with massive brick tower gives commanding views to the City and Docklands. Giles Gilbert Scott 1929. Entry: tower, grounds, assembly hall.
Rail: Denmark Hill; 40,42,68,176,185,468,484

WALKS/TOURS

artouride cycle tour ●
■ Meet: Sun 2pm at Canada Water Station (outside) SE16 7BB Pre-book ONLY on info@artouride.com – max 12 on tour. Duration 3 hours. Bring own bike. T
Cycle tour with a local guide from artouride around SE16 landmarks. Celebrating this year's Thames Festival (Totally Thames), the tour will be exploring the rich history and architecture around the river front.
Tube/Rail: Canada Water, Surrey Quays; Ferry: Greenland Pier; C10

Bankside Urban Forest ●
■ Meet: Sat 12noon and 3pm at Bankside Community Space, 18 Great Guildford Street SE1 0FD. T G
Guided walk of Bankside Urban Forest, a public space partnership and strategy with an ecological approach. Learn about recent and emerging public space and urban greening projects within one of London's oldest neighbourhoods. Witherford Watson Mann, Adams & Sutherland, Gort Scott, VOGT Landscape, Wayward Plants and more 2008-present.
Tube/Rail: London Bridge, Blackfriars; Tube: Southwark, Borough; RV1,381,344

Blackfriars Arts Treasure Hunt ●
■ Sat/Sun 10am-4pm. First come basis. Trail contains many kids activities. D C. Drop in treasure hunt. Maps can be picked up from ASC Studio Erlang House or Blackfriars Station South Side, next to The Founders Arms on the Riverside. Download a treasure map at www.cityhunt.co.uk.
Trail bringing the heritage and history of Blackfriars to life through oral histories and interventions. Visit City hunt website for further details. Funded by Southwark Council.
Tube/Rail: Blackfriars, London Bridge; 63,100,45,168,1,68

Supported by

Southwark
Council

Key. A Architect on site **B** Bookshop **C** Children's activities **d** Some disabled access **D** Full wheelchair access **E** Engineer on site **G** Green Features **N** Normally open to the public **P** Parking **Q** Long queues envisaged **R** Refreshments **T** Toilets

Sutton

See openhouselondon.org.uk/sutton
to find out more about this area

All Saints Carshalton
High Street, Carshalton SM5 3AQ
■ Sat/Sun 10am-5pm. Regular tours. Max 50 at one time. N R P d
12C south aisle and former chancel. Blomfield nave, chancel, baptistry. Kempe glass, Bodley reredos and screen, spectacular Comper decorations, monuments and brasses, award-winning lighting scheme, fine modern benches. A & R Blomfield 19C.
Rail: Carshalton; 127,157,407,x26

BedZED and Regeneration of Hackbridge ● ●
24 Helios Road, Wallington SM6 7BZ
■ Sat 12pm-4pm. Guided tours on the hour, first come basis. Max 15 per tour. R T B A G d
Come explore the UK's first large-scale mixed use eco-village and sustainable community. Completed in 2002, BedZED is still an inspiration for low carbon neighbourhoods that promotes One Planet Living across the world, developed in partnership with Peabody Trust and Bioregional. Details about the public realm improvements in Hackbridge by architects Adams & Sutherland will also be included in the tour. Bill Dunster Zedfactory Architects/Adams & Sutherland 2002. Entry: show-home.
Rail: Hackbridge, Mitcham Junction; 127,151

Carshalton Water Tower and Historic Gardens
West Street, Carshalton SM5 2QG
■ Sat/Sun 1pm-5pm. First come basis. Quiz sheets for children. If disabled access required, call 020 8647 0984 in advance. Last entry 4.30pm. R T B C d
Early 18C Grade II listed building incorporating plunge bath with Delft tiles, Orangery, saloon and pump chamber with part-restored water wheel. Hermitage and sham bridge in grounds. 18C. Entry: Orangery, saloon, bathroom, pump chamber.
Tube: Morden; Rail: Carshalton; 157,127,407,X26,154

Charles Cryer Studio Theatre
39 High Street, Carshalton SM5 3BB
■ Sun 10am-5pm. Regular tours. Duration 30 mins, with special live performances at 12noon and 2pm. Last tour 4.30pm. Exhibition on history of area and building. Max 10 at one time. T d
Originally built as a public hall in 1874 for Carshalton village this building has since been used as a cinema, a theatre and later, as a roller skating rink. The venue was redesigned by Edward Cullinan Architects and re-opened again by Prince Edward as a theatre in 1991. Edward Cullinan Architects 1991.
Rail: Carshalton; 127,157,407

Honeywood
Honeywood Walk, Carshalton SM5 3NX
■ Sat/Sun 10am-5pm. Last entry 4.45pm. N R T B C d
Chalk and flint house dating to 17C with many later additions including major extensions of 1896 and 1903 when owned by John Pattinson Kirk, a London merchant. Rich in period detail and the interior recently restored and back stairs opened up with funding from the Heritage Lottery Fund. Now a local museum.
Rail: Carshalton; 127,157,407,X26

Little Holland House
40 Beeches Avenue, Carshalton SM5 3LW
■ Sat 2pm-5pm. First come basis, queuing outside if necessary. Max 25 at one time. N T B d
Grade II* listed building whose interior was created entirely by Dickinson, inspired by the ideals of John Ruskin and William Morris and contains Dickinson's paintings, hand-made furniture, furnishings, metalwork and friezes, in Arts and Crafts style. Frank Dickinson 1902-4. Entry: ground floor, master bedroom, back bedroom, bathroom, garden.
Tube: Morden, then 154 bus; Rail: Carshalton Beeches; 154

Lumley Chapel
St Dunstan's Churchyard, Church Road, Cheam SM3 8QH
■ Sat/Sun 2.30pm-4.30pm. N
Medieval former chancel of parish church. All that remains after church was demolished in 1864, part 12C, with many important post-Reformation memorials. 12C.
Rail: Cheam; 151,213,293,X26

Nonsuch Gallery and Service Wing at Nonsuch Mansion
Nonsuch Park, Ewell Road, Cheam SM3 8AL
■ Sat/Sun 2pm-5pm. Regular tours. Last entry 4.30pm. D R T B P
Georgian mansion, designed in Tudor Gothic style, later used at Windsor Castle. Built for wealthy merchant Samuel Farmer. Restored Service Wing includes dairy, kitchen, scullery, larders and laundries. Gallery has timeline and first ever model of Henry VIII Nonsuch Palace, scale drawings and archaeological dig artefacts. Jeffrey Wyatt 1806. Entry: service wing museum, gallery (not inside mansion itself).
Rail: Cheam; 213,151,293,X26

Russettings
25 Worcester Road, Sutton SM2 6PR
■ Sun 10am-12.30pm. First come basis, queuing outside if necessary. Last entry 12.45pm. Max 25 at one time. N D T P
A double-fronted red brick upper-middle class house, Russettings is one of a few Victorian villas to survive in Sutton. The well-preserved interior includes an entrance hall with a mosaic tiled floor and an oak galleried staircase. Frederick Wheeler 1899.
Rail: Sutton; 470,S4

The Circle Library ● ●
Green Wrythe Lane, Carshalton SM5 1JJ
■ Sat 9.30am-5pm. 'The Making of an Estate' St Helier 1935-50 exhibition. D T P
An inviting, accessible contemporary social space. Full of air and natural light with spacious free-flowing areas, the building incorporates a range of environmental features designed to keep carbon footprint to a minimum including ground-source heating, sedum roof and rainwater harvesting. Curl La Tourelle Architects 2010. Entry: library, courtyard garden, multi-purpose room, heritage meeting space.
Tube: Morden; Rail: Carshalton; S1,151

The Sutton Life Centre ●
24 Alcorn Close SM3 9PX
■ Sat 9.30am-5pm. Tours at 11am, 3pm, first come basis. Max 25 per tour. E D R T C G P
Multi-purpose community building awarded BREEAM Excellent for its use of sustainable energy. Key features include a unique learning facility for children aged 10-13, library, eco-garden, sports pitch and climbing wall. Curl La Tourelle Architects/Elliott Wood Partnership 2010. Entry: library, eco-garden, life skills zone, media lab. Arts and crafts for kids.
Tube: Morden; Rail: Sutton Common; S3,80,470
www.elliottwood.co.uk

BedZED and Regeneration of Hackbridge

Whitehall
1 Malden Road, Cheam SM3 8QD
■ Sat 10am-5pm/Sun 2pm-5pm. House model-making for children. N R T B C d
Originally a farmer's house dating to 1500, with jettied upper storey. Later additions through the centuries reflect the changing lifestyles of the owners, including the Killicks for over 2 centuries. Now houses scale model of Henry VIII's Nonsuch Palace. Restored by John West & Partners 1974-76. c1500.
Rail: Cheam; X26,151,213

WALKS/TOURS

Revealing Eco Structures ●
■ Meet: Sun at 1.30pm or 3.30pm at the cross roads at the top of Sutton High Street outside Barclays Bank and Cafe Nero SM1 1LD. Walks timed to coincide with the Imagine Eco arts festival. Duration 75 mins.
Tour will uncover the impact of a living wall of plants and take visitors to the Straw cafe. Tour led by Enjoy Sutton and Sutton Council and visitors will learn about the sustainable work of the borough. For more information see www.suttontheatres.co.uk/imagine
Rail: Sutton; 407,420

> ### Imagine
> IMAGINE is Sutton's largest festival of the Arts, running from September 13th – November 2nd 2014. This year will host all things ECO, from cycle powered films to recycled puppets. For more information please visit **www.suttontheatres.co.uk/imagine**

Supported by

●AJ Library Building　●Green Exemplar　Landscape/Public realm　●Infrastructure/Engineering　■Open Saturday　■Open Sunday　■Open Saturday and Sunday

openhouselondon.org.uk | Sutton | 63

Tower Hamlets

See **openhouselondon.org.uk/towerhamlets**
to find out more about this area

20 Winkley Street
20 Winkley Street E2 6PT
■ Sat 10am-5pm. Regular tours, first come basis. Max 6 per tour. A G

A contemporary open plan house is hidden behind a traditional brick façade. Three small storeys are connected by vast glazing, open voids, folded metal stairs and the vertical garden. The internal interplay of space, light and materials creates a voluminous residence in a dense mews setting. Kirkwood McCarthy 2014. Entry: House, garden.
Tube: Bethnal Green; 48,55,388,254,8

Balfron Tower
Balfron Tower, St Leonard's Road E14 0QT
■ Sat 1pm–5pm. Half-hourly tours, first come basis. Last tour 4.30pm. Max 12 per tour. G d

Trellick Tower's older, shorter, and lesser known sister. Grade II listed 27-storey block designed in the brutalist style for the London County Council. Erno Goldfinger 1965. Entry: entry area, lifts/stairs, access bridges & corridors, a flat.
DLR: All Saints, Langdon Park; 15,115,D6,D7,D8

Boundary
2-4 Boundary Street E2 7DD
■ Sat/Sun 8am-11pm. D R T G

The original building, a late Victorian warehouse, was carefully converted over a period of 3 years. Special attention was given to preserving attractive industrial features, from the double-height basement to the original brickwork and sash windows. Prescott & Conran Ltd 2009.
Tube: Old Street; Rail: Shoreditch High St; Tube/Rail: Liverpool St

Bow Arts
183 Bow Road E3 2SJ
■ Sat 11am-4.30pm. Hourly tours at 11am, 12noon, 1pm, 2pm, 3pm and 4pm. Max 15 per tour.

New headquarters of Bow Arts. The building consolidates the charity's activities at the heart of its Bow Road studio complex. Located in a set of historic warehouse buildings grouped around a courtyard, the scheme provides offices, meeting facilities and a flexible event space. Delvendahl Martin Architects 2014. Entry: Offices and private courtyard.
Tube/DLR: Bow Road, Bow Church; Tube/Rail: Stratford; 8,25,108,276,425,D8

Bow School
Bow School, Gillender Street E3 3JY
■ Sat tours at 10.15, 11.15 and 12.15, pre-book ONLY at kate@vhh.co.uk giving preferred tour time. Max 15 per tour. Visitors should arrive 15 minutes before tour start. D R T A G

Completing LBTH's Building Schools for the Future programme, the new school provides great facilities for 1600 pupils, in 3 blocks around a landscaped playground facing the Limehouse cut. van Heyningen and Haward Architects (vHH) 2014. Entry: whole site, inc 3 buildings, interior, roof and external landscaped areas.
Tube: Bromley-by-Bow; Tube/Rail: Stratford; 108,488,323,309

Canary Wharf Crossrail Station Construction Site ●
Entrance from the North Colonnade opposite 1 Canada

Square, between the Financial Conduct Authority and Bank of America buildings E14 5HS
■ Sat/Sun 9.30am-5pm. First come basis. Self-guided walk through the site using designated segregated walkways. NB Sensible clothing – jeans and closed sturdy shoes. Unsuitable for under 5s. Last entry 4pm. E N d

This is a unique opportunity to view the Canary Wharf Crossrail site ahead of station completion in 2018. The structure is built in a reclaimed dock and is 6 storeys high, making it large enough to accommodate One Canada Square on its side. Due 2018. Entry: Tour will include viewing of platform level, ticket hall, retail areas and roof gardens. www.mottmac.com **ice**
Tube/DLR: Canary Wharf; 277,135,D3,D7,D8

Chrisp Street Market
The Clocktower, Chrisp Street Market E14 6AQ
■ Sat/Sun 10am-6pm. Regular tours to Clocktower. Sat 12noon tour of Festival area and related points of interest.
A beautiful Modernist "practical folly" designed as part of the site for the 1951 Festival of Britain live architecture exhibition. Sir Frederick Gibberd 1951.
DLR: All Saints; D8,15,115,D6,108,309

Christ Church Spitalfields
Commercial Street/Fournier Street E1 6LY
■ Sat 10am-4pm/Sun 1pm-4pm. First come basis. N C d
Grade I listed masterpiece of English Baroque, restored to its 18C splendour. Refurbished and restored by Whitfield Partners 1978-2002 and Purcell Miller Tritton from 2002. RIBA Award Winner 2006. Nicholas Hawksmoor 1714-1729. Entry: nave, vestibule, galleries.
Tube: Aldgate East; Tube/Rail: Liverpool Street; 67,8,149,78,26

Coborn House
1a Tredegar Square E3 5AD
■ Sat 10am-2pm. First come basis. Tours taking places every half hour. Max 10 per tour. A
Previous factory/office in a conservation area, transformed into two high-end unique dwellings, exposing King truss rafters, insertion of a 'hidden' roof terrace and stunning interior specification. Clear Architects 2013.
Tube: Mile End; 25,205,339,425

East London Central Synagogue
30-40 Nelson Street E1 2DE
■ Sun 10am-5pm. Half-hourly tours. Last tour 4.30pm. Max 40 per tour. T d
Only remaining purpose-built synagogue in Stepney/Whitechapel area. Most original features intact, having survived the Blitz. Ornate eastern wall (focal point) with Corinthian, Doric and Ionic pillars. Neo-classical style, oak panelling and pews. Excellent acoustics. Lewis Solomon & Son 1923. Entry: main hall.
Tube: Aldgate East, Whitechapel; Rail/DLR: Shadwell; 115,15,135,25,254

Four Corners ● ●
121 Roman Road E2 0QN
■ Sat 10am-5pm. Half hourly tours and presentations on the history of the project. R T G d
Refurbished building with extension and a clear circulation route forming the spine of building. A central courtyard or integrated 'hub' allows light and air to filter through. New loft conversion to create studio and work space. Sustainable features include natural light and ventilation, sedum roof to reduce rainwater run-off and provide heat saving and summer cooling. JaK Studio (refurb) 2007/2011. Entry: gallery, darkrooms, offices, garden, green roof.

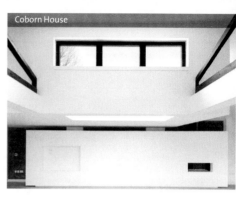
Coborn House

Tube/Rail: Bethnal Green; 106,8,277

Glamis Adventure Playground ●
10 Glamis Road E1W 3EG
■ Sat 2pm-4pm. Talks by Mark Halden engineer 2pm, 3pm. E N T C d
Continually evolving self-built structures hark back to the golden days of adventure play. Join Mark Halden in a visit to one of London's most distinctive adventure playgrounds in action and meet staff, parents, volunteers and users. 1969/2002.
DLR/Rail: Shadwell, Limehouse

Half Moon Theatre
43 White Horse Road, E1 0ND
■ Sat/Sun 10am-5pm. Half-hourly tours, first come basis. Last entry 4.15pm. N D R T B C
Half Moon Theatre is a highly decorated stucco-rendered building in the York Square conservation area which has recently been renovated. The building was originally constructed as Limehouse District Board of Works in 1864. C. R. Dunch 1864. Entry: Foyer, auditorium, backstage.
DLR/Rail: Limehouse, Shadwell; 135,115,15,D3,D7

Hermitage Community Moorings
16 Wapping High Street E1W 1NG
■ Sat/Sun 10am-4pm. First come basis. Information regarding history of the vessels. Special visiting boats open to the public. Cruise under open Tower Bridge on sailing barge Volharding. Prior booking recommended on www.hcmoorings.org – last entry 3pm. R T d
An exciting new development of residential and recreational moorings for historic vessels on the Thames. The architectural scheme has been designed as a model for river dwelling that takes into account its tidal location. The unique Pier House, built to a high specification, provides a floating community centre just downstream from Tower Bridge. Anna Versteeg & Ollie Price 2010. Entry: The Pier House, possible access to some historic vessels.
Tube: Tower Hill; 100,RV1

Idea Store, Whitechapel – In.Vi.Te @ The Gallery ● ●
4th floor, 321 Whitechapel Road E1 1BU
■ Sat 10am-4pm/Sun 12pm-4.30pm. First come basis. E N D R T G
Exploring the role of the Architect, a display of drawings and research materials will highlight the evolution of the building from concept to creation. RIBA Award Winner 2006. Adjaye Associates 2005. Entry: 4th floor gallery.
Tube: Whitechapel, Aldgate East; 25,106,205,254

Kingsley Hall
Powis Road, off Bruce Road E3 3HJ

Key. A Architect on site **B** Bookshop **C** Childrens' activities **d** Some disabled access **D** Full wheelchair access **E** Engineer on site **G** Green Features **N** Normally open to the public **P** Parking **Q** Long queues envisaged **R** Refreshments **T** Toilets

The Tree House

■ Sat 11am-6pm. Hourly tours from 12noon. History and archives exhibition. Last tour 5pm. Max 18 per tour. R T P d
Grade II listed, Pioneer East End community centre founded by peace campaigners Muriel and Doris Lester. Includes main hall and 5 rooftop cells for community volunteers. Links with Gandhi, George Lansbury, R D Laing's Philadelphia Association 1965-1970. Set for Attenborough's Gandhi 1983. Charles Cowles Voysey 1928. Entry: Gandhi's cell, Peace garden.
Tube: Bromley-by-Bow; DLR: Bow Church; 8,25,108,488

Lansbury Estate
Grundy Street E14 6DR
■ Sat/Sun 10am-5pm. First come basis, queuing if necessary. Public Housing Estate built as part of 1951 Festival of Britain. Named after George Lansbury, social reformer and MP for Poplar, who died in 1940. Sir Frederick Gibberd and others 1949-82.
DLR: All Saints; D6,D7,D8,15,115

Limehouse Town Hall
646 Commercial Road E14 7HA
■ Sat/Sun 1pm-5pm. Information on history of building and plans for future developments. Last entry 4.30pm. R T
White brick palazzo-style former town hall with stone dressings, vast arched moulded windows and grand Portland stone staircase with 11m high stairwell. A & C Harson 1881. Entry: lobby, main staircase, main hall (former council chamber), side stairs, workshop spaces.
Tube: Canary Wharf; DLR/Rail: Limehouse; 15,115,D6,D7,277,D3

London Buddhist Centre
51 Roman Road E2 0HU
■ Sun 11am-5pm. First come basis. Tours at 11am & 4pm to section of normally inaccessible 1st floor. Last entry 4.45pm. Max 20 per tour. N R T B G P d
Ornate vernacular red brick Victorian former fire station (1888). Grade II listed. Now a Buddhist Centre with 3 beautiful shrine rooms with Buddha figures and paintings. Robert Pearsall 1888.
Tube: Bethnal Green; Rail: Cambridge Heath; D6,8,309,106,388

Mint Street ● ◉ ◉
Mint Street, Bethnal Green E2 6JL
■ Sat 10am-1pm. Tours every 45 mins. Places available on the day on first come basis but also places can be pre-booked on admin@pitmantozer.com – last tour 12.15pm. A G
A new housing development of 67 flats for Peabody, close to the railway creating a new pedestrian link. An example of how to combine affordable, shared ownership and market sale homes on a noisy urban site creating a pleasant environment. Pitman Tozer Architects 2014.
Tube/Rail: Bethnal Green; 8,254,106,205,388

One Bishops Square ◉
One Bishops Square E1 6AD
■ Sun 10am-5pm. Last entry 4.30pm. Max 150 at one time. D R T G
An efficient, flexible, user-friendly and supportive working environment. 'Intelligent' building with many sustainable features including London's largest office-based solar installation and inbuilt computer system aimed at efficiency and energy conservation. Lights and air conditioning operate only when area is populated. Triple glazing and blinds reduce solar gain on all south-facing windows. Foster + Partners 2006. Entry: 6th floor coffee bar, office area, terrace, lobby.
Tube/Rail: Liverpool Street; 8,11,26,35,42

One Canada Square, Marketing Suite and Level 39
Meet: Lobby, One Canada Square E14 5AB
■ Sat 10am-5pm. Tours on the hour with talks around architectural models of marketing suite and Level 39, Europe's largest technology accelerator space. Pre-book ONLY at openhouse@canarywharf.com for details & preferred time. Last entry 4pm. Max 20 per tour. D R T
In just over 20 years, Canary Wharf Group plc has achieved one of the greatest feats of civic transformation – an iconic urban regeneration – designing and constructing 34 office buildings and 4 retail malls across a 97 acre business and shopping district with a workforce of 100,000 people. Level 39 is a sophisticated accelerator, social and event space, designed in 'tech industry' style by Gensler. Cesar Pelli 1991.
Tube/DLR: Canary Wharf; DLR: Heron Quays; D3,D7,D8,135,277

Oxford House in Bethnal Green
Derbyshire Street E2 6HG
■ Sat 10am-12pm. Regular tours. Victorian chapel will be open. Max 15 per tour. N D T
First "University Settlement", now a multi-purpose community centre with recently opened extension providing visual and performing arts space. Arts events taking place. Sir Arthur Blomfield/All Clear Designs 1891/2003.
Tube/Rail: Bethnal Green; 8,254,106,388

Phoenix School
49 Box Road E3 2AD
■ Sat 10am-1pm. Tours at 10am & 11.30am, first come basis. Max 15 per tour. T
Original school building was designed by LCC as an 'open air school', Grade II listed. Major new school building provides a prominent new entrance and reception, teaching space and green roof. Farquharson & McMorran/Patel Taylor (new building) 1952/2013. Entry: school.
Tube: Mile End, Bow Road; DLR: Bow Church; 8,25,108,205

Providence Row Arts and Activity Building at the Dellow Day Centre
82 Wentworth Street E1 7SA
■ Sat 1pm-5pm. Hourly tours. Last entry 4pm. Max 8 per tour. T A d
The new building sits opposite the original centre providing improved facilities for the homeless charity Providence Row. The charity offers an integrated service of crisis support, advice, recovery and learning programmes from this site, helping homeless and vulnerably housed people. The new building strengthens connections with the courtyard and the main centre, providing light and views in and out through a faceted facade. RIBA Award Winner 2012. Featherstone Young Architects 2011.
Tube/Rail: Liverpool Street; Tube: Aldgate East; 149,67,25,253,205

Roominaroom ◉
1 Narrow Street E14 8DP
■ Sat architect-led half tours at 10am, 10.45, 11.30am and 12.30pm. Pre-book ONLY on https://openhouselondon14-roominaroom.eventbrite.co.uk/ Max 10 per tour. T A
A digitally-fabricated gem – a highly sculptural and bespoke installation to create an extra bedroom within its host house that magically swells from the walls to create a beautiful nook. atmos 2012.
DLR/Rail: Limehouse; 135,277,C10,D3,D7
www.atmosstudio.com

Sandys Row Synagogue
4 Sandys Row E1 7HW
■ Sun 12pm-4pm. Regular tours, first come basis. Films will also be shown. Last entry 3.45pm. Max 100 at one time, max 40 per tour. N R T B d
Hidden gem at the very heart of London. Built originally as Huguenot chapel in 1763, this extraordinary building has been in continuous use as a synagogue since 1860. Oldest Ashkenazi synagogue in London. 1763. Entry: synagogue sanctuary, vestry, ladies gallery.
Tube/Rail: Liverpool Street; Rail: Shoreditch High Street; 100,214,205,23,153

Society for the Protection of Ancient Buildings (SPAB)
37 Spital Square E1 6DY
■ Sat 10am-5pm. Tours at 10am, 11am, 12 noon, 1pm, 2pm, and 3pm, each tour lasting about 30-45mins. Pre-book ONLY by emailing info@spab.org.uk specifying preferred timeslots. Last entry 3pm. Max 12 people per tour. T B C
The panelled 1740s former Huguenot silk merchant's house is the only building of its kind still on historic Spital Square. Explore this Georgian gem, now a working office and home to the SPAB, the country's oldest and most respected charity advising on historic buildings. We will be offering children's activities, craft demonstrations, free technical advice and a glimpse into our extensive archives. 1740s. Entry: Tours of ground floor and courtyard.
Tube/Rail: Liverpool Street; Tube: Moorgate; 8,26,35,47,48,78,149,242,344

SS Robin
2d & 2e Royal Victoria Place
■ Sun 10am-1pm. Tours at 10am, 11am and 12noon. Pre-book ONLY on ssrobinengagement@outlook.com – max 10 per tour.
The world's oldest complete steam coaster conserved on a purpose built pontoon. The SS Robin is not currently open to the public and is being refitted. Graham Gollar 1890. Entry: vessel and pontoon.
DLR: Custom House; 474

St Andrew's
Devas Street, Bromley-by-Bow E3 3LS
■ Sat 10am-4pm. Architect led tours at 10am, 11.30am, 2pm, 3pm. Pre-book ONLY on rsvp@alliesandmorrison.com – Last tour 3pm. Max 15 per tour. A
The St Andrew's masterplan for Barratt London provides 964 residential units, a health centre and a network of communal open spaces. The high density scheme includes three urban courtyard blocks arranged to form streets and clear boundaries between public and private space. Roof levels vary in height, creating generous outdoor terraces and a distinctive skyline. Allies and Morrison 2014. Entry: external public areas, internal access to residential courtyards. NB no entry to flats.
Tube: Bromley-by-Bow; DLR: Devons Road; 108,488,323

St Anne's Church, Limehouse
Commercial Road, London E14 7HP
■ Sat 10am-1pm/Sun 1pm-5pm. Regular tours, first come basis. N T P
St Anne's Limehouse is an imposing Hawksmoor church in brick and Portland stone completed in 1725. It is home to an active church congregation today. Nicholas Hawksmoor 1730.
DLR: Limehouse, Westferry; 15,115,135,D3

St Matthias Old Church – Community Centre
113 Poplar High Street E14 0AE
■ Sun 11am-6pm. Regular tours, first come basis. N D R T P
Oldest building in Docklands built in the Gothic and Classical styles, with original 17C stonework and fine mosaics. One of only three churches built during the Civil War, it was originally the East India Company Chapel. John Tanner 1649.
DLR: Poplar, All Saints; 15,115,D6,D7,D8

St Paul's Bow Common
Cnr Burdett Rd/ St Paul's Way E3 4AR
■ Sat 10am-5pm/Sun 12pm-5pm. First come basis. N D R T P
Described as 'the most significant church built after the 2nd World War in Britain' – Brutalist, inclusive and influential signpost for future church design. Robert McGuire & Keith Murray 1960s. Entry: All areas of church.
Tube: Mile End; DLR: Westferry, Limehouse; 277,D6,D7,205,15

St Paul's Old Ford
St Paul's Church, St Stephen's Road E3 5JL
■ Sat 10am-5pm. Regular tours, first come basis. Pictorial treasure hunt for children. Last entry 3.45pm. N D R T C
Victorian church, rehabilitated to include 'a building within a building' – a stunning Ark or Pod of tulipwood situated in the nave. "Stylish...thrilling..." Jay Merrick in The Independent. Winner of RICS Community Benefit Award, London Region 2005. Matthew Lloyd Architects LLP 2004.
Tube: Bow Road, Bethnal Green; DLR: Bow Church; 8,276,488

Sundial Centre
11 Shipton Street E2 7RU
■ Sat/Sun 10am-5pm. First come basis. Last entry 4.30pm. R T
Light-filled building for Peabody, established with a vision of providing a beacon of best practice in integrated, multi-disciplinary services for older people. Adjoining Shipton House recently refurbished. Building is recognised as an example of good practice incorporating functionality with design to aid dementia recovery. Peabody Trust 2000. Entry: cafe/dining hall, IT suite, therapy room.
Rail: Hoxton, Cambridge Heath; Tube/Rail: Liverpool Street; 22,48

Thames River Police
98 Wapping High Street E1W 2NE
■ Sat/Sun 10am-5pm. Regular tours, first come basis. Last entry 4pm. Max 25 at one time. E N T d
A unique ex-carpenters' workshop (1910), contained within a working police station. The workshop space now displays a history of Thames River Police. 1910. Entry: museum.
Rail: Wapping; 100

The Floating Cinema: The International Village Shop Workshop and Tour ●
Embark: 90 Wallis Road, Hackney Wick E9 5LN
■ Sun 2pm-6pm. Pre-book ONLY on www.floatingcinema. info/events
UP Projects' extraordinary floating structure designed by Duggan Morris Architects and programmed by artists/ filmmakers Somewhere. The 2014 theme is 'Extra-International' and opening will contain talks, workshops and films as the vessel is transformed into 'The International Village Shop'.

Duggan Morris Architects 2013.
Rail: Hackney Wick

The Kiosk, Bethnal Green Gardens
The Shelter in Bethnal Green Gardens E2 0HL
■ Sat/Sun 10am-5pm. First come basis. Talk on Sun with David Lawrence at 3pm.
An excellent example of mid-20th century London Underground architecture, originally a park shelter built to disguise Central line air vent, come to life again as The Kiosk, restoring it as a model of civic and community amenity. 1950.
Tube/Rail: Bethnal Green; 8,388,106,254

The Tree House ●
200 Jubilee Street E1 3BP
■ Sat tours at 11am, 12noon, 2pm, 3pm, 4pm. Pre-book ONLY on https://www.eventbrite.co.uk/e/open-house-london-the-tree-house-tickets-12277122203.
The tree house is a timber framed and reclaimed timber-clad addition to two 1830s terraced cottages. Its ramped interior reframes the activities of the house around the garden, absorbing the storey level differences. The mother of a busy family remains central to activity whether in her wheelchair or resting. RIBA London Small Project Award 2014. Shortlisted for Manser Medal. RIBA London Award 2014. 6a Architects 2013. Entry: 6a extension.
Tube/Rail: Whitechapel, Bethnal Green; 25

Tower Hamlets Cemetery Park ●
Tower Hamlets Cemetery Park, Southern Grove E3 4PX
■ Sat 10am-4pm. Guided history walks at 10.30, 12.30pm and 2.30pm; nature walk at 2pm. N R T B C G P d
One of the 'magnificent seven' cemeteries, opened 1841. Burials ceased 1966, now 33 acres of mature woodland, glades meadows and ponds including the Soanes Centre educational facility (Robson Kelly 1993). It is of outstanding importance for plant and animal biodiversity, set amongst a wealth of funereal monuments, some listed. Thomas Wyatt & David Brandon.
Tube: Mile End; DLR: Bow Church; DLR/Rail: Limehouse; 25,277,D6,D7,425,339,323

Tower Hamlets Local History Library and Archives
277 Bancroft Road E1 4DQ
■ Sat tours at 10.30am and 3pm. Pre-book ONLY on 020 7364 1290 or localhistory@towerhamlets.gov.uk – max 15 per tour. N T B d
Ornate classical building originally a Vestry Hall for the Hamlet of Mile End Old Town. A library since 1901 it was extended in 1905 and 1935-37. Currently under refurbishment as a Tower Hamlets Heritage Centre. James Knight/MW Jameson/ BJ Delsher 1861/1905/1935/7. Entry: Reading room, former Vestry hall, archive store.
Tube: Stepney Green, Mile End; Rail: Whitechapel; 25

Town Hall Hotel & Apartments
Patriot Square E2 9NF
■ Sun 10am-4pm. Access by hourly tours, first come basis. Last tour 3pm. Max 20 per tour. D R T
Beautiful redevelopment of former Grade II listed town hall incorporating sensitive contemporary design complementing the original Edwardian/Art Deco features. A modern extension is covered in a metal laser-cut 'skin', in a pattern inspired by the Art Deco metal ornamentation still evident in the remaining council chamber. RIBA Award Winner 2011. Percy Robinson & W Alban Jones/ECP Monson/Rare (refurb) 1909/1939/2010. Entry: lobby, bedrooms, event spaces, pool.
Tube: Bethnal Green; Rail: Cambridge Heath, Shoreditch High Street; 254,106,D6,388

Trinity Buoy Wharf/Container City ●
64 Orchard Place E14 0JY
■ Sat/Sun 11am-4pm. History & art and regeneration tour 12noon. First come basis, meet at lighthouse. Last entry 3.30pm. N R T A d
Home to London's only lighthouse, fine stock buildings and examples of the innovative Container City buildings including the new Olympic Legacy – Clipper House. This former buoy manufacturing site is now a centre for the creative industries with Thames views and various sculptures and installations. 500th anniversary of Trinity House. Eric Reynolds/Buschow Henley/ABK Architects/Lacey and Partners 1822-75/1950s-2014. Entry: Trinity Buoy Wharf, Container City, lighthouse, historic buildings, pier, lightship.
DLR: East India; DLR/Tube: Canning Town; 277

West India Dock Impounding Station ●
Western end of Marsh Wall E14 8JT
■ Sat 10.30am-4pm. First come basis, queuing if necessary. Displays on history and current workings. Last entry 3.45pm. E G
The recently automated impounding station controls the water level in the docks using the original Worthington Simpson pumps driven by Lancashire dynamo. 1929. Entry: Pump room.
Tube: Canary Wharf; DLR: Heron Quays; D3,D7,D8,135

Whitechapel Gallery
77-82 Whitechapel High Street E1 7QX
■ Sat tour 3pm, pre-book ONLY on 020 7522 7888, meet in the foyer. Architect Chris Watson of WWM Architects introduces the gallery's recent expansion and its architectural history. Max 35 on tour. N D R T B A
For over a century the Gallery has premiered world-class artists from modern masters to contemporaries. RIBA Award Winner 2010. Charles Harrison Townsend/Robbrecht en Daem/ Witherford Watson Mann 1901/2009. Entry: entire gallery.
Tube: Aldgate East; 250,135,254,115,25

Wilton's Music Hall
Graces Alley, Ensign Street E1 8JB
■ Sat 12noon-11pm. First come basis, queuing outside if necessary. Audio tours available. Max 50 at one time. N R T P d
The oldest music hall in London to survive in its original form, complete with papier-mâché balconies, barley sugar iron columns and unique atmosphere. Hall is fronted by five terrace houses; four Georgian and one 1990s. Maggs 1859. Entry: main hall, foyer, upstairs foyer.
DLR: Shadwell, Tube: Tower Hill, Aldgate East; Rail/Tube: London Bridge; 100

WALKS/TOURS

Canary Wharf Public Art Tour ●
■ Meet: Sat 10.30am, 1pm, 3.30pm in Lobby, One Canada Square E14 5AB. First come basis. Duration 1 1/2 hours. Max 15 per tour. N D R T B
Canary Wharf's commitment to a high quality environment is demonstrated in 65 works by 40+ artists acquired over the last 20 years, making London's largest public art collection. Illustrated art map also available free.
DLR/Tube: Canary Wharf; Boats to Canary Riverside; D3,D7,D8,135,277

Supported by

TOWER HAMLETS

Key. A Architect on site **B** Bookshop **C** Childrens' activities **d** Some disabled access **D** Full wheelchair access **E** Engineer on site **G** Green Features **N** Normally open to the public **P** Parking **Q** Long queues envisaged **R** Refreshments **T** Toilets

Waltham Forest

See openhouselondon.org.uk/walthamforest
to find out more about this area

All Saints Church (The Old Church)
Old Church Road, Chingford Mount E4 8BU
■ Sat 10am-3pm/Sun 11am-2pm. D R T P
Original parish church of Chingford, with Norman
foundations and interesting monuments. C12-C13.
Tube: Walthamstow; Rail: Chingford then 97 bus

Annexe for the Haven House Children's Hospice
The White House, High Road, Woodford Green, IG8 9LB
■ Sat 10am-4pm. First come basis, tours every 30mins.
Last entry 3.30pm. Max 15 per tour.
New annexe to children's hospice, the existing building, the
White House, is locally listed and in a conservation area. New
annexe is contemporary in design and clad in timber shingles.
Clear Architects 2014 Entry: annexe and grounds.
Tube: Woodford; 123

Aveling Centre/Cafe at Lloyds Park ● ●
Winns Terrace E17 5JW
■ Sat/Sun 10am-5pm. First come basis. N D T
Standing as a natural gathering point, the pavilion comprises
a gallery, 6 artists' studios and a cafe run by Waltham Forest
College. architecture plb 2012. Entry: art gallery.
Tube/Rail: Walthamstow Central; 275,123,230,357,215

Blackhorse Workshop
1-2 Sutherland Road Path. Just off Blackhorse Lane E17 6BX
■ Sat 10am-5pm. First come basis. Tours at 10am and 2pm.
N d R T C A P
Blackhorse Workshop is a new public space dedicated to
making and mending, with open access to a fully equipped
wood and metal workshop and on site technicians. Assemble
2014. Entry: cafe, bench space, machine rooms.
Tube: Blackhorse Road; Rail: St James Street; 158

Highams Green
Repton House, Larkshall Road, E4 9JD
■ Sun 10am-1pm. First come basis. Entry to communal areas,
flats by appointment. Pre-book ONLY by email Ana to book:
anac@isha.co.uk). N D G
The 11.43 acre (462) industrial site is now a mixed use
development including shops, cafes, offices and workshops
and 253 homes. Highams Green is an example of a 'New
London Vernacular' promoted by the Mayor's London Housing
Design Guide. Collado Collins Architects 2013.
Rail: Highams Park; 212,275

Highams Park Signal Box ●
Level Crossing, Hale End Road, Higham E4 9PT
■ Sat/Sun 10am-5pm. First come basis. Last entry 5pm. N B
The Signal Box dates from 1925. It is one of the few boxes
remaining in London and has recently been refurbished by a
local builder, Dendales. 1925.
Rail: Highams Park; 212,275,W16

Leyton Sports Ground Pavilion ●
Crawley Road, Leyton E10 6PY
■ Sat/Sun 11am-3pm. First come basis. D R T C G P
Home of Essex County Cricket Club 1886-1934, host to
W.G. Grace, Don Bradman and Denis Compton. Displays and
literature on history of the ground, sports activities to view.

Grade II listed. Richard Creed 1886.
Tube: Leyton; Rail: Leyton Midland Road; 69,97

Queen Elizabeth's Hunting Lodge
Rangers Road, Chingford E4 7QH
■ Sat/Sun 10am-5pm. Tours at 12noon, 1pm, 3pm, 4pm. Last
entry 4.45pm. N T B P d
Unique Grade II* listed atmospheric timber-framed hunt-
standing, commissioned by Henry VIII, set amongst ancient
pollards of Epping Forest. 1589 fireplace and Tudor food
displays. 1543. Entry: three floors. Special viewing of the
construction of the Tudor stairs.
Rail: Chingford; 97,179,212,313,379,444

St Margaret with St Columba
Woodhouse Road E11 3NG
■ Sat 9am-4pm/Sun 8am-4pm. First come basis. N T G P d
Large Grade II listed late gothic revival 19C brick-built church
intended for Anglo-Catholic worship, retaining many original
features. Described in Pevsner as 'a mighty basilica'. 5 windows
by Gordon Beningfield. WJT Newman and W Jacques 1892-3.
*Tube: Leyton, Leytonstone; Tube/Rail: Stratford; Rail:
Leytonstone High Road; 58,257*

The View: Epping Forest Visitor Centre ●
Rangers Road, Chingford E4 7QH
■ Sat/Sun 10am-5pm. Tours at 12noon & 4pm, first come
basis. Last entry 4.45pm. N D T B G P
The coach house and stable block to the 1880s Royal Forest
Hotel (J Ebenezer Saunders and Edmund Egan) has been
developed as the main visitor centre for Epping Forest
combining a minimalist glass box linking the buildings and
raised oak galleries, with lift access for visitor panoramic view
of the Forest enjoyed from the adjacent Tudor hunt standing.
Freeland, Rees, Roberts 19C/2012. Entry: public areas.
Rail: Chingford; 97,179,212,313,379,444

The Walthamstow Pumphouse Museum
10 South Access Road E17 8AX
■ Sat 10am-4pm. First come basis. Displays on industrial
heritage of Lea Valley. Last entry 3.30pm. E N R T B d
Grade II listed Victorian engine house (1885) remodelled in
1897, still in working order. Entry: pump house, functioning
Victorian workshop, cafe.
Tube/Rail: Blackhorse Road; Rail: St James Street; 58,158,230,W19

Vestry House Museum
Vestry Road E17 9NH
■ Sat/Sun 10am-5pm. First come basis. Sat 11am guided tour,
pre-book tour ONLY on 020 8496 4391. N D T B C
Built as a workhouse in 1730, the date plaque warns 'if any
should not work neither should he eat'. From 1840-1870 a
police station, private house, and from 1931 the Museum for
Waltham Forest. Interior contains early 17C panelling and over-
mantel from nearby demolished Essex Hall. 1730.
Tube/Rail: Walthamstow Central; W12, W16

Walthamstow Assembly Hall
Waltham Forest Town Hall Complex, Forest Road, E17 4JF
■ Sat 9am-12pm. First come basis, queuing if necessary. Last
entry 11.45am. T d
Grade II listed subsidiary building of the Town Hall built
in a restrained style in Portland stone. Art Deco interior.
P D Hepworth 1942. Entry: main hall, foyer, balcony.
*Tube/Rail: Walthamstow Central; Rail: Wood Street;
123,34,97,212,357,W11*

Walthamstow Library
206 High Street E17 7JN
■ Sat 9am-6pm/Sun 10am-4pm. Tour Sat 11am, book at
www.walthamstowtour.eventbrite.com. Explore restored
Edwardian splendour of Walthamstow's Central library,
post-war buildings by F.W. Southgate and survivals of the
earliest phases of the town's transformation from elite
rural idyll to Victorian suburb. N D T C
The Reading Room and 'Wren'-style red brick building with
stone dressings were refurbished in 2006 creating a new 8m
high glass foyer with terracotta cladding and new children's
library. JW Dunford/FaulknerBrowns 1909/2006.
*Tube: Walthamstow; Rail: Walthamstow Central;
20,212,215,230,257,34,357,48*

Walthamstow Town Hall
Waltham Forest Town Hall Complex, Forest Road, E17 4JF
■ Sat 10am-4pm. Last entry 12noon. Max 20 at one time. D T P
Impressive civic centre, built in Portland stone with a classical
layout in Swedish influenced popular inter-war style. Art Deco
internal design. PD Hepworth 1937-42.
Tube/Rail: Walthamstow Central; Wood Street; 123,275

William Morris Gallery ●
Lloyd Park, Forest Road E17 4PP
■ Sat/Sun 10am-5pm. Sat/Sun 11am tour 'Water House and
its owners', limited places, first come basis. N D R T B C
Handsome 1740s Georgian Grade II* listed former Water
House with original features. Now refurbished and with new
extension by Pringle Richard Sharratt Architects. Formerly the
home of the designer, craftsman, poet and socialist William
Morris (1834-1896), now a museum of his work and that of his
followers in the Arts and Crafts Movement. 1740s.
*Tube/Rail: Walthamstow Central (then bus 34,97,215,275,357 to
Bell Corner); Blackhorse Road (123 bus to Lloyd Park)*

WALKS/TOURS

High Road Leyton Tour ●
Meet in front of Leyton Technical Pub, 265 High Road Leyton,
E10 5QN
■ Sat/Sun tours at 11am, 12pm. Max 20 per tour.
In the lead up to the 2012 Olympics, Waltham Forest Council
commissioned this award-winning regeneration scheme
to celebrate the local identity and idiosyncrasies of this East
London high street. Jan Kattein Architects 2012.
Tube: Leyton; 58,69,97,158

Walthamstow Wetlands ● ●
■ Meet: Sat 1pm at Walthamstow Reservoir entrance, Ferry
Lane N19 9NH. First come basis, tour led by London Wildlife
Trust and William Mann of Stirling Prize winning architects
Witherford, Watson, Mann. T G d W
Walthamstow Wetlands will be the most significant urban
nature reserve development in Britain for many years.
This largely hidden, working landscape has evolved into a
distinctive wild space, where the Victorian engineering which
once supplied London's water is now designated as a Site of
Special Scientific Interest. Historic buildings on site include
the Grade II listed Coppermill and the Old Marine Engine
House built in the 1850s. Witherford Watson Mann.
Tube: Tottenham Hale, Blackhorse Road; 41,192,123,230

Supported by

Waltham Forest

Wandsworth

See openhouselondon.org.uk/wandsworth
to find out more about this area

BAC (Battersea Arts Centre)
Lavender Hill SW11 5TN
- ■ Sat tours at 11am, 3pm, first come basis. Max 30 per tour.
  N R T P d

Designed and built as Battersea's Town Hall and home to BAC for the last 30 years. Striking features include a glass bee mosaic floor, marble staircase and stained glass dome. See the plans which are underway to develop a 21C arts centre in this 19C town hall. E Mountford 1893.
Tube: Clapham Common; Rail: Clapham Junction; 87,77,156

Brandlehow Primary School
Brandlehow Road SW15 2ED
- ■ Sat 10am-4pm. Regular tours. Last entry 3.30pm. Max 25 at one time. D T A

Series of extensions to a listed modern school by Erno Goldfinger formed from prefabricated timber elements clad with cedar boards. Franziska Wagner/team51.5° architects 2006/2011/2014. Entry: all 3 buildings.
Tube: East Putney; Rail: Putney; 270,220,337,14,74

Burntwood School
Burntwood Lane, SW17 0AQ
- ■ Sat/Sun 1pm-5pm. Tours 2pm, 4pm each day. First come basis. T D A

Recently completed striking precast concrete-clad buildings, refurbishment of Leslie Martin-designed pool and assembly hall, and a new landscape plan for the school's original 1950s Modernist educational campus. Allford Hall Monaghan Morris 2013.
Tube: Tooting Bec, Tooting Broadway; Rail: Earlsfield; G1
www.ahmm.co.uk

Clapham House ⓐ
Address given on booking
- ■ Sat half-hourly tours. Pre-book ONLY on https://openhouselondon14-claphamhouse.eventbrite.co.uk. Max 6 per tour. T A G d

Award-winning sensual, sculptural transformation of Victorian family home, interweaving house and garden. Of particular note is an iconic, lavishly-carved and digitally-fabricated staircase. The house is inspired by the beauty of its central garden. atmos 1870s/2010. Entry: ground floor, main stairway.
Overground/Rail: Clapham Junction; 319, G1,219,337,35,37,49,77
www.atmosstudio.com

Emanuel School
Battersea Rise SW11 1HS
- ■ Sat 2pm-5pm. Regular 30min tours from 2pm to 4pm or longer 75min tours at 2.15pm and 3.45pm. Access to school's archives. T P d

Former Royal Patriotic orphanage by Henry Saxon Snell 1871, converted to school 1883, with 1896 additions. High Victorian style with stained glass by Moira Forsyth. Set in 12 acres. Henry Saxon Snell 1871. Entry: main building inc chapel, library, concert hall.
Tube: Clapham South; Rail: Clapham Junction; 77,219,319,337

House for a Painter

Foster + Partners Studio ⓐ
Riverside, 22 Hester Road SW11 4AN
- ■ Sat 10am-5pm. Regular tours. Last entry 4.30pm. R T A

Single-space, double-height purpose-built architects' studio 60 metres long – part of a larger riverside building that has 30 apartments. Foster + Partners 1990. Entry: entrance and mezzanine (with view over whole studio).
Tube: Sloane Square, South Kensington; Rail: Clapham Junction; 19,49,170,319,345

House for a Painter
7 The Old Laundry, Haydon Way, London SW11 1YF
- ■ Sat 11am-5pm. Closed from 1.30-2.30pm. First come basis.

The project consists of the conversion of a 20th century workhouse laundry building into a studio and residence for an artist and his family. Price & Gore Architects 2013.
Tube: Clapham Junction; Rail: Wandsworth Town
www.pricegore.co.uk

National Tennis Centre Sports Canopy ●
100 Priory Lane, Roehampton SW15 5JQ
- ■ Sat 10am-5pm. Regular architect-led tours of canopy and exterior of National Tennis Centre. Last tour 4.30pm. Max 10 per tour. D T A G

The world's first composite demountable air-beam canopy, spanning 42m, to support player training and development on the Centre's clay courts. Timeless nature of the arched form provides an inspirational and 'clutter free' playing environment attuned to players' needs. ICE London Award Winner and British Construction Industry UK Small Project of the Year 2011. George Stowell 2010.
Tube: Putney Bridge; Rail: Barnes; 72,33,337,493

Skinner-Trevino House

Nine Elms: Riverlight
1 Riverlight Quay, Vauxhall SW8 5AU
- ■ Sun tours at 10am, 11am, 12pm and 1pm, Pre-book ONLY on chris.wade@stjames.co.uk. Max 15 per tour. T A G

Riverlight has six pavilions overlooking the river Thames that are built to maximise sunlight and optimise views. Inspiration came from the robust structures of industrial warehouses that formerly occupied the site. Rogers Stirk Harbour & Partners 2014.
Tube/Rail: Vauxhall, Battersea; 344

Oily Cart Theatre Treehouse
Smallwood School Annexe, Smallwood Road SW17 0TW
- ■ Sat 10am-5pm. First come basis. Last entry 4.45pm.

Oily Cart, a children's theatre company based in Tooting, has undergone a redevelopment which has seen increased access and efficiency and created an inspirational design, including a new mezzanine treehouse and a spectacular gold lift. Hawkins Brown 2013. Entry: all areas.
Tube: Tooting Broadway; Rail: Tooting; 44,77,270

Pump House Gallery
Battersea Park SW11 4NJ
- ■ Sat/Sun 11am-5pm. Regular tours, first come basis. Max 50 at one time. N T d

Beautiful Grade II listed Victorian ex-water tower overlooking Battersea Park lake. Now houses a contemporary art gallery. James and William Simpson 1861.
Tube: Sloane Square; Rail: Battersea Park, Queenstown Road; 137,19,44,49,239,344,345,452

Nine Elms: Riverlight

Quaker Meeting House
59 Wandsworth High Street SW18 2PT
■ Sat 12pm-4pm. Regular tours. Max 25 at one time. N T G d
Grade II listed, this is the oldest Quaker meeting house in Greater London (1778), with original panelling and a ministers' gallery. Secluded burial ground and garden. 1778. Entry: ground floor & garden, display of local Quaker history.
Tube: East Putney; Rail: Wandsworth Town; 28,39,87,156,337

Roehampton King's Head Pub
1 Roehampton High Street SW15 4HL
■ Sat/Sun 10am-5pm. First come basis. N D R T
The present building dates from at least the 1670s, but was most likely to have originated as a farmhouse in the Medieval period. It is certainly the oldest building in Roehampton, and is probably the oldest secular building in the whole of Wandsworth Borough. c1670. Entry: garden, main pub area.
Tube/Rail: Putney

Roehampton Uni – Southlands Chapel
80 Roehampton Lane SW15 5SL
■ Sat 11am-2pm. First come basis. D R T P
Circular Methodist chapel designed by Sheppard Robson for the new location of Southlands College in 1997. The brief was to create a sense of place for a vibrant community. Sheppard Robson 1997.
Tube: Hammersmith, Putney Bridge; Rail: Barnes; 72,265,493

Roehampton University – Parkstead House, Whitelands College
Holybourne Avenue SW15 4JD
■ Sun 11.30am-4.30pm. Tours at 12noon & 2.30pm, first come basis. T P d
Beautifully sited Grade I listed neo-classical Palladian villa built for the 2nd Earl of Bessborough by the royal architect William Chambers, to house the Earl's celebrated collection of classical artefacts. Sir William Chambers 1762.
Tube: East Putney, Hammersmith; Rail: Barnes; 72,85,265,493

Royal College of Art Dyson Building ●
1 Hester Road SW11 4AN
■ Sat/Sun 10am-5pm. First come basis. N D T
Centrepiece building of the RCA's Battersea Campus housing the Printmaking, Photography and Innovation RCA departments. Functional aesthetic derived from its concrete structure, exposed throughout and used expressively to form a series of dramatic interlocking spaces. Building references Andy Warhol's notion of the creative 'factory'. Haworth Tompkins 2012.
Tube: Sloane Square; 19,49,170,319,345

Skinner-Trevino House
67 Santos Road SW18 1NT
■ Sat 10am-5pm. NB. Closed between 1-2pm. First come basis, queuing outside if necessary. Top floor unsuitable for small children or those with vertigo. Last entry 4pm. Max 13 at one time. N Q A G d
A late Victorian house which has been almost completely gutted; the house is flooded with light by a new glass extension opening onto the semi open plan ground level and a glass box extension into the roof. This new level constructed of structural glass is accessed by glass stairs and includes a master bedroom suite with balcony and a sun deck. Luis Trevino 2009.
Tube: East Putney; Rail: Putney, Wandsworth Town; 37,170,337

St Mary's Church, Battersea
Battersea Church Road SW11 3NA
■ Sat 12pm-5pm/Sun 1pm-5pm. Regular tours. Fair on Saturday. D R T
Classic Grade I listed Georgian church with outstanding interior and monuments. New engraved glass doors by Sally Scott. Joseph Dixon 1775-7.
Tube: South Kensington, Sloane Square; Rail: Clapham Junction; 19,49,170,319,345

The Emma Thornton Building at Finton House School
Finton House School, 169-171 Trinity Road SW17 7HL
■ Sat 10am-2pm. First come basis, queuing outside if necessary. A D R T P
Innovative building featuring a glass-lined stairwell decorated with trees, which directs natural light into classrooms. 85 per cent of the building is below ground level with the design unveiling 400sqm of new teaching space, for a total of 320 pupils aged 4 to 11-years-old. Dinwiddie MacLaren Architects 2013.
Tube: Tooting Bec; Rail: Wandsworth Common; G1

The Garden House
163a Trinity Road, SW17 7HL
■ Sat 10am-10pm/Sun 10am-5pm. Hourly tours. Evening garden lounge and refreshments, weather permitting. Project illustrated through various phases. Max 8 per tour.
Seventies bungalow converted into a wide and spacious modern house, with a landscaped garden in a secluded area. Alpex Architecture Ltd 2014.
Tube: Tooting Bec, Wandsworth Common; 219,319,G1

WALKS/TOURS

New Covent Garden Flower Market – tour
■ Meet: Sat 7.30am New Covent Garden Market, Nine Elms Lane SW8 5NA. Pre-book ONLY on info@cgma.co.uk or 0207 501 3495. Further details provided upon booking. Max 25 per tour. R d T
Tour of London's wholesale flower market during market hours, covering its history and future plans for the site. 1974. Entry: Market Hall, Mezzanine and market floor.
Tube/Rail: Vauxhall; 156,344,77,87

Nine Elms Walk ●
■ Meet: Sat 1pm at Tea House Theatre, 139 Vauxhall Walk, Vauxhall Pleasure Gardens SE11 5HL, for refreshments and introductory talk, tour will begin at 2pm. Pre-book ONLY on www.vauxhallone.co.uk/news. Duration approx 2 hours. Max 50 on walk. A G
Nine Elms on South Bank is the largest regeneration zone in central London. Walk includes talk on history of Vauxhall and provides an insider look at progress on new landmark developments at Embassy Gardens, a Ballymore development designed through an exemplary collaboration between world class architectural practices: Terry Farrell and Partners, Feilden Clegg Bradley Studios and Allford Hall Monaghan Morris. Riverlight, a St James development, has been designed by world-renowned architects Rogers Stirk Harbour & Partners.
Tube/Rail: Vauxhall; 185,2,36,436
www.ahmm.co.uk

Supported by

Wandsworth
THE BRIGHTER BOROUGH

Westminster

See **openhouselondon.org.uk/westminster**
to find out more about this area

5 Merchant Square
5 Merchant Square West
■ Sat 10am-1pm. First come basis. E D T A G
With floorplates averaging 25,000 sq ft, the building is an elegant and distinctive response to the demand for quality office space in London's West End. The scheme incorporates primarily class A office space in addition to a public lobby. Its bold triangular volumes promote an open flow of pedestrians toward Paddington Basin. Mossession & Partners 2010. Entry: ground floor, 9th floor.
Tube/Rail: Paddington; Tube: Edgware Road; 208,23,8,98,11,6

10 Downing Street
10 Downing Street SW1A 2AA
■ Sat tours at 11am & 2pm, by ballot ONLY, see page 16 for more details. Background checks will be carried out on winning entries. Bring valid photo ID for entry. Max 20 per tour. D T
10 Downing Street has been the residence of British Prime Ministers since 1735. Behind its black door have been the most important decisions affecting Britain for the last 275 years. It functions as the official residence of the Prime Minister, their office and also where the PM entertains guests including Her Majesty the Queen. Every single room, every staircase and corridor has witnessed events that have shaped our nation. Sir Christopher Wren/William Kent 1684/1735. Entry: State rooms.
Tube: Westminster; Tube/Rail: Charing Cross, Waterloo; 12,24,53,88,253

26 Whitehall and Admiralty House
Ripley Courtyard, Whitehall SW1A 2DY
■ Sat/Sun 10am-4.30pm. Queuing outside if necessary. Last entry 4pm. Q
Grade I listed former Old Admiralty Building, behind Robert Adam's Admiralty Screen on Whitehall. Now owned by Department for International Development and Cabinet Office; works of art and antiques from Ministry of Defence Art Collection. Thomas Ripley (26 Whitehall)/Samuel Pepys Cockerell (Admiralty House) 1725/1785. Entry: Old Admiralty boardroom, state rooms in Admiralty House.
Tube: Embankment, Charing Cross, Westminster; Tube/Rail: Charing Cross; 11,12,24,88,159,453,53,87

37a Leamington Road Villas
37a Leamington Road Villas W11 1HT
■ Sat/Sun 10am-5pm. First come basis, queuing if necessary. Sun evening outdoor cinema in rear garden, weather permitting. Last entry 5pm. Q A
The use of exposed brickwork, concrete floors, skylights, exposed shuttered underpinning from which floating oak steps project, all give rise to this unique and stunning 3 bed home converted from a 1 bedroom Victorian flat. 3x3m glass doors give a seamless transition into the rear multi-levelled landscaped garden oasis with a cedar batten clad outbuilding. Studio 1 Architects 2013.
Tube: Westbourne Park; 27,31,7,328,70

55 Baker Street ●
55 Baker Street W1U 8EW
■ Sat 10am-5pm. Regular tours, first come basis, queuing

Burlington House

outside if necessary. Max 20 at one time. D T A. Audio Described Tours taking place as part of our VocalEyes partnership, see p.14 for details.
This radical renovation of a 1950s office building transforms the site into an important new urban amenity. The scheme enhances activity and interest at street level by offering an enriched mix of uses and introducing a substantial new public space to the streetscape. Three glass infills or 'masks' span the voids between existing blocks to create a new facade for the building, with the central glazed section enclosing a seven-storey atrium which is open to the public.
Make Architects 2007. Entry: ground floor and atria only.
Tube: Baker Street; Tube/Rail: Marylebone; 2,74,30,113,274

55 Broadway (London Underground Head Office)
55 Broadway SW1H 0BD
■ Sat/Sun tours at 10.30am, 11.30am, 12.30pm, 2.30pm, 3.30pm, 4.30pm, pre-book ONLY through https://www.tflevents.co.uk/55broadway. Max 20 at one time, minimum age 10 years. T d
Headquarters of London Underground described on its 1929 opening as 'the cathedral of modernity'. Its exterior features sculptures by eminent artists of the day, including Henry Moore, Jacob Epstein and Eric Gill. Charles Holden 1927-9. Entry: ground floor, office, roof terrace.
Tube: St James's Park; 11,24,148

68 Dean Street
68 Dean Street W1D 4QJ
■ Sat tours each hour (not 1pm), first come basis. Last tour 4pm. Max 15 per tour. T Q
Fine example of early 18C London domestic architecture by local carpenter/builder, with separate cesspits for the Meards and servants, and largely panelled hidden rooms. John Meard Jnr 1732.
Tube: Piccadilly, Leicester Square, Tottenham Court Road; Tube/Rail: Charing Cross

Antony Gormley Room at The Beaumont
The Beaumont, Brown Hart Gardens, W1K 6TF
■ Sat/Sun 1pm-5pm. Tours every 30mins by ballot ONLY. Please see page 16 for more details. Last entry 4.30pm. R T d
ROOM is a monumental, inhabitable sculpture by Antony

37a Leamington Road Villas

Gormley on the Listed façade of The Beaumont Hotel. The interior is as important as its exterior: a giant crouching cuboid figure based on the artist's body. Antony Gormley / Reardon Smith 2014.
Tube: Bond Street; 6,10,15,23,73

Argentine Ambassador's Residence
49 Belgrave Square SW1X 8QZ
■ Sat/Sun 12pm-5pm. First come basis, queuing if necessary. Max 80-100 at one time. D Q
Known as the 'Independent North Mansion' and christened by Sydney Herbert as 'Belgrave Villa' and then simply 'The Villa' by his successor the 6th Duke of Richmond. Owned by Argentina since 1936 and with sumptuous interiors still intact. Thomas Cubitt 1851. Entry: all main rooms.
Tube: Hyde Park Corner; Tube/Rail: Victoria; 19,22,14,38,10,8

Asia House
63 New Cavendish Street W1G 7LP
■ Sat 10am-5pm/Sun 11am-5pm. Regular tours, first come basis. Max 50 per tour. E N D R T C G
Grade II* listed town house originally planned by Robert and James Adam. Interiors designed by John Gregory in the 1770s. Library book shelves designed by Sir John Soane. Interior of the rooms is Adamesque with filigree plasterwork, inset classical paintings and elaborate marble chimney pieces. John Johnson 18C. Entry: library, cafe, fine rooms 1, 2 and 3.
Tube: Oxford Circus, Great Portland Street

Banqueting House
Whitehall SW1A 2ER
■ Sat/Sun 10am-5pm. Last entry 4.15pm. Max 500 at one time. R T B Q C
Stunning regal building originally part of Whitehall Palace, one of the first examples of the principles of Palladianism being applied to an English building. Ceiling paintings by Rubens. Inigo Jones 1619. Entry: main hall, undercroft.
Tube: Westminster, Embankment; Tube/Rail: Charing Cross; 3,11,12,24,53,87,88,159

Benjamin Franklin House
36 Craven Street WC2N 5NF
■ Sat/Sun 10.30am-4pm. Half-hourly tours, first come basis.

Key. A Architect on site **D** Bookshop **C** Children's activities **d** Some disabled access **D** Full wheelchair access **E** Engineer on site **G** Green Features
N Normally open to the public **P** Parking **Q** Long queues envisaged **R** Refreshments **T** Toilets

First tour 10.30am. Last tour 4pm. Max 15 per tour. T B
Grade I listed Georgian house, the only surviving home of
Benjamin Franklin, retaining many original features including
central staircase, lathing, 18C panelling, stoves, windows,
fittings and beams. Patrick Dillon Architect (refurb) 1732/2006.
Tube: Embankment; Tube/Rail: Charing Cross;
6,9,11,13,15,23,87,91,139,176

Burlington House
Burlington House, Piccadilly W1J 0BF
■ Linnean Society of London. Sat 10am–5pm. Last entry
4.30pm. d. Royal Astronomical Society. Sat tours 10am,
11.30am, 2pm, 3.30pm, first come basis. Tours include
Society's library. Max 25 per tour. T d. Royal Society of
Chemistry. Sat 10am–4pm. Last entry 3.45pm. D T. Society of
Antiquaries of London. Sat 12pm–4.30pm. Half-hourly tours,
first come basis. Last tour 4.30pm. Max 20 per tour. The
Geological Society of London. Sat 10am–5.30pm. Guided
hourly tours 10am to 4pm, early booking advised; email
receptionist@geolsoc.org.uk providing your name and
preferred tour time. Max 20 per tour. Self-guided tours
available.
■ Royal Academy of Arts. Sat/Sun 10am–6pm. Talks, tours,
family activities (including drawing in the historic RA
Schools Life Room) over the weekend. N D R T B C
1660s town-palace, remodelled in Palladian style by Colen
Campbell and William Kent for Lord Burlington. The main
building is at the northern end of the courtyard and houses
the Royal Academy, while five learned societies occupy the
two wings on the east and west sides of the courtyard and the
Piccadilly wing at the southern end.
Linnean Society of London – Part of the extension to
Burlington House to provide accommodation for learned
societies. Banks & Barry 1873. Entry: meeting room, 'double
cube' library, entrance hall.
www.linnean.org
Royal Academy of Arts – Main Galleries by Sidney Smirke
RA and also RA Schools Cast Corridor and studios, the latter
added to by Norman Shaw RA. The Sackler Wing of Galleries,
with glass stair and lift, by Foster + Partners opened in 1991.
The Keeper's House, newly transformed by Long & Kentish.
Burlington Gardens (1867–70) by James Pennethorne, RA's
new venue for expanded programme of art and architecture
currently being overseen by David Chipperfield RA. Entry: Royal
Academy Schools, The John Madejski Fine Rooms, Burlington
Gardens and all public areas.
www.royalacademy.org.uk
Royal Astronomical Society – Part of the extension to
Burlington House, the home of the Royal Astronomical Society since
1874 with recent refurbishment. Banks & Barry/Peregrine
Bryant Associates 1874/2007.
www.ras.org.uk
Royal Society of Chemistry – Enjoy a fascinating and historical
tour around the East Wing of Burlington House, home to the
Royal Society of Chemistry. Part of the quadrangle building
extension to Burlington House, purpose built for the learned
societies. Ground floor restoration by Hugh Broughton
Architects. Banks & Barry 1873. Entry: reception, ground floor
rooms, first floor rooms including council room and library.
www.rsc.org
Society of Antiquaries of London – Part of New Burlington
House, purpose built in 1875 for learned societies. Imposing
top-lit library with double galleries and marbled columns.
Ground floor now authentically restored. Banks & Barry 1875.
Entry: main stairs, library, meeting room, council room.
www.sal.org.uk

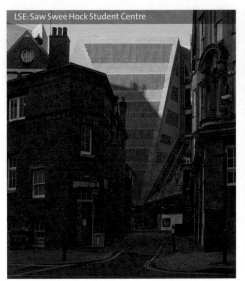
LSE: Saw Swee Hock Student Centre

The Geological Society of London – Part of the extension to
Burlington House built to provide accommodation for learned
societies. Recent refurbishment by Julian Harrap Architects in
2007. Banks & Barry 1873. Entry: entrance hall, meeting room,
galleried libraries, council room.
Tube: Green Park, Piccadilly; Tube/Rail: Victoria; 9,14,19,22,38
www.geolsoc.org.uk

Cabbies Shelters
■ Sat/Sun 11am–4pm. First come basis.
Originally built during the day of horse-drawn Hansom Cabs,
only 13 of the 60+ Cabmens' Shelters survive. Built between
1875 and 1914, these Grade II listed structures provide cabbies
with a place to eat and rest. Opening is part of wider project
that will see shelters transformed into spaces for art or art
works themselves.
Embankment Place – Embankment Place close to Playhouse
Theatre at bottom of Hungerford Bridge stairs, WC2N 5DE
Tube: Embankment; 6,9,11,13,15,23
Temple Place – Temple Place opposite side of road from
Swissotel Howard WC2R 2PR
Tube: Temple; Rail: Charing Cross; 6,9,13,87,139
Wellington Place – Wellington Place nr St John's Wood High
Street opposite Lord's Cricket Ground NW8 7PE
Tube: St John's Wood; 13,46,82,113,187

Caledonian Club
9 Halkin Street SW1X 7DR
■ Sun 10am–5pm. Hourly tours. Pre-book ONLY on 020 7333
8712. Last tour 4pm. Max 12 per tour. T
Built 1908 in Neoclassical style by Detmar Blow for Hugh
Morrison (1868-1931), was the last mansion house of its kind
to be built in London. The club, founded in 1891, moved to the
premises in 1946. Detmar Blow 1908.
Tube: Hyde Park Corner; 38,22,C2,11,73

Chandos House – Royal Society of Medicine
2 Queen Anne Street W1G 9LQ
■ Sun 10am–3pm. Half-hourly tours, first come basis. Last
entry 2.30pm. Max 30 per tour. R T d
One of the finest surviving Adam houses, built in 1771 and
first occupied by the third Duke of Buckingham and Chandos.
Refurbished 2004 by the Howard de Walden Estate for the

Portcullis House

Society, used as members' accommodation and reception
rooms. Robert and James Adam 1769-71. Entry: ground and 1st
floor principal rooms.
Tube: Oxford Circus, Bond Street; Tube/Rail: Marylebone;
73,23,94,139,159
www.chandoshouse.co.uk

Channel Four Television ⒶⒿ
124 Horseferry Road SW1P 2TX
■ Sat 10am–5pm/Sun 10am–2pm. Pre-book ONLY on
openhouse@channel4.co.uk. NB No studios included in
this building. Max 25 per tour. E D T
Headquarters building with curving high glass and steel entry
atrium. RIBA Award Winner. Richard Rogers Partnership 1994.
Entry: reception, walkway, restaurant, drum.
Tube: St James's Park; Tube/Rail: Victoria; 11,24,211

Crown Court Church of Scotland
Russell Street WC2B 5EZ
■ Sat 11am–5pm/Sun 2pm–5pm. Max 50 at one time. D R T
Red brick with Portland stone dressings and slate roof.
Restrained, finely crafted Free Style. Three storeys, recessed
slated attic, mullioned and transomed windows. Fine stained
glass, most of which is by Farrar Bell. Eustace Balfour 1909.
Entry: sanctuary, hall.
Tube: Covent Garden, Holborn, Leicester Square; Tube/Rail:
Charing Cross; 6,9,15,188,RV1
www.crowncourtchurch.org.uk

Delfina Foundation
29 Catherine Place, Victoria, SW1E 6DY
■ Sat/Sun 11am–5pm. Hourly tours, book via eventbrite ONLY
www.eventbrite.co.uk/o/studio-octopi-6657106817. Last
entry 4.00pm. Max 10 per tour. T d A G
Founded in 2007, the foundation recently underwent a
major refurbishment and extension. The design exposes
the building's materiality and, through glass floors, the
foundation's ecosystem. Studio Octopi 2014.
Entry: Basement gallery.
Tube: Victoria, St James's Park; Rail: Victoria; 11,24,16,36,185

Dover House, Office of the Secretary of State for Scotland
66 Whitehall SW1A 2AU
- ■ Sat 10am-5pm. Pre-book ONLY on david.mott@ scotlandoffice.gsi.gov.uk. Last entry 4pm. Max 25 at one time. D

Elegant Whitehall facade and domed entrance commissioned by the Duke of York. Interesting original interiors. J Paine & H Holland 1754-8/1787. Entry: Ministerial rooms only.
Tube: Embankment, Westminster; Tube/Rail: Charing Cross; 3,11,12,24,53,87,88,159

Embassy of Belgium
Flanders House, 1a Cavendish Square W1G 0LD
- ■ Sat 1.30pm-6pm. Talk and tour at 2pm, 3pm, 4pm by Peter Guillery (Survey of London) on the history of Flanders House and Cavendish Square. First come basis. Max 30 at one time. T d

Grade II listed building, which together with other premises on Cavendish Square shares a rich history as the first development on the 2nd Earl of Oxford's London estate. Home to the Representation of the Government of Flanders, Visit Flanders and Flanders Investment and Trade. 1771.
Tube: Oxford Circus

Erco Lighting Showroom
38 Dover Street W1S 4NL
- ■ Sat 10am-5pm. Sequences of images and talks for visitors. N G d

Make's first completed interior fit-out project was the refurbishment of Architectural lighting company Erco. Conversion utilises restrained principles, allowing the use of light to define the space and create ambience. Structure and services are concealed behind simple, clean planes. Botschi Vargas Architects / Make 2004.
Tube: Green Park, Bond Street; 12,14,19

Fashion Space Gallery Roof Garden
Roof Garden, London College of Fashion, 20 John Prince's Street, W1G 0BJ
- ■ Sat 1pm-4pm. Pre-book ONLY, email events@fashion.arts.ac.uk. A T

The rooftop at London College of Fashion has been transformed by Studio Weave. The space is a homage to textiles and concrete. Conceived as an outdoor space for students to relax in, the new roof garden has been laid with brightly coloured decking in a herringbone pattern – a nod to the college's textile roots that has the dual role of emphasising the bold modernist concrete frame of the building. The mixture of planters, seats and tables will enable learning in small groups as well as the Fashion Space Gallery's events programme. Studio Weave 2014.
Tube: Oxford Circus

Foreign & Commonwealth Office
King Charles Street SW1A 2AH
- ■ Sat/Sun 10am-5pm. Last entry 4.30pm. R T B Q C d

Grade I listed Victorian government office buildings. Former India Office includes the magnificently decorated Durbar Court. Sir George Gilbert Scott & Matthew Digby Wyatt 1861-1868. Entry: Durbar court, India Office council chamber, Locarno suite and Foreign Office grand staircase.
Tube: Westminster; Tube/Rail: Charing Cross, Victoria; 3,11,12,24,53,87,88,159,453

Former Conservative Club (HSBC offices)
78 St James's Street SW1A 1JB
- ■ Sat 10am-2pm. Timed entry every half hour, pre-book ONLY on 020 7024 1255. Last entry 1.30pm. Max 40 at one time. E T d

Foreign & Commonwealth Office

Grand and monumental building with rich carvings and spectacular decorated saloon at its heart. Conserved and refurbished to replace 2 wings and provide new glazing to atrium at junction of new and old sites. Grade II* listed. Sidney Smirke & George Basevi/Squire & Partners 1844/2004. Entry: Grade II* listed areas.
Tube: Green Park; Tube/Rail: Charing Cross, Victoria

Gap House ●
28D Monmouth Road W2 4UT
- ■ Sun 10am-12pm. Half-hourly tours. Pre-book ONLY on admin@pitmantozer.com. Last tour 11.30am. Max 10 per tour. A G

New family home with a minimal carbon footprint on a very narrow site (8ft wide), once the side alley and garden of adjacent house. Each room has good natural light whilst fitting in between two listed buildings in conservation area. Cost effective design methods achieved an environmentally friendly house, utilising amongst many eco-friendly devices ground source heat pump heating and rainwater harvesting. RIBA Manser Medal Winner 2009. Pitman Tozer Architects 2007.
Tube: Bayswater, Queensway; 70,23,7,27,52

Hayes Davidson Studio
Studio A, 21 Conduit Place, Paddington W2 1HS
- ■ Sat 10am-1pm. First come basis, informal tours. D R T

21 Conduit Place was converted by architects Toh Shimazaki in 1996-7 to provide bespoke studios for architectural illustrators Hayes Davidson. Toh Shimazaki Architects 1997. Entry: Main studio, workspace, garden, meeting room.
Tube/Rail: Paddington; 7,23,27,205,436

HM Treasury
1 Horse Guards Road SW1A 2HQ
- ■ Sat/Sun 9am-5pm. Film of refurbishment of building. Last entry 4pm. D R T Q

Grade II* listed Government offices, Great George Street constructed 1900-17 in two phases. Refurbishment completed 2002, now occupied by HM Treasury. John Brydon & Sir Henry Tanner/Foster + Partners 1917/2002. Entry: reception, auditorium, inner courtyard garden, drum.
Tube: Westminster, St James's Park; Tube/Rail: Charing Cross, Victoria; 3,11,12,24,53,87,88,159,211

Home House
19, 20 & 21 Portman Square W1H 6LW
- ■ Sun tours at 3pm, 4pm, 5pm, pre-book ONLY by email on openhouse@homehouse.co.uk, confirmation sent by email. Max 12 per tour. D T

Built in 1776 by Wyatt with very fine interiors by Adam. Was the London base of the Countess of Home and is probably the greatest surviving Georgian town house. James Wyatt & Robert Adam 1776. Entry: Drawing rooms.
Tube: Marble Arch; Tube/Rail: Paddington; 2,13,82,139,159

Horse Guards
Whitehall SW1A 2AX
- ■ Sat/Sun 10am-3.30pm. Half hourly tours. Duration 45 mins. Approx waiting time 1.5-2hrs at peak. Last tour 3.30pm. Max 20 at one time. Q

Grade I listed beautifully-detailed Palladian composition at the heart of Whitehall, for a hundred years HQ of the British Army. Duke of Wellington's office as it was c1842. William Kent 1745-55. Entry: Horse Guards Arch, south side.
Tube: Westminster; Tube/Rail: Charing Cross; 3,11,12,24,53,87,88,91,139,159

Isis Education Centre at The LookOut ●
Hyde Park (north of the Serpentine, south-west of Speaker's Corner) W2 2UH
- ■ Sat 10am-4pm. Tours on the hour 12pm-3pm. Max 20 per tour. Nature-based play and crafts. E D T C A G

Old meets new at this award-winning eco-friendly building. Emulating the canopy of a tree, the green oak frame building blends into its listed surroundings of Hyde Park. With many sustainable features it sits proudly on top of a re-instated Victorian reservoir with an Edwardian Gatehouse at its entrance. David Morley Architects 2012. Entry: grounds, main building area.
Tube: Marble Arch, Hyde Park Corner; Tube/Rail: Victoria, Paddington; 10,137,148,16,2,36,414,436,73,74,82,452,52,9
www.supporttheroyalparks.org/explore/isis_education_centre

Italian Cultural Institute
39 Belgrave Square SW1X 8NX
- ■ Sat 10am-5pm. First come basis. N T d

Key. A Architect on site B Bookshop C Childrens' activities d Some disabled access D Full wheelchair access E Engineer on site G Green Features
N Normally open to the public P Parking Q Long queues envisaged R Refreshments T Toilets

Grade I listed stucco-fronted Belgravia town house. Library extension built 1960s. George Basevi c1825. Entry: reception area, conference room, library, reading room, main reception rooms.
Tube: Hyde Park Corner; Tube/Rail: Victoria; 9,16,36,38,52,82

Iyengar Yoga Institute, Maida Vale
223a Randolph Avenue W9 1NL
■ Sun 10.30am-5pm. Last entry 4.45pm. Max 6 at one time. D T
The first purpose-built yoga centre in Europe. Yoga's philosophy is translated into the crisp simplicity of the design, with light pouring in through a grid of square lightwells in ceiling. Two yoga studios with underfloor heating. Shiva Design 1994. Entry: reception area, corridor, viewing of 2 studios.
Tube: Maida Vale, Kilburn Park; Rail: Kilburn; 16,31,98,316,328

Lindo Wing, St Mary's Hospital
South Wharf Road, W2 1NY
■ Tour on Sunday at 10.30am. Pre-book ONLY on 020 8383 5226 or email Julia Weiner on ajw65@aol.com. Max 20 per tour. D R T
The Lindo Wing reopened in 2012 following refurbishment and the installation of more than 40 works by artist Julian Opie. Sir Edwin Cooper 1937/2011.
Tube: Edgware Road; Rail: Paddington; 7,15,23,27,36

London School of Economics: Saw Swee Hock Student Centre ●
1 Sheffield Street WC2A 2AP
■ Sat/Sun 1pm-5pm. Regular tours, pre-book ONLY by email: estates.admin@lse.ac.uk. Max 12 per tour.
Home to the LSE Students' Union, this newly constructed award winning building has dramatic sculptural form and unusual perforated brick façade achieving BREEAM Outstanding status. O'Donnell + Tuomey 2014.
Tube: Holborn, Temple; Tube/Rail: Charing Cross; 1,168,521,15,26
www.lse.ac.uk

London Victoria Railway Station ●
London Victoria Station SW1V 1JU
■ Sat/Sun 9am-5pm. Half-hourly tours, pre-book ONLY on www.networkrail.co.uk/VicOpenHouse. Last entry 4pm. Max 4 per tour. T E
A fully guided tour on top of London Victoria Station's Grade II listed roof. Designed by engineer Sir John Fowler and renovated by May Gurney/WSP in 2011 as part of a £35m upgrade. Sir John Fowler 1862/2011.
Tube/Rail: Victoria; 2,170,C10,185,136

Marlborough House
Pall Mall SW1Y 5HX
■ Sat 10am-5pm. Last entry 4.30pm. Max 150 at one time. R T d
Originally home of the Dukes of Marlborough, and later of Edward VII and Queen Mary. Now HQ of the Commonwealth Secretariat and Commonwealth Foundation. Sir Christopher Wren & Sir James Pennethorne 1709-11/1861-3. Entry: all fine rooms on ground floor.
Tube: St James's Park, Green Park, Piccadilly; Tube/Rail: Victoria, Charing Cross; 23,12,9,15,159,88,6,38,14,24

Methodist Central Hall Westminster
Storey's Gate SW1H 9NH
■ Sun 1.30pm-5pm. Regular tours, first come basis. Organ recital and historical footage. N D R T B
A masterpiece of Edwardian neo-baroque architecture opposite Westminster Abbey. Great Hall was the venue for the Inaugural General Assembly of the United Nations in 1946. Lanchester & Rickards 1906-1912. Entry: Great Hall, roof balcony, dome, café.
Tube: St James's Park, Westminster; Tube/Rail: Victoria, Waterloo; 11,24,88,159,87,453,148

New West End Synagogue
St Petersburgh Place W2 4JT
■ Sun 10am-1.30pm. Regular tours. N T d
Magnificent Grade I listed high Victorian synagogue, Audsley's masterpiece building. Includes metalwork, stained glass and a mosaic by Audsley; stained glass by NHJ Westlake. Further enrichment 1894/5 included ornate lighting believed to have been designed by George Aitchison. George Ashdown Audsley 1877-79.
Tube: Queensway, Bayswater, Notting Hill Gate; Tube/Rail: Paddington; 7,23,27,36,70,94,148,390

One Great George Street – Institution of Civil Engineers ●
One Great George Street SW1P 3AA
Monday 15th Sept tours at 2pm, 3pm and 4pm led by ICE archivist, pre-book ONLY on www.ice.org.uk/london. Duration 1 hour. Max 30 per tour. E D R T
Grade II* listed HQ building of the world's premier engineering institution, the first of its kind. Fine example of Edwardian architecture. James Miller 1913. **ice**
Tube: Westminster, St James's Park; Tube/Rail: Charing Cross; 3,11,12,24,53,77A,88,91,139,159

Oriental Club
11 Stratford Place W1C 1ES
■ Sat 10am-5pm. Four tours in the day, pre-book ONLY by email on events@orientalclub.org.uk. T d B
Grade 1 Listed Stratford House, designed by Richard Edwin and built by Edward Stratford 1770-1776. Forms centrepiece of noble Robert Adam Design and home to Oriental Club founded by Major-General Sir John Malcolm and Duke of Wellington since 1962. Richard Edwin 1770-1776. Entry: drawing room, small drawing room, smoking rooms, library, dining room.
Tube: Bond Street; Tube/Rail: Marylebone

Peabody Avenue ● ●
Peabody Avenue SW1V 4AT
■ Sat 10am-5pm. First come basis. D T Q
Victorian social housing estate with striking 200m long avenue. Designated Conservation Area. 55 new flats created in 2011 with landscaping and community facility. New design seeks to draw on the scale and material texture of the historic estate. Haworth Tompkins 2012. Entry: community centre, external areas, no entry to flats.
Tube: Victoria, Sloane Square, Pimlico; 360,C10,24,44,452

Pimlico District Heating Undertaking (PDHU) ● ● ●
The Pumphouse, Churchill Gardens Road SW1V 3JF
■ Sat/Sun 10am-5pm. Regular tours, first come basis. Last entry 4.30pm. Max 25 at one time. R T G P d
Churchill Garden Estate used energy from waste heat from Battersea Power Station when it was functional. The Pumphouse still provides low carbon heating to Pimlico from combined heat and power engines and has the UK's largest thermal store. Powell and Moya 1950.
Tube: Pimlico; Tube/Rail: Victoria; 24,36,137,360,C10

Portcullis House
Victoria Embankment SW1A 0AA
■ Sat 10am-5pm. Last entry 4.30pm. Max 300 at one time. E D R T B Q
Portcullis House contrasts its imposing facade with a generous light-filled courtyard covered by a glass roof at second level and surrounded by a 2-storey cloister. Extensive collection of parliamentary portraiture from Gilray to Scarfe. RIBA Award Winner. Hopkins Architects 2001. Entry: ground floor courtyard and 1st floor. Entry to Portcullis House only via

main entrance on Victoria Embankment.
Tube: Westminster; Tube/Rail: Charing Cross; 3,11,12,24,53,87,88,159,211

Reform Club
104 Pall Mall SW1Y 5EW
■ Sat 10am-5pm/Sun 10am-3pm. Pre-book ONLY by email on paul.austin@reformclub.com. NB. Regret no children under 12 admitted. Max 15 per tour. E N G d
Built as a Whig gentleman's club and inspired by Italian Renaissance palaces. Lobby leads to an enclosed colonnaded courtyard with complementary glazed roof and tessellated floor. Tunnelled staircase leads to upper floor. Sir Charles Barry 1841. Entry: ground & 1st floor principal public rooms.
Tube: Piccadilly Circus; Tube/Rail: Charing Cross

Regent Street Block W4
10 New Burlington Street, W1S 3BF
■ Sat/Sun 10am-4pm. Architect led tours and talks at 10am, 12pm, 2pm. A
New office and retail accommodation that sensitively balances preservation of the characters of Regent Street and New Burlington Street with the insertion of contemporary buildings, forming a distinctive new contribution to the neighbourhood's built heritage. Allford Hall Monaghan Morris 2014.
Tube: Oxford Circus, Piccadilly Circus; Bus: 3,6,12,13,88,94,159,453
www.ahmm.co.uk

RIBA
66 Portland Place W1B 1AD
■ Sat 11am-4pm. Guided tour of RIBA's stunning art deco headquarters: 11.30am & 1.30pm. Curator-led tours of the Architecture Gallery and exhibition Ordinary Beauty: The Photography of Edwin Smith: 12.30 & 2.30pm. Be inspired by views from the top of 66 Portland Place in our 'Build a Skyline' family workshop: 11am-4pm (drop-in). See original drawings, models and photographs of Open House favourites, including Battersea Power Station and the Houses of Parliament: 11am-4pm (drop-in). Max 20 per tour. N R T B C d
Fine example of Grade II* listed 1930s architecture with many original features and fittings. Grey Wornum 1932-4. Entry: Council chamber, Aston Webb room, Jarvis hall, Lutyens room and all public areas.
Tube: Great Portland Street, Oxford Circus, Regent's Park; 88,C2
www.architecture.com

Romanian Cultural Institute
1 Belgrave Square SW1X 8PH
■ Sat/Sun 11am-5pm. Last entry 4.30pm. N D T A
Situated in one of the grandest and largest 19th century squares in London, 1 Belgrave Square was acquired by Romania in 1936 and is now home to the Romanian Cultural Institute. Thomas Cubitt 1828. Entry: ground and first floors and 'Auspicious Absents' exhibition.
Tube/Rail: Victoria; Tube: Hyde Park Corner; C2,2,9,14,82,137,148,73,436

Royal Academy of Music
Marylebone Road NW1 5HT
■ Sun 10.30am-2.30pm. Tours at 10.30am & 12.30pm. First come basis. Duration approx 1hr 45mins. Max 25 per tour. N R T d
A mix of historical Grade I and II listed buildings by John Nash and Ernest George alongside innovative developments. The site has been extended over the past 9 decades, most recently the museum and concert hall (2001) and additional practice rooms (2010) both by John McAslan + Partners, the latter with a no-maintenance bronze roof. Entry: Foyer, Duke's

● AJ Library Building ● Green Exemplar ● Landscape/Public realm ● Infrastructure/Engineering ■ Open Saturday ■ Open Sunday ■ Open Saturday and Sunday

openhouselondon.org.uk | Westminster | 73

Hall, museum (including student demonstrations of historic keyboards and exhibition 'War Music') and the theatre.
Tube: Baker Street; Tube/Rail: Marylebone; 27,30,205,453,74

Royal Albert Hall
Kensington Gore SW7 2AP
■ Sun 9.30am-3pm. First come basis, self-guided tours. Entrance times may be staggered when demand is high. Max 20 per tour. N D R T G d
One of Britain's most iconic buildings, the Royal Albert Hall was designed by Royal Engineers Captain Francis Fowkes & General Henry Scott. Completed in 1871 and now a Grade I listed building, it hosts over 370 main events every year including a full range of music, sport and films. Captain Fowkes & General Scott 1871. Entry: via door 12.
Tube: South Kensington, Gloucester Road, High St Kensington; Tube/Rail: Victoria; 9,10,52,360,452

Royal College of Nursing
20 Cavendish Square W1G 0RN
■ Sat 10am-5pm. First come basis, queuing outside if necessary. Half-hourly tours of period rooms. Last entry 4pm N D R T B
A cleverly integrated mixture of architectural styles and periods, incorporating a late 1720s house with rare and Baroque painted staircase and the purpose-built college of nursing (1926). George Greaves/Sir Edwin Cooper/EPR Architects/Bisset Adams Architects 1729/1921/2001/2013. Entry: library and heritage centre, painted staircase. 1720s rooms, Cowdray Hall, Glass Walkways only accessible on guided tours.
Tube: Oxford Circus; 3,12,25,55,73

Royal Courts of Justice
Strand WC2A 2LL
■ Sat 10am-4pm. Activities and displays until 3.30pm, doors close promptly at 4pm. NB. Any knives brought in will be confiscated. N R T C d
Street's masterpiece and one of Victorian London's great public buildings. 13C Gothic given a Victorian interpretation. G E Street 1874-82. Entry: main hall, selected courts, cells and areas of interest.
Tube: Temple, Holborn, Chancery Lane; Tube/Rail: Waterloo, Charing Cross; 4,11,15,23,26,76,172,341

Royal Geographical Society (with IBG)
1 Kensington Gore (Exhibition Road entrance) SW7 2AR
■ Sat 10am-5pm. Pavilion exhibition 'London Lives' and self-guided tours. N R T B d
Originally a private home in R Norman Shaw's Queen Anne style, with later additions for the Society. Richard Norman Shaw/Kennedy and Nightingale/Studio Downie 1874/1930/2001-4. Entry: pavilion, Stanfords travel bookshop, Ondaatje Theatre, Council room, Map room, education centre, Lowther room, Members' Room, terrace and garden.
Tube: South Kensington; Tube/Rail: Paddington, Victoria; 9,10,52,452

Royal Institution of Chartered Surveyors
12 Great George Street, Parliament Square SW1 3AD
■ Sat 10am-5pm. Regular tours covering building highlights. Max 25 at any one time. D R T B
Historic Grade II listed gabled Victorian building purpose built for the RICS in Franco-Flemish style. Only surviving Victorian building in the street. Alfred Waterhouse 1899. Entry: ground, 1st floor, 5th floor suite & terrace.
Tube: Westminster; Rail: Waterloo; 11,12,24,148,221

Royal Over-Seas League
Park Place, St James's Street SW1A 1LR
■ Sat/Sun tours 10.30am, 12noon, 2.30pm, pre-book ONLY on elocke@rosl.org.uk or 0207 408 0214 ext 215. Max 20 per tour. R T d
Over-Seas House is an amalgamation of two Grade I listed houses – Rutland House (James Gibbs, 1736) and Vernon House (1835 rebuilt 1905). It is now the International Headquarters of the Royal Over-Seas League. James Gibbs 1736/1905. Entry: period style function rooms.
Tube: Green Park; Tube/Rail: Victoria; C2,9,14,19,22,38
www.rosl.org.uk

Rudolf Steiner House
35 Park Road NW1 6XT
■ Sun 2pm-5pm. Tours every 15 mins. Last entry 4.30pm. N D R T B P
Unique example of Expressionist architecture in London with sculptural staircase based on organic plant forms. Grade II listed. New cafe and renovations in 2008. Montague Wheeler/Nic Pople 1926-37/2008. Entry: all areas except offices.
Tube: Baker Street; Tube/Rail: Marylebone; 2,13,18,27,30,82,274,113

Serpentine Gallery Pavilion ●
Kensington Gardens W2 3XA
■ Sat/Sun 10am-6pm. Last entry 5.45pm. Max 200 at one time. N D R T B C
Semi-translucent, cylindrical structure, designed to resemble a shell, resting on large quarry stones. Radic's Pavilion has its roots in his earlier work, particularly The Castle of the Selfish Giant, inspired by the Oscar Wilde story. Designed as a flexible, multi-purpose social space with a cafe inside. Smiljan Radic 2013.
Tube: Knightsbridge, South Kensington, Lancaster Gate; 9,10,52,94,148

St Anne's Tower
St Anne's Churchyard, Wardour Street W1D 6AF
■ Sat 10am-5pm. Regular tours, first come basis. Historians on site, museum display with video. Last entry 4.30pm. Max 25 at one time. R T d
Extraordinary brick, stone and copper Grade II listed church tower with bulbous lead spire. Clock by Gillett and Johnston 1884. S P Cockerell 1803. Entry: tower, clockroom, church, community centre.
Tube: Piccadilly Circus, Leicester Square; Tube/Rail: Charing Cross; 14,19,38,24

St Mary's Hospital, Paddington
Praed Street W2 1NY
■ Sun tour 12.30pm. Access via tour only. Pre-book ONLY on 020 8383 5226 or email Julia Weiner on ajw65@aol.com. Max 20 on tour. D R T
Tour of the hospital to include the original entrance foyer and chapel by Hopper & Wyatt (1843-51) with fine Victorian stained glass, the board room, the Queen Elizabeth the Queen Mother Wing and Sporborg Link Bridge (1980-7) by Llewelyn-Davies Weeks which includes new mural by Bridget Riley. Hopper & Wyatt/Sir Edwin Cooper 1843-51/1937. Entry: chapel, entrance foyer, board room, historical display area, Queen Elizabeth the Queen Mother Wing.
Tube: Edgware Road; Tube/Rail: Paddington; 7,15,23,27,36

The British Academy
10-11 Carlton House Terrace SW1Y 5AH
■ Sat 10am-5pm. Hourly tours, first come basis. Last tour 4pm. Max 15 per tour. D R T
Grade I listed Nash-designed terraced houses described as one of London's finest Georgian treasures. Interiors in No.10 by Bonomi later altered by Billery and Blow in 1905-07; No.11 interiors by Pennethorne, Nash's pupil. The British Academy, the UK's national body for the promotion of the humanities and social sciences, moved to the building in 1998. 2010 refurbishment includes state of the art auditorium. John Nash/Feilden & Mawson 1833/2010. Entry: ground and first floor rooms.
Tube/Rail: Charing Cross; Tube: Piccadilly Circus; 11,24,29,87,91

The British Library of Political and Economic Science (LSE Library)
10 Portugal Street WC2A 2HD
■ Sun 12pm-3pm. Half-hourly tours, first come basis. Last entry 2.30pm. D d
Preserving the Grade II listed 1916 exterior, a £30m interior transformation and lozenge-shaped footbridge were completed in 2001. The Women's Library Reading Room completed in 2014. Houses the world's largest library specialising in social and political science. Foster + Partners 2001. Entry: lower ground floor to 4th floor.
Tube: Holborn, Temple; Tube/Rail: Charing Cross; 1,59,68,91,168,171,188

The College of Optometrists
42 Craven Street WC2N 5NG
■ Sun 1pm-5pm. Last entry 4.45pm. Max 20 at one time. T B C d
HQ of professional and examining body for UK optometrists occupying two terraced houses, no. 41 (Flitcroft c1730 with later additions) and no. 42 (rebuilt by Tarmac plc, c1989). Henry Flitcroft c1730. Entry: Council room, Panelled room, Sutcliffe room, Print room, Giles room, Library.
Tube: Embankment; Tube/Rail: Charing Cross; 3,6,11,12,24

The Connection at St.Martin in the Fields
12 Adelaide Street WC2N 4HW
■ Sun 2pm-5pm. Architect-led tours of entire building including exhibition of art by homeless people and introduction to the work of The Connection. Pre-book only on events@cstm.org.uk with Open House in subject of email, or call on 0207 766 5555. Last entry 4.45pm.
Grade II* listed ex-school building, now a centre for homeless people. Rare opportunity to see inside historic building delivering modern solutions to an old problem. John Nash/Eric Parry (refurb) 1830/2007. Entry: Ground floor.
Tube: Leicester Square, Embankment, Charing Cross; Rail: Charing Cross; 23,11,15,29,24
www.connection-at-stmartins.org.uk

The House of St Barnabas
1 Greek Street, Soho Square W1D 4NQ
■ Sun 10am-5pm. Tours on the hour. Pre-book ONLY by email on mary@hosb.org.uk. Last tour 4pm.
Soho's grandest Grade I listed Georgian townhouse. Fine Roccoco plasterwork commissioned 1754. Victorian Oxford Movement Chapel built 1862 by Joseph Clarke. Owned by charity supporting the homeless back into the workplace. Joseph Pearce 1746. Entry: house, private members club, chapel, gardens.
Tube: Tottenham Court Road, Leicester Square; Tube/Rail: Charing Cross; 14,19,24,29,38,176

The Learning Centre at The Mall Galleries
The Mall, SW1
- Sat tours at 12noon and 2pm. Pre-book ONLY on info@mallgalleries.com or 0207 930 6844.

Explore the Mall Galleries refurbished 19th century vaults and find out more about the history of The Mall and Carlton House Terrace. John Nash / Corrigan + Soundy + Kilaiditi Architects 1863/2013. Entry: refurbished Grade I listed Victorian cellars.
Tube: Piccadilly Circus; Tube/Rail: Charing Cross; 9,15,23,88,453

The London Library ●
14 St James's Square SW1Y 4LG
- Sat 10am-4pm. Hourly tours. Pre-book ONLY on 020 7766 4704. Last tour 4pm. Max 20 per tour. T

The world's largest independent lending library, housing 1 million books in atmospheric Victorian cast-iron bookstacks. A labyrinth of disparate buildings have been recently remodelled and restored and new features include an award-winning lightwell over a newly created reading room and contemporary but sensitive finishes. James Osborne Smith / Haworth Tompkins 1896-8/2010. Entry: bookstacks, reading room, art room, main hall. NB. Many stairs. Please wear flat shoes due to grille flooring.
Tube: Piccadilly Circus, Green Park; Tube/Rail: Charing Cross; 9,14,19,22,38

The Photographers' Gallery ●
16-18 Ramillies Street, W1F 7LW
- Sat 10am-6pm/Sun 11.30am-6pm. Sat tours at 11am and 3pm, first come basis. Last entry 5.30pm. Max 25 per tour. N R T B d

An elegantly redeveloped Edwardian red-brick warehouse, linked to a steel-framed extension through an external sleeve of black render, terrazzo and Angelim Pedra wood. O'Donnell and Tuomey 2012.
Tube: Oxford Circus; 159,3,12,73
http://thephotographersgallery.org.uk

The Queen's Chapel (St James' Palace)
St James' Palace, Marlborough Road, SW1A 1BG
- Sat/Sun 10am-5pm. Pre-book ONLY for tickets. royalcollection.org.uk/queens-chapel, last entry 4pm. D

The first Palladian style post-Reformation Church in England and private Chapel of Charles I's bride Henrietta Maria; later extensively refurbished by Sir Christopher Wren in 1682-3. It is one of the facilities of the British monarch's personal religious establishment, the Chapel Royal. Inigo Jones 1623.
Tube: Green Park, St James's Park; Rail: Victoria; 8,9,14,19,22,38

The Royal Society
6-9 Carlton House Terrace SW1Y 5AG
- Sat 10am-7pm/Sun 11am-4pm. Tours every 20 mins, first come basis. Max 15 per tour. D T

Grade I listed Nash-designed town houses, refurbished in the 1890s before conversion into the German Embassy. 2004 refurbishment provided additional facilities for the home of the UK's national science academy. Nash/Speer/William Holford & Partners/Burrell Foley Fischer 1828/2004. Entry: lecture theatres, reception rooms, library.
Tube: Piccadilly Circus; Tube/Rail: Charing Cross; 29,91,24,9,6,13

The UK Supreme Court (formerly the Middlesex Guildhall)
Parliament Square SW1P 3BD
- Sat/Sun 9.30am-4.30pm. Queue likely to close at 4pm. Last entry strictly 4.30pm. N D R T Q C

Sensitive refurbishment of this neo-gothic Grade II* listed building enhances the historic fabric whilst reversing more recent adaptations that had left it feeling gloomy. The north

and south light wells were cleared bringing light back into the building, improved orientation, and greatly enhanced the appearance of original features such as stained glass windows, wood panelling and ornate ceilings. J S Gibson/Feilden + Mawson 1913/2009. Entry: courts, library, reception area, lobbies, exhibition, cafe.
Tube: Westminster, St James's Park; Tube/Rail: Victoria, Charing Cross; 11,24,29,88,159

Two Temple Place
2 Temple Place WC2R 3BD
- Sun 11am-4.30pm. Pre-book ONLY by email to tours@twotempleplace.org. Max 30 per tour. T d

Finished in 1895 for the first Viscount Astor, William Waldorf Astor, to the elaborate architectural specifications of John Loughborough Pearson. The house sits on reclaimed land overlooking the River Thames. It embodies much of the outstanding workmanship and architecture of the late Victorian period. J L Pearson 1895. Entry: main part of house.
Tube: Temple; Tube/Rail: Charing Cross, Waterloo; 6,9,13,87,139

Westminster Academy at the Naim Dangoor Centre ●
255 Harrow Road W2 5EZ
- Sat 10am-2pm. Architect-led tours at 11am and 1pm, first come basis. Last entry 1.30pm. T A G

A colourful, dynamic Academy for 1,175 students including a dramatic glazed atrium, integrated supergraphics, separate sports hall, and extensive landscaped playground. Since the building opened in 2007, results have increased from 17% A*-C including English and Maths, to 75% in 2012, and in 2013 the Academy was judged Outstanding by Ofsted. RIBA Award Winner 2008. Allford Hall Monaghan Morris 2007.
Tube: Warwick Avenue, Royal Oak, Queensway, Bayswater; Tube/Rail: Paddington; 18,36
www.ahmm.co.uk

Westminster Archives Centre
10 St Ann's Street SW1P 2DE
- Sat 10am-5pm. Hourly tours. Last tour 4pm. Max 15 per tour. N D R T B C

Modern red brick building purpose-built to house City of Westminster's historic records. Opportunity to visit the conservation studio and strongrooms. Tim Drewitt 1995. Ground floor public library facilities.
Tube: St James's Park; Tube/Rail: Victoria; 11,24,88,211,148

Westminster Hall
House of Commons (Cromwell Green entrance) SW1A 0AA
- Sun 10am-5pm. Last entry 4.30pm. R T Q d

One of the finest and largest Medieval halls in Europe with a magnificent hammerbeam ceiling. Work began in 1097. The architect for the 14C rebuilding was Henry Yevele, with Hugh Herland who designed the roof. Henry Yevele 14C.
Tube: Westminster; Tube/Rail: Victoria, Charing Cross, Waterloo; 11,77A,12,53,24,109,159

WALKS/TOURS

'Do the West End Walk' with Atkins ●
- Meet: Sat 11am at Caffe Nero, 48 Oxford Street W1D 1BF Walking tour with landscape architects, pre-book ONLY on neil.manthorpe@atkinsglobal.com. Duration 2 hours.

A walking tour exploring the West End's landscape and public realm from Oxford Circus through to the NLA via Regent Street, Trafalgar Square and Covent Garden.
Tube: Oxford Circus; 3,6,7,8,10,12

Brunel's Paddington: Then and Now ●
- Meet: Sat at 10.30am, 1pm, 3.30pm outside Paddington, Hammersmith and City underground station on canalside, W2 1FT. Pre-book ONLY on 0203 145 1200 or email walks@inpaddington.com. Max 30 per tour. E N G d

Meet Isambard Kingdom Brunel for a tour of Paddington. Find out about the history of the Great Western Railway, the great man's life and work, and explore his Paddington then and our Paddington now. See stunning bridges, hear about Crossrail and visit Paddington's newest quarter, Merchant Square.
Tube/Rail: Paddington; 23,15,36,27,436

David Kohn Architects Mayfair Galleries Walking Tour
11 Old Burlington Street W1S 3AN
- Sat tours, first come basis. Tours at 11.30am, 2.00pm. Max 20 per tour. A

Architect led tour of two recent gallery refurbishments by David Kohn Architects. Meet at Stephen Friedman Gallery, tour continues to Thomas Dane Gallery. David Kohn Architects 2011.
Tube: Piccadilly Circus, Green Park; 14,19,88,38,139

Leicester Square ●
- Meet: Sun 11am at Leicester Square Gardens WC2H 7NA Tour duration 1 hour. Max 25 per tour. D A

The new design is based on the creation of a coherent city block and includes intrinsic landscape qualities of a London square with contemporary and unique design features found nowhere else in the UK. Burns + Nice 2012.
Tube: Leicester Square; Tube/Rail: Charing Cross; 24,12,38,29,176

The Northbank Revealed
Meet at St Martin-in-the-fields (steps)
- Sat tours at 10am and 12noon. Duration 90 mins. Pre-book ONLY at http://openhousenorthbank.eventbrite.co.uk or call 0203 697 9270. Experts at each stop with amenities available on the way. Max 20 per group.

Take in the wonders of London's architecture through time on the Northbank, with tours of prominent historical buildings. Explorers will travel through time from Roman to Art Deco British spectacles along the Strand and Aldwych with a focus on Two Temple Place, a "hidden architectural gem" built by William Waldorf Astor in 1895.
Tube: Embankment; Tube/Rail: Charing Cross; 24,29,176

The Northbank Revealed – St Clement Dane Church & St Mary Le Strand
- Meet: Sun tours at 12noon and 2pm at St Martin-in-the-fields (steps). Tour duration 2hrs 30 mins. Pre-book ONLY at http://openhousenorthbank.eventbrite.co.uk or call 0203 697 9270. Max 20 per group.

Tour to take in St Clement Dane Church and St Mary Le Strand, both marvels of the Northbank. Enjoy a guided tour of the churches after a walk through Trafalgar Square, Strand and Aldwych; a historical destination revealed.
Tube: Embankment; Tube/Rail: Charing Cross; 24,29,176

Supported by

City of Westminster

Programme index

Listed here are special events, and buildings by type. The website search facility at **openhouselondon.org.uk/london** enables you to use different criteria such as location, architect and period, as well as additional special activities taking place.

Image copyright credits

Cover: Cover: Chandos House - The Royal Society of Medicine, The Ismaili Centre – VIEW Pictures, Villa Caroisla – Hamish Par, Queens Chapel - Royal Collection Trust, Her Majesty Queen Elizabeth II 2014 - Cliff Birtchwell, The Leadenhall Building - Richard Bryant, Ravensbourne - Morley von Sternberg; p1 Gasholder no.8, Kings Cross - Andrew McKelvie; p7 Fulham Palace – credit Justin Piperger and copyright Fulham Palace Trust, The Leadenhall Building - Richard Bryant, Stockwell Street, Greenwich School of Architecture – Luxigon and Heneghan Peng, The Ismaili Centre – VIEW Pictures, ORTUS – Jack Hobhouse, Lullaby Factory – Studio Weave, HM Treasury – Kevin Sansbury, Otts Yard – Helene Binet, p9 Forest Mews - Tim Crocker, Mint Street – Kilian O'Sullivan, Otts Yard – Helene Binet; p12 King's Cross Public Realm - John Sturrock; p19 Phoenix Cinema - Phoenix Cinema Trust ltd; p20 Wembley WC Pavilion – David Grandorge; p22 JW3 - Hufton + Crow; p23 Royal College of Physicians - Hufton+Crow; p24 Robin Grove music room & library extension - Kilian O'Sullivan; p27 The Leadenhall Building - Richard Bryant; p31 Whitehorse Manor Primary and Junior Schools – Hayhurst &co, Kilian O'Sullivan; p33 North London Hospice - Timothy Soar, Suburban Studio - Ashton Porter Architects; p35 Royal Greenwich UTC - Dennis Gilbert; p38 Writer's Shed - Weston Surman & Deane; p41 Clyde Rd – Will Pryce; p43 West Drayton Primary School –Anthony Coleman; p47 The Yellow Building - Timothy Soar; p48 The Ismaili Centre – VIEW Pictures; p49 West Norwood Health and Leisure Centre - Timothy Soar; p51 Bateman Mews – Ioana Marinescu, p52 Spring Gardens - Morley von Sternberg, Surrey Canal Roof Top Box - Robin Forster; p53 Green Man (Phoenix Community Housing) - Timothy Soar; p54 40a Dawlish Avenue – Will Pryce; p55 Chobham Academy – Timothy Soar; p56 Lee Valley Hockey and Tennis Centre – Hufton + Crow; p57 Valentines Mansion & Gardens – Paul Riddle Photographer; p59 Style Council – KSKa, Kew House - Jack Hobhouse; p61 City Hall – Ian Hadingham; p63 BedZED – BioRegional; p65 The Tree House – 6a architects; p68 House for a Painter - Ioana Marinescu; p70 37a Leamington Road Villas - Daniel Rowland; p71 LSE Saw Swee Hock - Dennis Gilbert.

Disclaimer: Neither Open-City nor the leader or organiser of any event, activity or walk advertised here or on the Open-City website nor any other programme listing, print or electronic, shall be held liable for the death or injury, accident or damage to the person or property (including theft or loss) of any event participant or any guest or any person occurring during or arising from participation in any of the events advertised in the Open House London events programme.

Please help keep Open House weekend free for all by donating at open-city.org.uk/ donate

Use the **iPhone app** to store your favourites in advance, find 'buildings nearby me' and get what's new this year

Take part in our survey and be in with a chance to win tea for two at the Gherkin

About the event:
Which buildings/events did you visit this year?

_____

Did Open House London make you think differently about any part of the city?
Yes / No If yes, where and how?

_____

Did you go to an area you hadn't been to before? **Yes / No** If yes, where?

_____

Have you learnt more about the role of and/or landscape architects?
☐ Engineers ☐ Landscape architects

How important is Open House London in engaging you with the city's architecture?
☐ Essential ☐ Very important ☐ Important ☐ Not important ☐ Don't know

Please tell us about you:
Where did you see or hear about Open House London this year? Please circle as many as apply :
OHL website   other website/newsletter   magazine/newspaper   local library   Radio/TV
Leaflet/poster   Transport advertising   word of mouth   Facebook   Twitter

Was this your first ever time at Open House London? **Yes / No** If No, when?

What were your reasons for taking part? **Leisure / Professional / Both**

Nationality _____ Occupation _____

Age _____ Gender _____

Thinking Green: Where do you make the most effort to be sustainable, at work or at home? ☐ Home ☐ Work   Why and how?

_____

Are you willing to be contacted by us in future for a more detailed research exercise?
Yes / No

DETAILS (please complete for both survey and/or purchases):

Name: _____

Address: _____

_____

London Borough or County: _____ Postcode: _____

E-mail: _____

Tel: _____

Order next year's Open House London guide

I would like to order the following: Cost

1   **Annual Open House London Event Programme**
    19 & 20 September 2015 Event (published 08 August 15).   £7.99 (incl p&p)

2   **Open House London: An Exclusive Insight into 100 Architecturally Inspiring Buildings in London**
    The first hardback illustrated book on Open House London, celebrating its 20th anniversary.
    Published by Ebury Press.   £23.30 (incl p&p)

3   **Mapguide to Contemporary Architecture (2014 edition)**
    A map of 270 contemporary London buildings with details of address, architect & year.   £3.95 (incl p&p)

4   **London's Contemporary Architecture: A Visitor's Guide**
    Ken Allinson, Victoria Thornton – full colour, 6th edition, 2014. Map-based guide to London's new buildings.   £23.95 (incl p&p)

    Sub Total   £

    Donation to support and sustain Open-City's education programmes for young Londoners
    TOTAL   £

GIFT AID Please tick here ☐   **Signature**
(Gift Aid is a simple scheme that enables charities to reclaim the tax you pay on your donations at no extra cost to you. Please provide address below left and sign above. You must pay tax at least equal to the tax that we will reclaim on your donation.)

The charity's education initiatives are funded solely through individuals, companies and trusts donations

Registered Charity No.1072104

METHOD OF PAYMENT (if making a purchase above):

Cheque: £_____ (made payable to Open-City)
Credit card details:

I authorise Open-City to charge £_____to my *VISA/MASTERCARD/SWITCH/DELTA
(*delete as appropriate) SORRY NO AMEX

No. ☐☐☐☐ ☐☐☐☐ ☐☐☐☐ ☐☐☐☐

Expiry date_____ Issue date_____

Issue Number (Switch/Delta only) _____

Date: _____

Do you want to receive our free enewsletter. If yes please tick here ☐

Visit open-city.org.uk/shop for more books and products
Find us on Facebook and Twitter @openhouselondon

Tear out page and send to:
FREEPOST RRXR-UBCB-ZKYC, Open House, 18 Ensign Street, London E1 8JD